THE RUSSIAN ARMY

AND THE FIRST WORLD WAR

by

Nik Cornish

SPELLMOUNT

British Library Cataloguing in Publication Data:
A catalogue record for this book is available
from the British Library

Copyright © Nik Cornish 2006

ISBN 1-86227-288-3

First published in the UK in 2006 by
Spellmount Limited
The Mill, Brimscombe Port
Stroud, Gloucestershire. GL5 2QG

Tel: 01453 883300
Fax: 01453 883233
E-mail: enquiries@spellmount.com
Website: www.spellmount.com

1 3 5 7 9 8 6 4 2

Printed in Great Britain by
Oaklands Book Services
Stonehouse, Gloucestershire GL10 3RQ

Contents

	Acknowledgements	vi
	Introduction	vii
Chapter 1	Russia to 1914	1
Chapter 2	1914: The Shock of War	21
Chapter 3	1915: A Time of Mixed Fortunes	39
Chapter 4	Winter 1915–16	57
Chapter 5	The Caucasian Front	75
Chapter 6	1916, Brusilov's Summer	99
Chapter 7	Romanian Winter 1916–17	119
Chapter 8	1917: The Hopeful Revolution	141
Chapter 9	1917, Kerensky's Offensive: The Last Gamble	163
Chapter 10	Epilogue: September–November 1917, Russia's Exit	183
Appendix 1	The Russian Navy	203
Appendix 2	The Russian Military Air Fleet	215
Appendix 3	TAON: The Heavy Artillery of Special Duty	225
Appendix 4	Conscription and Casualties	235
Appendix 5	Chemical Warfare	237
	Bibliography	241
	Index	243

Acknowledgements

Thanks and acknowledgements are due to the following splendid people: Stephen Perry, Dmitry Belanovsky, Norbert Hofer, August Blume, Lt Col Tom Hillman (US Army), Steve Locker-Lampson and Angie Meyrick-Brown.

This book is dedicated to my mother, Dorothy Gardner, for always being there and to my children Alex and Charlotte for being who they are.

Introduction

I have written this book with the simple purpose of providing a reasonably clear introduction to the Russian Army of 1914–18 and events on the Eastern Front during that period. Militarily this was the era of many new technologies and industrial warfare but set in the minds of many soldiers, of all nations, were the ideas of glory, a noble cause and victory in under a year. These men were not fools, but rather products of their training, societies and modes of thinking. There had been several wars during the fifty years before 1914 but no one influential person was gifted with the powers of a seer to be able to anticipate what the First World War would be like.

Three events dominate much of the western literature that covers this subject: the battle of Tannenberg and the revolutions of March and November 1917. The Russian defeat at Tannenberg was important and certainly the revolutions of 1917 were world-changing events, but they were not the only things to happen. During the two and a half years that separated the outbreak of war from the outbreak of revolution the Russian Army had learnt the facts and bitter realities of modern warfare through a mix of bloody experience, success and failure. These lessons were common to every other belligerent: what varied from nation to nation was how they were applied and the human cost.

Please note that the dates throughout are given using the Gregorian as opposed to the Julian calendar so that direct parallels may be kept with events elsewhere without continually adding thirteen. Throughout the text the term army will be used to include the navy and air fleet as both were subject to the authority of the Army Headquarters – *Stavka*.

As there is sometimes more than one Russian personality sharing a surname, initials will be given to avoid confusion other than in the case of major characters. I have deviated from accepted practice by referring to the Austrian Chief of Staff, Conrad von Hotzendorf, not as Conrad but as von Hotzendorf. Austria-Hungary will be Austria; Poland refers only to that area of the Russian Empire, not the state that re-emerged at the war's end.

The Tsar, Nicholas II (seen here reviewing the *Konvoi*) loved his army. The *Konvoi* was the Tsar's personal bodyguard and was composed of Cossacks from the Kuban and Terek regions of the north Caucasus. Nicholas' birthday (6 May 1868) was the festival of the prophet Job which was regarded as highly inauspicious.

In 1914 the provinces of Austria, Galicia and the Bukovina where much of the fighting took place were still almost unknown lands, undeveloped and populated by peasant farmers whose lifestyle had changed little during the previous 500 years. Across the frontier in Russia life was little different. Neither the Russians nor the Austrians had provided much in the way of roads and railways and this lack of infrastructure was to play havoc with troop and supply movements during the war years. When it rained, the earth tracks turned to mud and any movement slowed to a crawl. Moving north into Poland conditions were similar, although the population density was greater and rail links marginally better. It was only across the border in East Prussia that conditions improved significantly, here the German government had overseen the development of strategic roads and railways to facilitate the rapid movement of their army in all weathers.

A final point regarding the Central Powers, Austria and Germany. Although they were allies they did not enjoy a unified plan or command structure. Certainly for the first year of the war Austria pursued a semi-independent strategy: it was only from mid-1916 that the Germans exercised almost complete control over operations.

CHAPTER 1

Russia to 1914

Background

During the century leading up to 1914 Russia's military experience had been mixed. Having effectively destroyed Napoleon's Grand Army during the winter of 1812–13, the army of Tsar Alexander I emerged as the most powerful in Europe. However, during the reign of Tsar Nicholas I (1825–55) the fear of a revolution led by army officers tainted with western-style liberalism created an atmosphere that discouraged innovation and initiative. This stifling of independent, creative thought produced an army that was plagued by a determination to perform well on the parade ground and translate this precision onto the battlefield. Consequently the army that faced the Turkish-British-French alliance during the Crimean War was defeated by generals whose performance was only marginally less inept than their Russian opponents.

Alexander II, who succeeded his father in 1855, recognised that military reform was vital when informed by his War Minister that it would take up to six months to assemble four army corps on the border with Austria. Yet things moved slowly in imperial Russia and it was only with the appointment of General D. A. Miliutin as War Minister in 1862 that things began to improve.

Throughout the 1860s and 1870s the army was engaged in a series of campaigns in the Caucasus and Central Asia which impeded the reform process and consumed the military budget. Furthermore in 1861 Alexander II had emancipated the serfs and this colossal piece of social engineering, involving over ninety per cent of the population, was more than enough to deal with, certainly in economic terms. Nevertheless, by 1865 the empire was divided into fifteen military districts. Each of these areas was, in effect, a small state answerable to the Tsar and the War Ministry in St Petersburg. The War Minister was chief military adviser to the Tsar and controlled the Imperial Headquarters, the Military Council, the High Military Council, the War Ministry Staff and the Main Staff. Despite this profusion of bureaucrats there was no General Staff and all decisions remained the prerogative of the Tsar. In 1868 a new Field Regulations Manual was issued. It noted that the army (in this was included the navy) was to be led by a Supreme Commander in Chief who, "represented the person of the Tsar and was invested with Imperial authority". It was assumed that, in time of war, the War Minister would lead the armies in the field regardless of his command experience. This situation was to remain unchanged until the fall of the Romanov dynasty in 1917.

Following the Franco-Prussian War (1870–71) General N. N. Obruchev reported that Austria and the newly united Germany would be the most likely enemies of Russia in any future conflict. And due to the excellent railway networks at their disposal they could mobilise their forces in half the time it took the Russians and that they would outnumber the Russian army by a considerable margin. The area under immediate threat was Poland jutting peninsula-like between German East Prussia and Austrian Galicia. Poland west of the Vistula River was virtually indefensible, but a system of fortresses covered Warsaw and the shoulders of the Polish salient. Obruchev suggested investing £4,000,000, twenty-five per cent of the annual military budget, in upgrading the fortresses and extending the railways in that region as well as doubling the number of available troops within easy reach of Poland. At that time, 1873, Russia's army of theoretically 1,400,000 men was 500,000 understrength and could barely cope with its current responsibilities, let alone expand.

A conference chaired by the Tsar was convened and following a series of stormy meetings, it was agreed to introduce conscription but that the strengthening of the Polish railways and fortresses and, "other items [would have to] wait upon the financial means at hand" because the Finance Minister declared that any further military expenditure would bankrupt the empire. The basic idea of conscription was to create a body of time-served, trained men who at mobilisation would swell the ranks of the active or standing army and provide replacements.

With the introduction of universal military service on 1 January 1874 all males over the age of twenty-one were required to spend six years in the active army and nine in the reserve. Men who did not serve with the active army were to register for the Imperial Militia (*Opolchenie*) that could only be called to the colours by Imperial Decree (*Ukase*). In practice there was a multitude of exemptions that excused almost half of those reaching military age from peacetime service and a quarter from wartime service. Nevertheless Miliutin now had the manpower to expand the army.

The infantry grew to three Guards, four Grenadier and forty-one line divisions, each of four, four-battalion regiments. Distributed along the borders were twenty-nine rifle battalions. A battalion numbered one thousand officers and men. Each division was allotted an artillery brigade with sixty-four guns grouped in eight gun batteries.

The Grand Duke Nicholas Nicholaevich, pictured here in the uniform of a hussar regiment, shortly before becoming Supreme Commander in Chief of Russia's armed forces. The Grand Duke was an imposing figure, well over six feet tall, who reputedly enjoyed the confidence of the rank and file. Born in 1856 the Grand Duke retired to his estates in the Crimea in 1917 and took no further part in Russian politics. He died in exile in the south of France in 1929 where he was given a state funeral.

The cavalry, artillery and other branches of service expanded proportionately. The cavalry now consisted of two Guards, fifteen line and two Cossack divisions. A cavalry division comprised two brigades each of two regiments. The first brigade having a lancer and dragoon regiment, the second a hussar and a Cossack regiment. A regiment numbered almost 800 officers and men. However, Guards regiments were frequently home to more officers than their establishment due to the social cachet of such regiments and the selection procedure, including the candidate's capacity to hold his liquor like a gentleman, was scrupulous in the extreme.

The Cossacks perceived themselves as a military caste and were treated as irregulars enjoying different terms of service established decades before. They were divided into two groups; hosts, those of the steppe, the *Stepnoy*, and those of the Caucasus, the *Kavkas*. In 1914 there were nine *Stepnoy* hosts and two *Kavkas*. The largest *Stepnoy* host was that of the Don, the Kuban the largest of the *Kavkas*, between them they provided over fifty per cent of the Cossack manpower. Other than a small number of Kuban Cossack infantry battalions, the *plastuni*, Cossacks were cavalry with their own horse artillery formations. Each Cossack regiment was backed by two more composed of older men: these second and third line regiments would, in time of war, be attached to army corps for escort, reconnaissance and other duties. This structure would remain the basis on which the Russian Army went to war in 1914. Finns and native Caucasions were exempt from conscription as were all the Tsars Moslem and Asiatic subjects.

In 1874 it was announced that the Polish fortresses, particularly the major ones at Novo Georgievsk, Ivangorod, Warsaw and Brest-Litovsk would undergo a rolling programme of modernisation over the next thirty years at a cost of £6,500,000. The value of the changes was tested during the Russo-Turkish War, the first serious challenge Russia's reforming army would face.

The Russo-Turkish War, 1877–78

On 24 April 1877 Russia declared war on Turkey. The causes and course have no place here but the effect on the Russian Army does.

Russia's mobilisation and deployment to the main theatre of operations (modern day Bulgaria) was carried out efficiently. But the region lacked roads and railways and those through Romanian territory were primitive. The supply route was long and tortuous as Russia lacked a significant naval presence on the Black Sea and was thus confined to the land. The Turks had adopted a defensive strategy based around the town of Plevna that was defended by hastily thrown up earthworks. The Russian plan of campaign had anticipated that the fighting would be over before Christmas. However, Plevna's stout defence prolonged the war into the next year.

A Cossack outpost on Manchurian front during the Russo-Japanese War enjoys a tea break. The small size of their ponies is evident but deceptive as they were hardy, strong and capable of finding forage in the most inhospitable of conditions. The casual pose of the men is rare in photos of this period, as the camera was not common in the front line.

The entrenched Turkish infantry were presented with the opportunity to use their excellent Peabody-Martini rifles against Russian and Romanian infantry who advanced in neat formations across almost open ground with inadequate artillery support. Inevitably the attackers were mown down, but Plevna eventually fell. The victory was regarded as clear proof of the value of fortresses and the Russian belief that bravery and the bayonet would always triumph over the rifleman. What their analysis would have been had the Turks deployed machine guns in their trenches is unknown. As it was Russia had suffered over 100,000 casualties and the losses amongst officers had been particularly high as they had to expose themselves to retain control over a battlefield that lacked communications and cover and where they were expected to lead very clearly from the front.

Miliutin established a commission to compile an accurate history of the war. However, the assassination of Alexander II in 1881 and Miliutin's resignation led to the commission's report being delayed for twenty years by which time its conclusions were almost redundant.

The new Tsar, Alexander III was a parsimonious reactionary as was his War Minister General P. S. Vannovski. The officer corps and the men were discouraged from study as in the time of Nicholas I and the heroes of Russia's Napoleonic campaigns were chosen as more appropriate role models than contemporaries such as Germany's von Moltke or the Confederacy's Lee or Jackson.

Despite the economic retrenchment of Alexander's reign, he did allow for the introduction of a new rifle, the Mosin-Nagant M1891 7.62mm, that was to remain in service for over 50 years. Alexander disliked the growing western influence that was creeping into Russian life and undertook a wholesale "Russification" of the army's uniforms which led to the adoption of a very simple style of dress; a loose tunic, trousers and knee boots which reflected traditional peasant attire. All regular cavalry regiments were converted into dragoons reflecting their new role as mounted infantry. Unpopular as these changes were, the Tsar had spoken and therefore the decisions were beyond question. Diplomatically the picture was gloomy; Russia stood alone until, in 1894, the Tsar signed a defensive treaty with France that was to draw republic and autocracy closer and closer during the next 20 years.

The empire now reached from the Pacific Ocean to the middle of Europe and from the Arctic to the deserts of central Asia and it was this vast expanse, one sixth of the Earth's landmass, which Alexander bequeathed to his son Nicholas II on his death in 1894.

Nicholas II

Nicholas II was, for a variety of reasons, ill-prepared for the role he was to play. Nevertheless he was committed to the idea of preserving the monarchy as it was at the time of his father's death so he married a woman, Alexandra of Hesse-Darmstadt, who was equally if not more committed to this ambition. Both Nicholas and Alexandra disliked court life and withdrew from the capital city of St Petersburg to live at Tsarskoe Selo some 24kms (15 miles) away. However, despite their belief in the common people's devotion to the dynasty, the imperial couple's unpopularity began with the aristocracy and seeped downwards through society over the course of the next twenty years.

To those of a liberal persuasion Nicholas was a tyrant, indifferent to the lives of his people and devoted to the maintenance of his family's position. To those of the right he was the living symbol of the state wherein the characteristics of warlord, spiritual leader and political patronage were manifest. To the mass of his subjects he was simply the Tsar, the all-powerful, all-seeing ruler in whose name policies were formulated, laws passed and wars fought. The Tsar was the embodiment of the state and his word brooked no opposition. Simplistic as these perceptions may appear they were the essence of imperial Russia, which during the early years of the twentieth century was viewed by foreigners as being a snow-bound enigma: on the one hand cruel, unpredictable and threateningly xenophobic, while on the other mystical, immensely wealthy, ripe for economic exploitation and a potentially unconquerable ally. Tsarist Russia could provide evidence for any label an observer chose to hang on her, depending on need or political standpoint. Nicholas inherited from his father a multi-ethnic, multi-faith land-based empire. But although over eighty per cent of the people were peasant farmers there was a growing urban population, a tiny but rising mercantile and entrepreneurial class and the beginnings of an industrial revolution. However, many of the recently conquered lands in the Caucasus and Asia were not assimilated into the empire. Similarly, despite intensive Russification programmes, Poland, the Baltic provinces and Finland had nationalist – often socialist – underground movements. In the words of Count Sergei Witte, President of the Tsar's Council of Ministers, Russia was, "essentially a military empire." Indeed civil servants wore uniforms and were, to the untutored eye, virtually indistinguishable from the military on gala occasions. The Council of Ministers was the body that advised the Tsar on all matters of policy and below them a vast bureaucracy carried out the decisions thus made. But there was no elected body to represent the interests of society at large. A degree of local government had been established some years before but these bodies, the *Zemstvos*, had limited powers and were elected by a very exclusive group of voters.

Nicholas' first military test was to come in 1904 with a war against people he described as, "long-tailed monkeys" – the Japanese.

The Russo-Japanese War, 1904–05

Again the causes and course are out of place here but the effects on Russia and its army are not. In 1903 the army numbered over 750,000 infantry and 70,000 cavalry with 5,500 guns. When fully mobilised some 70,000 Cossacks would swell the ranks to almost 1,000,000 without calling on the reserves or the *Opolchenie*. As a British commentator remarked, "The Russian army must always be a very formidable foe from its great numerical strength." But the majority of these troops were quartered within European Russia, west of the Ural Mountains; the war with Japan was to be fought thousands of miles to the east in Manchuria.

The war began on 8 February 1904 with a surprise Japanese naval attack on the Russian Pacific squadron in their base at Port Arthur. The Russians

The Russian Army's standard issue machine gun the 7.62mm M1910 Maxim mounted on its signature *Sokolov* wheeled carriage. Drag ropes were attached to the metal loop at the rear. The thin metal shield is not in use on this example. As with all Russian equipment it was simple to produce and maintain and regarded as "soldier-proof."

initially relied on units of the Pri Amur and Siberian military districts, which amounted to just over 140,000 men with 120 guns operating from Mukden. Reinforcements, drawn from the Kiev, Moscow and Kazan military districts, would be sent via the incomplete, single track Trans-Siberian Railway along which everything from bullets to bandages would also travel. Separated from the munitions factories in the west, the Russian forces in Manchuria were in a potentially critical situation.

The War Minister, General A. N. Kuropatkin journeyed east to take command but from the beginning was at loggerheads with the regional Viceroy who was theoretical commander of the land and sea forces in the area. The Viceroy wanted to wage an offensive war from the outset whereas Kuropatkin intended to build up his forces and choose his time and place. The result was a compromise and a string of defeats for the Russians. Port Arthur surrendered on 2 January 1905 after a siege lasting for several months during which the Japanese suffered huge casualties as they attempted to storm its entrenchments. Two months later the Russian field army suffered another defeat and Kuropatkin resigned. Nine years to the day after Nicholas' coronation on 27 May, the Russian Baltic Fleet having steamed from St Petersburg to the Korean coast was destroyed by the Japanese at the battle of Tsushima. Nicholas sued for peace. On 5 September 1905 the war officially ended in the American town of Portsmouth. It is interesting to note that by April 1905 the Japanese treasury and armies were exhausted whereas the Russian field army, despite its losses, had increased in strength and held very strong positions putting Japan's ultimate victory in doubt. Russia's domestic problems and the naval defeat at Tsushima brought the war to an end.

The 1905 Revolution

Nicholas firmly believed that, "he was accountable to God for the country entrusted to his care," and that, "he believed it to be his duty to direct governmental policy according to his own conscience and understanding." Membership of the Council of Ministers was in his gift and his power was enshrined in the Fundamental Laws, which only he could alter. The deteriorating situation in Manchuria and problems in Poland, along with the deaths of hundreds of civilians who were shot down in St Petersburg on "Bloody Sunday" 22 January 1905 while peacefully attempting to petition the Tsar, led to an empire-wide outburst of sympathy strikes and demonstrations which cut across the social strata. The naval disaster at Tsushima only added to this tale of woe. In June the mutiny of the crew of the battleship *Potemkin* provided an ominous glimpse of things to come while across the non-Russian areas of the empire nationalist movements were stirring, demanding various degrees of autonomy.

By the autumn of 1905 passions were riding high and a general strike was called. Nicholas finally yielded to the urgings of his Ministers and issued the October Manifesto which granted a range of civil liberties and the establishment of an elected legislature to be known as the *Duma*. However, the Tsar retained his power over military and foreign affairs and crucially over when the *Duma* should be called. The October Manifesto effectively satisfied the demands of all but the most militant of revolutionaries. To maintain control the Council of Ministers had dispatched troops to support the police in major trouble spots. Ironically the soldiers were paid more to quell domestic difficulties than to fight a war. Towards the end of 1905 the *Semenovsky* Guards Regiment, with artillery support, was deployed on the streets of Moscow where it brutally suppressed an armed uprising leaving hundreds dead. For the next eighteen months the army was engaged in hundreds of similar actions but was itself not immune to outbreaks of trouble. During the summer of 1906 the first battalion of the *Preobrazhensky* Guards Regiment, in which Nicholas himself had served when young, refused to obey orders. This mutiny ended rapidly and without bloodshed but demonstrated that politics had spread even to the ranks of the army's élite. Dozens of similar instances of unrest occurred in the army and navy and were dealt with by a combination of tact and repression, and discipline was gradually restored. Nevertheless such incidents were a clear warning that the armed forces were no longer an obedient, unthinking mass that could be relied upon to obey any order from the sovereign no matter how harsh.

Military reform post-1905

Humiliated by the Japanese, engaged in police actions across the empire and lacking funds to replace lost equipment, the Russian armed forces presented a sorry spectacle in 1906. This crisis prompted the Tsar to listen to his advisers and take action. To increase the pool of trained men the length of service was reduced for the infantry to three years and four in the other branches of service. A new War Minister, General G. F. Rediger, was appointed and a Council of State Defence (CSD) was created and led by the Tsar's uncle the Grand Duke Nicholas. The CSD's mission was to oversee military policy and it enjoyed direct contact with the Tsar, bypassing the War Ministry. Furthermore a General Staff, again outside the thrall of the War Ministry, was set up with undisputed power over planning and mobilisation.

With stability returning to Russia revenue became available to provide resources for the military. The CSD proposed a reduction in the size of the army using the savings made to improve its efficiency. However, the War Ministry and both staffs made other proposals. The Tsar took the opportunity to reassert his power and demonstrate his renewed self-confidence by playing one group off against the other. Nicholas decided to allocate the lion's share of the money to re-equipping the navy splitting the funds between the Black and Baltic Sea fleets.

The *Duma* was also prey to the Tsar's rediscovered confidence, its powers were curbed and the franchise narrowed. By 1908 the return of stability firmly convinced Nicholas that reform was unnecessary and it was time to show that he still ran the empire. That year the Grand Duke Nicholas was transferred from the CSD to take charge of the St Petersburg Military District and the powers of the General Staff curtailed. Finally, in 1909 the CSD was abolished and the General Staff brought under the control of the new War Minister General V. A. Sukhomlinov. Happily for Sukhomlinov his appointment coincided with an upturn in the empire's economic fortunes and significant loans from France, consequently he had money to spend on the armed forces.

With money available to spend on the armed forces one of the measures brought in was the re-introduction of the different classifications of cavalry. Here three NCOs of the 13th *Narvski Hussar* Regiment pose in the parade, in the field uniforms of their unit. The parade uniform was mid-blue with white frogging.

Choices

Expansion and modernisation would all take time and choices would have to be made. With the benefit of a century of hindsight we can see that Sukhomlinov had a mere five years but at the time this was not obvious. However, as time was not apparently a problem the bureaucratic machinery could grind on at its own pace. A plethora of committees could assemble, negotiate and discuss for example whether to import a new type of heavy gun or create a factory to produce one. New uniforms were introduced and the old cavalry descriptions of hussar and lancer were reintroduced in an effort to improve morale.

But there were undercurrents and disputes, particularly in planning for a future war. The empire's border was roughly 40,000kms (25,000miles) in length and therefore, with the possibility of war in remote districts, where to deploy was problematic.

Planning

For decades Russian planning had been based on the understanding that its mobilisation would be slower than either Austria or Germany due to their superior railway networks. Therefore the Russian Army would assemble well within its borders covered by the fortress system of Poland that would prevent any surprise attack. When mobilisation and deployment were complete a short campaign would decide the issue.

In 1906 General M. V. Alexeyev, a member of the newly created General Staff, reviewed Russia's strategic position identifying the Central Powers (Germany and Austria) as the main threat with Germany as the driving force. Alexeyev reiterated the need to adopt an initially defensive posture but argued that Russia's main effort should be directed against Germany. He reinforced this proposal by declaring that, as the bulk of Germany's forces would be committed against France, an offensive against Germany, before Russia's mobilisation was complete, was a risk worth taking.

In 1908 **Plan 18** acknowledged the Central Powers as the main threat and determined that the Russian Army would await events until its enemy's strength and objectives were clear. Two years later **Plan 19** was drafted. It called for an "active defence" and allowed for the deployment of units from Siberia to the west as the threat from Japan was believed to have diminished. Fifty-three divisions would face Germany but only nineteen Austria. Most of Poland, including Warsaw and the fortress system would be abandoned, as the troops would deploy further to the east. Both fleets would be subordinated to *Stavka* (the Supreme Headquarters).

Plan 19 caused uproar. Its opponents, including Alexeyev, argued that such a weak force facing Austria would be unable to prevent Austrian cavalry threatening the rear and communications of the forces facing Germany and capture Warsaw. Furthermore as the loyalty of the Poles was questionable what other trouble might ensue?

The plan's author, General I. N. Danilov, argued that despite Russia's increasing military power the army was still comparatively weak and that French support would be inadequate. To quell dissension a compromise was reached resulting in **Plan 19 (revised)** which came into force in June 1912. As it was mainly under the terms of this plan that Russia went to war in 1914 a deeper examination is justified.

Plan 19 (Revised)

The revision had two variants: **A** with the main thrust at Austria, or **G** with the main thrust at Germany. It was understood that **A** was the most likely scenario even if Germany deployed more troops than anticipated.

Variant A
In this case the plan was, "to go over to the offensive against Austria and Germany with the objective of taking the war into their territory". Forty-five infantry divisions, divided between Third, Fourth and Fifth armies would comprise the South Western (SW) Front to invade Austria. Twenty-nine infantry divisions, First and Second armies, had the task of, "the destruction of German forces in East Prussia…with the goal of creating an advantageous assembly area for further operations".

Variant G
The intent in this case was, "to go over to the attack against German forces threatening us from East Prussia, paralysing the enemy on the remaining fronts". The First, Second and Fourth armies, grouped as North Western (NW) Front, with forty-three infantry divisions would face Germany and only Third and Fifth with thirty-one would challenge divisions Austria.

By October 1913 **Plan 20** had been devised which changed the forces committed to **Variant A**. Eighth Army was added to the line up and SW Front would be split into two groups. Fourth and Fifth armies would invade Austria from the shoulder of the Polish salient, Third and Eighth armies would advance from the east. This deployment would envelop the Austrian army in Galicia, capture the regional capital Lemberg (Lvov), isolate (if not take) the railway junction and fortress of Przemysl, occupy the Carpathian passes and invade Hungary and probably capture the vital railway centre of Cracow. NW Front, First and Second armies, would invade East Prussia and move towards the mouth of the Vistula River west of the great fortress of Konigsberg.

Under the terms of all plans the Army of the Caucasus was deemed to be capable of containing any threat from Turkey, a single corps would monitor Sweden (which the Russians considered likely to cause trouble in Finland). Sixth and Seventh armies would protect the Baltic coastline and the capital St Petersburg and cover Romania respectively. The movements for both variants were the same for the first week of mobilisation so there was a period of grace before final commitments were made. Unfortunately the debates about which enemy to face first created two schools of thought which were not to be reconciled and the discord was to continue beyond 1914.

A further complication was the promise made to the French in 1913 that, "Russia would begin operations against Germany with 800,000 men on M [mobilisation] +15." The French, in the same year, approved a loan to Russia that was to be used to build or upgrade 5300km (3293 miles) of railway lines in Poland to facilitate a move against Germany. This project had hardly left the drawing board by 1914 but **Plan 20** was designed with it in mind.

Another strategic controversy was over whether to retain the Polish fortress system. It was decided to keep it and improve its artillery stock although its value was debatable. Much would depend on how it was used and the weight of artillery an enemy deployed against it. The Plevna and Port Arthur definitive systems had worked effectively and very significantly the fortresses were a potent symbol of imperial power in Poland.

Army reform, 1910–14

The modernisation overseen by Sukhomlinov did not fundamentally alter the structure of Miliutin's army that rested on the army corps and cavalry division. The standing army was divided into thirty-seven corps; the Guards, the Grenadiers, I–XXV line, I–III Caucasian, I and II Turkestan and I–V Siberian. These included all the infantry divisions with their attached artillery. The usual structure of a corps was comprised of two infantry divisions, two field artillery brigades (each of two *divizions* or half regiments) of six, eight-gun batteries, a sapper battalion, telegraph and telephone sections and one *divizion* of light howitzers, two, six-gun batteries. The 208 line infantry regiments recruited from specific areas, the Guards, the Grenadiers and all other branches of service from across the empire.

Even though the Russo-Japanese War had highlighted the difficulties of command, communications and control across a large combat zone, the infantry retained the four-battalion regiment, including an eight-gun machine gun section and specialist scouting and communications personnel. In total the wartime strength of a regiment was 4000 officers and men.

During this period it was decided to disband the fortress troops and reserve formations. Instead cadres, trained with the standing army, would form the basis of thirty-five reserve divisions which would be numbered from fifty-three to eighty-four and from the 12th to the 14th Siberian. These divisions would have the same structure as those of the standing army but the artillery would not be as modern. An additional seven infantry divisions for the standing army were to be raised and the *Opolchenie* would provide 640 battalions.

The cavalry establishment in 1913 stood at twenty-four divisions; including the Guards and the Cossacks with a further eight separate brigades. Each division included eight machine guns and specialist scouting, communications and demolition sections as well as two six-gun horse artillery batteries. The military districts of the Caucasus, Siberia, Finland, Turkestan and Kiev all had two batteries of mountain artillery, the latter for use in the Carpathian Mountains. Artillery ammunition was stockpiled at 1000 rounds per gun, a third more than the total expended during the Russo-Japanese War but less than the French who maintained 1390 for their field artillery.

Industrialisation

Field artillery, rifle and small arms production and stock in hand were deemed to be adequate for a future war. However, Russia lacked the capacity to produce heavy artillery. To overcome this, negotiations were under way with Vickers of Britain to build and manage a factory in Tsaritsyn (later Stalingrad/Volgograd) to produce guns for the army and possibly the navy. The negotiations were protracted as the Russians were seeking to expand their domestic industrial capacity. Therefore to fill the gap one hundred and twenty-two 152mm (6-inch) guns were bought from Schneider of France and a similar order was placed in Germany for 122mm (4.8-inch) guns. Tooling and skilled workers were also brought in to allow for the licensed production of heavy artillery. Aircraft, aero engines and motor vehicles had been imported from a variety of suppliers again with an eye to creating Russian-based production facilities. It must be understood that government and private investment was viewed as long term and decisions were made on the basis that speed was not of the essence before or even after 1914.

A Junior Under Officer (corporal) of the *Pavlovski* Guards Regiment. The piping on the tunic front is white but the main distinguishing feature of this regiment was the turned up noses of the men. All the Guards regiments jealously protected their traditions and were very selective when choosing recruits. A British commentator described the Guards infantry during 1916 as, "The finest human animals in Europe."

The Russians had experimented with armoured cars for several years before 1914. Pictured here is one of the first tested. Made by the Charron Automobile Company of France it was armed with a single 8mm Hotchkiss machine gun in the turret. The gun barrel is protected in the usual Russian manner with thin sheet metal. One vehicle of this type saw service with a cavalry formation in 1914.

Training and debate

Following the 1905 revolution the army's training had taken second place to internal security missions. During the years that followed some efforts were made to expand the men's skills beyond parade ground necessities but the quality of training depended on the enthusiasm and motivation of the Military Districts' staffs which were sometimes lacking.

The officer corps was variable in quality and an inordinate amount of their time was taken up with paperwork. Although the number passing through the Staff Academy was rising and professionalism was growing, there were still many who regarded a military career as less than serious – after all, war was still perceived across much of Europe as a great adventure that would be brief and glorious.

Amongst the more serious students of military theory was Colonel A. A. Nezmanov who was closely involved in the writing of the new

Artillery officer cadets under training with the Schneider M1910 122mm (4.8 inch) howitzer in the months before 1914. This piece was imported from France and licensed to be built in Russia. Served by 8 men, it fired a 22.7kg (50lbs) shell 7,680m (8,400 yards). With modifications it served with the Red army during the Second World War.

field regulations. Nezmanov believed that the army command needed a unified doctrine for conducting a war and questioned many traditional Russian military theories. He became such a figure of controversy that the Tsar intervened personally to end the resultant disputes with the words, "Military doctrine consists of doing everything I order."

Many of those younger staff officers who shared Nezmanov's iconoclastic views found themselves sidelined and promoted to the provinces by their more conservative superiors. Money for new technology and more men coupled with the long established prowess of a Russian soldier wielding a bayonet would be more than enough to see off any enemy. The Tsar approved a further round of spending in November 1913. The "Great Programme for Strengthening the Army" would provide more men, including a further six cavalry divisions, more artillery and more equipment than ever before. Eight months later the *Duma* also gave its approval to the Great Programme which it was anticipated would take three years to complete.

Tsarist Russia did not have three years. The assassination of the Austrian heir apparent on 28 June 1914 set Europe on the slippery path to war and

The citizens of St Petersburg greeted Germany's declaration of war at the beginning of August with a vast demonstration of loyalty. But in the countryside Milukov (leader of the Kadet–Liberal party) remembered, "…eternal silence reigned". At the end of August 1914 St Petersburg became Petrograd, a more Slavonic name.

just over five weeks later the sunny avenues of Paris, Berlin, London, Vienna and St Petersburg would be ringing with the measured tread of men marching into battle.

Although Sukhomlinov had just a few months earlier declared, "Russia is ready", had the right choices been made? Nezmanov had written, "We must know what we want" about the lack of a common military doctrine. That question suddenly took on a new urgency. The realities of war would mean that incorrect choices and indecision would have to be paid for in flesh and blood. The campaigns of 1914 would be a testing time.

CHAPTER 2

1914: The Shock of War

Mobilisation and deployment

During the early summer of 1914 the Russian empire had been experiencing wave after wave of strikes and unrest. In St Petersburg itself demonstrations were an almost daily occurrence, presenting the picture of a state divided against itself. As the Balkan crisis deepened, the government authorised the armed forces to assume the condition of the Period Preparatory for War under which the class of men who were due to complete their military service was retained. As the diplomatic services attempted to prevent war, the Tsar telegraphed his cousin Kaiser Wilhelm II in a last ditch effort to resolve matters. However, when this appeal to family feeling proved useless, Nicholas issued the order for general mobilisation at 1800 hours on 31 July. Six hours later Germany declared war on Russia, followed by Austria on 6 August. Almost by magic the strikes and demonstrations ceased to be replaced by crowds declaring their unswerving loyalty to the dynasty and giving practical expression to their feelings by sacking the German embassy under the Nelsonian eye of the police.

The response to the mobilisation order was, on the whole, satisfactory: ninety-six per cent of those summoned answered the Tsar's call without a qualm. The scattered instances of trouble were generally contained without too much difficulty although at least 225 people, including sixty policemen, died. But as Sir George Buchanan, Britain's ambassador to Russia remarked, "What would be the feelings of these people for their 'Little Father' (the Tsar) were the war to be unduly prolonged?"

As his men travelled to their regiments Nicholas was dissuaded from taking the post of Supreme Commander in Chief and that honour passed to his uncle the Grand Duke Nicholas on 3 August. The Chief of Staff, General N. N. Yanushkevitch, was not the Grand Duke's choice but the first of many appointments that the Tsar would make to demonstrate his authority. When Romania and Italy declared their neutrality on 3 August the battle lines were clearly drawn. Oddly, the Romanian General Staff were

One of several Russo-Balt armoured cars that formed part of 1st Automobile Machine Gun Company leaves Petrograd shortly after the unit's formation in August 1914. This was the first such formation of its type in the world and consisted of 10 armoured vehicles. The men wore a practical all-leather uniform with a flatter than usual peaked cap.

still asking the Austrians where they should deploy as late as 8 August. Clearly news travelled slowly in Bucharest. The *Duma* was summoned to declare its solidarity with the Tsar and to vote through war credits, both objectives were achieved although with opposition from the extreme left, on 8 August. That same day Yanushkevitch visited the French ambassador, Maurice Paleologue, to inform him that the garrison of St Petersburg would be leaving for the front as, "The Government has every confidence in the maintenance of order" in the capital.

From the outset the French had been pressing for the Russians to invade not only East Prussia but also the eastern German province of Silesia. To invade Silesia the Russians would have to march across western Poland, a region virtually devoid of railways. On 14 August Nicholas declared to his Foreign Minister, "I have told the Grand Duke Nicholas to force his way to Berlin at the earliest possible moment and at any cost. I regard our operations against Austria as of secondary importance only. Our primary objective is the destruction of the German army." The Tenth (General F. V. Sievers) and Ninth (General P. A. Lechitski) armies, ordered into being on

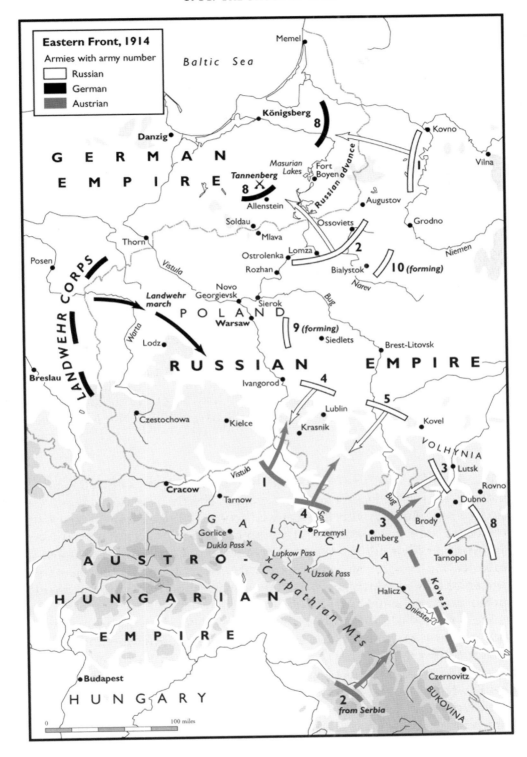

8 August, were the forces chosen for this task with their assembly points north and south of Warsaw respectively.

Meanwhile the SW Front (General N. I. Ivanov, Chief of Staff General M. V. Alexeyev) with the Third, Fourth, Fifth and Eighth armies drew up some distance inside Russia's borders, forming an arc from Lublin to the Romanian frontier. The First and Second armies of the NW Front (General I. G. Zhilinski, Chief of Staff V. A. Oranovski) gathered in another arc from Kovno to a point north west of Warsaw facing East Prussia and again well within Russian territory. By assembling thus, the risk of being surprised during the deployment phase was minimised but the distance the men would have to march to contact was, in some cases, considerable. Indeed some corps of Second Army (General A. V. Samsonov) had 128kms (80 miles) to go before they reached the border.

Communications between NW and SW fronts all had to be routed through the staff at *Stavka*, which was creating a headquarters at the railway junction of Baranovitchi, a central point to the east. However, when the Grand Duke left St Petersburg on 14 August, the communications system had not yet been set up, obliging him to travel from place to place to ensure that things flowed as smoothly as possible. At this time there was little to co-ordinate as the mobilisation and deployment were proceeding remarkably well, especially considering the distances and the lack of railways as well as the fact that neither front depended on the other. However, the almost complete freedom of action enjoyed by the front commanders was to generate problems in the not too distant future.

NW Front, Tannenberg and the Masurian Lakes

On 15 August First Army (General P. Rennenkampf) began to move on East Prussia from the east and three days later Second Army moved from the south. Neither army was completely formed and many units marched without field kitchens and other necessities. Nevertheless the invasion was underway. The Russian plan was, on paper at least, simple. First and Second armies would attempt to outflank the German Eighth Army's position by moving separately around the Masurian Lakes which, with large areas of dense forest and marshland, formed a natural line of defence. Although the combined strength of the two Russian armies was double that of the Germans, they left themselves open to defeat if they risked leaving one Russian army to its own devices and the Germans took advantage of their rail network.

Rennenkampf's First Army, having defeated two German corps (I and XVII) at Gumbinnen on 20 August, allowed the Germans to retreat without maintaining contact while informing *Stavka* that the Germans were retreating in disorder. On 26 August Zhilinski ordered Rennenkampf

№ 9. Пѣхота въ походѣ.

Men of the 13th *Belozersky* Infantry regiment on a route march in the summer of 1914. As part of 4th Division, VI Corps in Samsonov's Second Army the regiment suffered badly during the invasion of East Prussia. The 4th Division lost 73 officers and over 5000 men on 26 August. Rolled around the men's chests are their greatcoats and the officers are wearing the dark green parade trousers.

to invest the fortress of Konigsberg with, "two corps, while the remainder [two corps plus five and a half-cavalry divisions] should continue the pursuit to the Vistula." A second telegram instructed Rennenkampf to, "co-operate with Second Army by moving your left flank…". Rennenkampf then began a leisurely pursuit of some 17kms (10 miles) per day, despite the Russian field service regulations which (based on a rate designed for dirt roads) specified a distance of over 25kms (16 miles) per day for the infantry alone. The cavalry did virtually nothing. However, the Guards Cavalry Corps, in an action reminiscent of the charge of the Light Brigade, dispersed a brigade of second line infantry and captured a couple of guns at the cost of fifteen officers in a single brigade. Contact was not established with Samsonov's Second Army.

Two days later Rennenkampf was ordered to send two corps to support Second Army only to have the order rescinded as, "Second Army has withdrawn." In fact Second Army, having advanced on a front some 217kms (135 miles) wide, was in deep trouble. Lateral communications had almost completely broken down within a couple of days of the advance beginning due to a lack of sufficient telegraph or telephone cable and Samsonov was hard-pressed to control his corps' movement. The dispositions ordered for 24 August were transmitted uncoded via radio to the units concerned and intercepted by the Germans who took full advantage of the situation when making their own dispositions.

Despite a period of panic, which resulted in the replacement of the German Eighth Army's commander and Chief of Staff, the transfer of men to encircle Second Army was put in motion. A weak force remained to cover First Army. Samsonov's left was the first German target and the force of their attack shattered it. Unfortunately the centre continued to advance as it had achieved success against the Germans to its front. The Russian right was the next to go and by 28 August the Germans had drawn a slender noose around Second Army. Samsonov, his communications in tatters, knew little of these events. Although Zhilinski ordered both flank corps to attack it was to no avail. With the centre of Second Army, upwards of 100,000 men, boxed into a bewildering rectangle of marsh and forest, Samsonov attempted to join XV Corps. Wandering vaguely from unit to unit, he separated from his escort and apparently committed suicide. Some of his men fought on and others broke out of the encirclement but most were captured. By 31 August 10,000 had escaped back over the border and the Germans claimed 90,000 prisoners. The battle of Tannenberg had destroyed Second Army and now it was the turn of First Army to face the Germans who had received two corps of reinforcements plus a cavalry division from the west.

Although Rennenkampf had taken up a strong position, misleading German communications and his own instincts about the direction of the attack caused him to position his reserves in the wrong place. When two German corps hit his left flank on 7 September, First Army's rear was wide open. Although Tenth Army was gathering on Rennenkampf's left it was too weak to intervene effectively. Despite the best efforts of the First Army's central corps, retreat was inevitable. The retreat was well organised but brought no credit to Rennenkampf who according to Gourko (commander of one of First Army's cavalry divisions), "lost all self-control, and, leaving his staff departed by motor car for the Russian frontier. He eventually arrived in Kovno, abandoning all power over his forces and leaving them to get through the hazards of the retreat on their own account." Zhilinski exercised no influence over First Army, a situation exacerbated by Rennenkampf's practice of relocating his headquarters without warning.

On 13 September the Germans crossed the border into Russia and four days later Zhilinski was replaced by General N. V. Ruzski. As the Grand Duke Nicholas reported to the Tsar, "I am inclined to think that General Zhilinski has lost his head and in general is not capable of controlling operations."

But as Russian units were still moving into their concentration areas and the Germans were outrunning their supply lines the tables began to turn. First and Tenth armies mounted a successful counterattack which drove

Marching in Eastern Europe was a dry, dusty matter during the heat of the summer. The sandy soil of Poland and East Prussia threw up clouds of dust, which enabled the columns to be seen for many miles as well as increasing the men's need for rest and water.

the Germans back across the frontier so that by the end of September the line had stabilised.

On 14 September the French military attaché, in a telegram to Sukhomlinov, praised the Russian army's efforts and finished with "bravo and thanks." As a French historian succinctly remarked, "When the fronts were stabilised, the Russian army, had in the final analysis, done what was expected of it."

SW Front, Lemberg

The four armies of SW Front were made up of thirty-four infantry, and twelve cavalry divisions with some 2,100 guns. Fourth Army (General Baron A. E. Salza) with Fifth Army (General A. E. Pleve) on its right was to advance from Lublin in Poland against the left flank of the Austrian armies, which it was believed would be marching almost directly eastwards on Tarnopol. Pleve and Salza would cut the line of retreat to the fortress of Przemysl or Cracow. Third (General N. V. Ruzski) and Eighth (General A. A.

Brusilov) armies would carry out the main Russian offensive with Lemberg as their objective. The Austrian province of Galicia, of which Lemberg was the capital, was cut by a series of rivers and rolling hills. Well aware that they would have to shoulder the main burden on the Eastern Front until the arrival of the bulk of the German army from the west, the Austrians also planned to take the offensive from the outset. They anticipated linking up with a German advance from East Prussia to the east of Warsaw and it was in this direction that their First Army was moving when it encountered Russian Fourth Army moving south.

The Grand Duke Nicholas ordered the SW Front to advance on 18 August; troops who had not reached their units were to catch up on the march. Again Russian troops marched to war without their full compliment of equipment. There was not a continuous line and a screen of cavalry filled the gaps between the armies. It was to be the cavalry that fought the first divisional-sized engagement on this front at the village of Jaroslawice. The Austrians and Russians engaged in a re-enactment of an eighteenth-century battle complete with swords and knee-to-knee charges. The Russians won the day and that evening the officers of both sides engaged in an after battle dinner discussion in French. It was an extremely civilised affair, but was symbolic of a rapidly vanishing world. Further to the north at Krasnik the first real battle on this front was to unfold as Russian Fourth met Austrian First Army on 23 August. After two days of vicious fighting the Russians withdrew and Pleve's Fifth Army was ordered to wheel right in order to hit the Austrian flank, thus opening a gap of some 80kms (50 miles) with Third Army on its right. Ivanov insisted that the Grand Duke Nicholas release Ninth Army to his support. Several corps, including the Guards, were thus diverted to SW Front. Apparently the Austrians were about to pounce on the rear of First and Second armies as predicted. The Austrian Chief of Staff, von Hotzendorf, began to incline his forces to the north-west as he was unaware of the steady advance of Third and Eighth armies from the east. Russian Fifth Army was now in danger of encirclement by the rapidly moving Austrians but following the defeat of part of his army at Komarow, Pleve recognised the danger he faced and began to withdraw.

What followed next was a series of battles, again reminiscent of the eighteenth- and nineteenth-centuries, with both sides attempting to outflank one another whilst inclining their entire line to the north. With increasingly exhausted and depleted units von Hotzendorf, who was beginning to understand the full extent of the Russian invasion, attempted to lure the Russians into a trap. Although reinforcements arrived from the Serbian Front, the Austrians were unable to prevent the Russians from pouring across the provinces of Galicia and Bukovina. Attempts to counterattack or defend the river lines east of Lemberg all failed and on 3 September Ruzski's Third Army marched triumphantly into the abandoned city. The

The Cossack hero Kozma Krioutchkov pictured here having just received the first
St George Cross of the war. A member of 3rd Don Cossack Regiment, Krioutchkov
was the subject of much publicity. Thousands of patriotic postcards were sold to
commemorate his fight on the German border, each edition exaggerating the episode
more than the last.

Officers of the 17th *Arkhangelogorodsky* Infantry Regiment, in field service dress complete with swords. This regiment was part of the IX Corps in Ruzski's Third Army that invaded Austria-Hungary in August 1914. The officer in the centre has a map case attached to his waist belt. There is an interesting variety of tunics shown here.

Grand Duke Nicholas announced the victory to the Tsar, "with extreme joy and thanking God that Lvov (Lemberg) is ours."

Now it was the Austrians turn to face disaster as their First Army found itself increasingly isolated on the left. Interestingly, a corps of Silesian *Landwehr* had joined First Army on 4 September having marched, almost unchallenged, over 320kms (200miles) across Poland. The *Landwehr* were to suffer thirty per cent casualties over the next five days as First Army retreated from the vicinity of Lublin.

After the failure of his men to beat Third and Eighth armies along the Wereszyca River, von Hotzendorf gave the order for a general withdrawal behind the San River. Luckily for the battered Austrians the heavens opened and the Russians failed to pursue them vigorously. Ivanov's armies rested and prepared to advance on the Carpathian passes and Cracow.

As both fronts drew breath and Ruzski hastened to take over command of the NW Front, the Grand Duke called a conference at Cholm on 26 September. Much as *Stavka* might dictate strategic necessities, it was fast becoming impotent as much of its power lay in the allocation of resources with which to carry them out, and by now the majority of the army was in place. The transfer of units from one front to another was fraught with difficulties: not only the problems of the railway network but also the unwillingness of front commanders to relinquish control of resources.

At the Cholm conference the dilemma that was to haunt Russia throughout the war surfaced with blinding clarity – which enemy should be dealt with first? Which front should be given priority to complete a task? Nezmanov's words, if anyone recalled them, were proving all too prophetic, "We must know what we want." After the failure of the East Prussian invasion Ruzski insisted that NW Front be allowed to withdraw to a line running from the fortress at Novo Georgievsk to Kovno possibly abandoning Warsaw in the process. Such a move would expose the northern flank of SW Front at the very moment when Ivanov was pressing for a renewed offensive against the Austrians. The Grand Duke Nicholas, still under the Tsar's order to invade Silesia, decided to press ahead with this option as the Ninth and Tenth armies were almost fully assembled.

The Russian armies were now marshalled thus: First and Tenth armies covered the East Prussian border while Fifth moved north to cover their left flank. The reconstituted Second Army was to form part of the Silesian invasion group gathering around Warsaw including various formations from SW Front and commanded by Ivanov. Fourth Army would hold its position near Ivangorod, as would Ninth Army at Lublin. Brusilov's Eighth Army would screen the Carpathian Mountains and the fortress of Przemysl that contained over 100,000 men.

A Russian infantry regiment rests on the march in southern Poland during August 1914. The soldier in the centre of the image holds the regimental flag. Infantry units carried their standards into the combat zone where it remained with the reserve company. There were several instances of standards being captured during the early days of the war. The standard is wrapped in a cover to protect it from the dust.

As the Austrians fell back on Cracow the Germans, resentfully, provided support with the five corps of the newly created Ninth Army. German Ninth Army was expected to regain the initiative by advancing against, "the flank and rear of the first group of armies pursuing the Austrians who came in reach" i.e. those following up towards Cracow.

On 29 September the Germans began their march into south western Poland having re-assembled their forces by a remarkably good piece of staff work that exploited their railway system to its utmost. However, the following day the Russians discovered a set of orders on the corpse of a German officer that gave them sufficient information to modify their dispositions to face this new threat. Russian Tenth Army would undertake a series of attacks to pin the remains of Eighth Army defending East Prussia. Fourth and Ninth armies would attack the German Ninth across the Vistula River near the Ivangorod fortress bridgehead, First Army would move west and (co-operating with Second and Fifth armies) fall onto the left flank of German Ninth Army. Hindenburg would later describe this as "the Grand Duke's greatest plan".

By early October the dirt roads of Poland were blending into the fields as rain turned everything into a quagmire of knee-deep mud. As the Russians

№ 33 Наблюдательный пунктъ Командира батареи.

A splendidly posed shot of a Russian artillery spotting and communications unit. The artillery regarded itself as the cream of the Imperial army and far superior to the infantry who they disparagingly referred to as "the cattle". Pre-1914 sophisticated optical equipment was almost all imported but domestic production made up for the shortfall from 1915 onwards.

re-jigged their forces the Austrians struck across the San River and relieved Przemysl on 9 October.

Luckily for the German Ninth Army, radio intercepts indicated the extent of Russian progress on their left and again fate, this time in the form of a Russian corpse, gifted the Germans a set of plans for the Silesian invasion. The only German troops to arrive from the Western Front were committed to relieve the pressure on Eighth Army, so German XI Corps was transferred from the Ivangorod fighting to support Ninth Army's left. Arriving just in time XI Corps gave Hindenburg the opportunity to order Ninth Army to fall back to its start point at Czestochowa a distance of 97kms (60 miles) away. Austrian First Army withdrew on Cracow in line with the Germans and further south von Hotzendorf assigned units to cover the Carpathian passes where the first snows of winter were falling. Elsewhere torrential rain and the zeal of German engineers in destroying bridges and railway lines hampered the speed of their pursuers.

Once again the Silesian invasion assumed first place on the Grand Duke's priority list but now it was to be carried out by Second, Fourth, Fifth and Ninth armies and would be lead by Ruzski. The advance was to begin on

14 November. Indeed *Stavka* had due cause for optimism: the Germans had been driven from Poland, their Eighth Army was under severe pressure and the Austrians were apparently on the verge of collapse as Przemysl was once again cut off.

However, the complexity of the latest Russian deployment was time consuming and the Grand Duke was adamant that the flanks of the invasion force be secure. Consequently the Central Powers, alerted yet again by poor Russian radio discipline, were forearmed and by dint of another piece of transportation and staff wizardry transported Ninth Army into a position where it could hit the right flank of the invasion force. Incredibly, the Russians were completely unaware of their enemy's movements which were completed by 10 November. The Germans attacked the following day.

The battle for Warsaw

Ruzski and *Stavka* regarded the initial German attack as a feint and it was not until the 14/15 November that the full extent of their problems became apparent. Second and Fifth armies were ordered to fall back on Lodz and First Army was instructed to move to their support. Within a week Russian resistance had turned the situation around and German Ninth Army found itself in an increasingly difficult position as it attempted to encircle Lodz and fend off Russian relief efforts from the north and east. Ninth Army had reached the limits of its supply lines and was running short of munitions. However, the critical moment passed and the Germans were able to fight their way out of a threatened encirclement. Once again *Stavka's* plan for an invasion of Germany had come to nothing.

On the SW Front the situation looked more promising, the Austrian offensive that had begun on 18 November had achieved nothing and Cracow was now in clear danger as were the Carpathian passes from the steadily advancing Third (General Radko-Dimitriev) and Eighth armies. Such was the concern at Austrian HQ that consideration was given to the defences of the Budapest and the Danube River bridges.

On 29 November the Grand Duke chaired another front commanders' conference at which Ruzski again requested permission to withdraw east of the Vistula River and Ivanov asked for more troops to open, "the way to Berlin…through Austria-Hungary," Ivanov was given Ninth Army. It was now the turn of the Austrian staff officers to display their virtuosity as von Hotzendorf prepared to attack the left flank of Third Army at the point where its tenuous connections with Eighth Army's right were almost non-existent. In fact Eighth Army's advance into the Carpathian foothills had been reduced to a crawl by the transfer of several divisions to help contain the Austrian offensive of mid-November. Consequently, on 3 December,

One of the *Stavka* Rolls Royces, in pristine condition (given the season), is carefully driven aboard its special railway wagon. Facing the camera is General A. N. Kuropatkin and members of his staff and escort. Hundreds of private motor vehicles were commandeered during the first months of the war for use as staff cars or ambulances. The British manufactured Austin was a particular favourite.

when the Austrians attacked Third Army's left with troops moved from the Cracow defences, Brusilov had little to spare. As the Austrians transferred more men to support their initial successes, so did Ivanov. Austrian Third Army subjected Eighth Army, at a standstill, to an attack which pushed it back from the Carpathian passes. On 10 December Ivanov was obliged to order Third Army to retreat and align itself with Eighth Army. Nine days later Lodz fell to the Germans.

The route to Berlin via Austria-Hungary had proved to be as elusive as that through East Prussia or Silesia. The first four months of the war had come as an incredible shock to the nations of Europe and as ammunition stocks fell to what were perceived as catastrophically low levels, all the belligerents experienced what became known as "shell shortage": a phrase that included all forms of military necessities from caps to bayonets.

The vision of a short, glorious war had proved to be an illusion as men shivered and froze in their thousands among the Carpathians or

Not all regiments were as fastidious about their men's physical appearance as the Guards. The minimum height requirement was 1.54m (5.04 feet) which does not seem to have been applied to the man on the far right.

hauled their weary limbs through the soul-destroying morass of Poland. Incredibly, Russia's supply depots had insufficient winter uniforms but more worrying was the diminishing supply of small arms, ammunition and artillery shell. The appeals of first the front commanders and then *Stavka* had been viewed as absurd. The War Council had turned down a request for two million shells in September but by the end of the year it was decided to place substantial orders abroad mainly in Britain and the USA. As a stopgap 80,000 Arisaka rifles were bought from Japan but a request to return rifles captured during the Russo-Japanese War was refused as, "they had been destroyed". American and British manufacturers snapped up Russian orders but accorded them a low priority, as there were equal if not better profits to be made from the British government, which was more co-operative in the matter of supplying information and specifications. A Russian order for artillery fuses placed with a British manufacturer fell behind by a year due to a lack of guns on which to test the shells. This was along with other difficulties, including the natural desire of the British government to ensure that munitions production for their army received priority. American firms were unable to provide rifles within the specified time because they lacked the capacity to do so. Domestically the War Ministry had not developed a strong relationship with private industry before the war and at first did not see any reason to do so, believing that the state arsenals alone were capable of producing such sophisticated products as rifles. Imports would make up any shortfall as in the past.

As 1914 ended, Russian losses numbered over 1,500,000 men. From the four and-a-half million called to the colours and the officer corps, roughly 40,000 in August had been decimated. On 21 October an *Ukase* (a decree of the Tsar) had established special officer training schools providing short courses to refill the ranks with men chosen from student conscripts.

Shortcomings were becoming apparent across the spectrum from supply and procurement to care for the wounded. During the first month of the war two civilian organisations had come into being, the Union of Rural Councils, the *Zemstva*, and the Union of Towns. These two groups provided clothing, medicines and care for the wounded on a vast scale to supplement the inadequate efforts of the central government. Yet when a conference of *Duma* politicians, industrialists and private individuals gathered in late 1914 to discuss how they could contribute to the war effort the Interior Minister N. A. Maklakov accused them of fomenting revolution!

During December the Grand Duke had requested that the French make more effort on their front to prevent the transfer of German forces to the east. Shortly after this both the British and French ambassadors were told by the Chief of the War Ministry's Staff, General M. A. Beliaev, that the rifle shortage was critical. In another telegram to the French on 5 January the Grand Duke suggested he would have to go over to the defensive unless he received supplies of ammunition. Nevertheless, *Stavka* began planning another offensive, this time in East Prussia, which was to begin on 23 February to allow time for munitions to accumulate and be distributed. Distribution itself was becoming a problem as the number of serviceable locomotives and wagons was running dangerously low. But as Ruzski laid his plans, Ivanov, who should have gone over to the defensive, quietly prepared his own offensive.

On the home front the truce between workers and factory owners had begun to show signs of strain. The number of strikes had fallen to almost zero during the summer and early autumn but was now beginning to rise as inflation cut into the buying power of their wages. Many of the factories in Petrograd (as St Petersburg was patriotically renamed in August 1914) had relied on British coal to keep their furnaces burning but stocks were running short and transporting coal from the mines of southern Russia placed yet more strain on the railways.

Nicholas II's empire had weathered the first period of the war and, despite heavy losses in men and materiel, had survived. Almost everywhere the army stood on enemy soil and was planning, once again, to take the offensive. The Turkish invasion of the Caucasus, in December, was contained by the local forces with no transfer of men from either European front and had ended in disaster for the Ottoman forces involved. Maybe 1915 would prove to be a time of victories for the Tsar.

CHAPTER 3

1915: A Time of Mixed Fortunes

On 1 January 1915 von Hotzendorf met with his German opposite number Falkenhayn and requested support for his armies in Galicia to relieve Przemysl cut off since 11 November. The German Commander in the east, von Hindenburg and his Chief of Staff, Ludendorff, proposed a joint attack for which he too would need reinforcements from the west. In effect the plan was a revival of that which the Austrians apparently believed to have been in place in August 1914: a pincer movement from East Prussia and Galicia to drive the Russians from Poland. Falkenhayn regarded the Eastern Front as a distraction but was overruled and permission was given for men to go east. The first phase of the offensive would involve German Eighth and Tenth armies encircling Russian Tenth Army (General V. E. Flug) which occupied a position inside East Prussia similar to that of Rennenkampf in late August.

Russian preparations for their offensive involved the creation of a new army, Twelfth (General P. A. Pleve) to the left of Flug along the Narew River.

The battle of the Masurian Lakes

The Germans launched a series of local attacks to distract the Russians before the main offensive, one of which included the first use of gas by the Germans at the village of Bolimov on 31 January. The gas used was xylyl bromide (a tear gas) but it failed to react correctly due to the sub-zero temperature.

The main German attack struck the left of Flug's line on 7 February and due to the bad weather managed to take the Russians by surprise. When the right of the line was attacked the following day this sector began to crumble, as it was the weaker of the flanks. Ruzski, concerned for the assembly points of Twelfth Army, moved his reserves to the Narew River and granted Flug permission to withdraw to a line running from Kovno to

In the Carpathian Mountains during the winter of 1914–15 more troops of both sides died from illness or exposure than in combat. This bleak image captures the conditions after a bombardment.

Ossoviets fortress. However, this was easier said than done as Flug's right was in chaos, his rear under threat and XX Corps cut off in the Augustow Forest. A combination of appalling weather and the valiant defensive efforts of XX Corps slowed German progress and allowed much of Flug's army to escape. *Stavka* rushed men to Bialystok and Grodno but on 22 February XX Corps surrendered, bringing Russian losses to over 50,000 men and 185 guns. Much of German Eighth Army was then committed to besieging Ossoviets which, despite the weight of artillery ranged against it, held firm. By late February, the Germans had reached the limit of their endurance and supply lines and Russian counterattacks stabilised the line along the border. As the armies of the NW Front realigned themselves, events on SW Front were taking a more positive turn.

The fall of Przemysl

Von Hotzendorf's offensive had run into trouble almost from the start. Again the weather was appalling but this did not play to the Austrian's advantage: although they recaptured some ground it was at such a cost

A Russian outpost in the siege lines around Przemysl. The men appear to be *Opolchenie* judging by the colour of their tunics. Many of the units employed in the sieges were second line formations. The sandy soil of the region did not lend itself readily to the digging of solid trenches, which were often little more than deep ditches that afforded little protection.

that the relief of Przemysl became impossible and the prospect of linking up with the Germans sheer fantasy. Russian Eleventh Army (General A. N. Selivanov), mainly formed of reserve divisions, had completed the investment of Przemysl in December but guns capable of reducing the fortresses had only reached the area in the New Year. As von Hotzendorf's men struggled forward, the Russians began their bombardment and sapped towards the Austrian lines. During early March a height was taken, enabling the Russian guns to dominate a considerable portion of the defences. Although the Austrians attempted to break out they failed and pulled back to their fortifications. With its supplies almost exhausted, the garrison surrendered on 22 March and over 100,000 men went into captivity along with much equipment and artillery. Once again a success on the SW Front went someway to offsetting failure elsewhere. In the days immediately before the fall of Przemysl *Stavka* put NW Front on the defensive and chose to pursue an offensive to capture the Carpathian passes. Ruzski resigned in protest and was replaced by Alexeyev who had formerly been Ivanov's Chief of Staff.

SW Front made progress against increasingly demoralised Austrian forces provoking von Hotzendorf to make a further appeal to the Germans

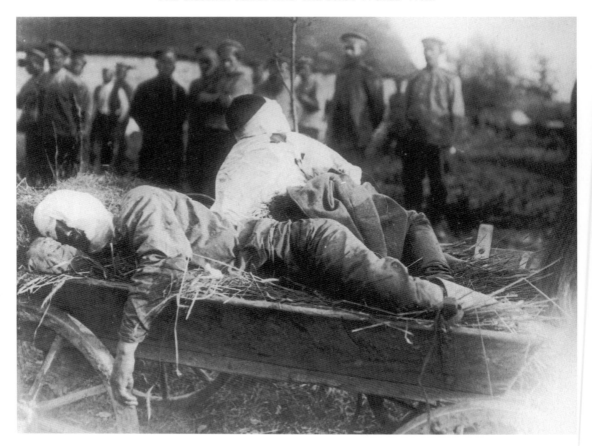

Casualty evacuation by *panji* wagon. Two men of 1st Caucasian Rifle Brigade (I Caucasian Corps). Voluntary organisations undertook much work for the wounded and by 1915 were operating in a very efficient manner. The local *panji* wagon despite being a delicate looking vehicle was well adapted to the mud and snow.

for support. On 10 April the thaw began and Ivanov halted the advance, as the roads were becoming impassable. Operations were to resume when the weather improved during May. To this end Eleventh Army moved to Eighth Army's right and Ninth Army to its left in the Bukovina to extend the scope of the offensive and possibly influence Romania to join the Allies. Italy was on the point of declaring war on Austria-Hungary and it was believed that these two new protagonists would spell doom for the Hapsburg Empire. The inclination of SW Front to the south left Third Army somewhat isolated and *Stavka* proved incapable of providing much in the way of support as NW Front refused to part with more than a single corps. If *Stavka* had believed that Alexeyev would prove more amenable to SW Front's requirements than Ruzski then they were sadly mistaken. Alexeyev's attitude was based on his concerns for an upcoming German

Everyday life in the front line could be intensely monotonous. Keeping watch and general housekeeping tasks were what passed the time. The three seated men appear to have received new undergarments: an event that often presaged an attack. A telephone line is strung precariously along the rear wall of the trench.

offensive on his front as the Germans had launched a series of small attacks at various points. Furthermore, French and British reports told of several German divisions leaving the west. Falkenhayn's offensive was to begin on 1 May against SW Front.

The breakthrough at Gorlice-Tarnow

The main target for the Central Powers was Third Army. In late April substantial German forces moved quietly into the lines opposite Radko-Dimitriev's army. The Germans had brought with them an overwhelming number of heavy guns. There had been little fighting in this area for some weeks and as the Catholic and Orthodox Easter celebrations had coincided an unofficial truce had been enjoyed by the men of both sides. Inconceivable as it may seem to minds attuned to the trenches of Flanders, the gap between the lines was up to 3.2kms (two miles) wide and often filled with grazing sheep. The local population was generally pro-Russian and provided news of the arrival of German troops. Nevertheless little or nothing was done to prepare for it. *Stavka's* commitment to the offensive had not encouraged the digging of trenches on an extensive scale and the bulk of its infantry was lodged in the front line. In addition, very few sectors of the line had much in the way of serious defence. Brusilov describes them graphically. "In practice our field works consisted of a single line of trenches made simply anyhow without any trenches communicating with the rear, and in the case of a prolonged bombardment of any kind, but especially by heavy guns, they were quickly blown in, and the men holding them were either wiped out by the hurricane of fire, or else surrendered in order to escape certain death."

When the German bombardment began, Third Army's central front line between the towns of Gorlice and Tarnow ceased to exist as did the best part of two divisions of reservists. Over the course of the next few days men were rushed forward in a desperate but vain attempt to stem the Austro-German advance which now entered open country where the only bar to a rapid advance was the establishment of dependable supply lines. Those elements of Third Army in the Carpathians withdrew in reasonably good order but the uncoordinated counter attacks in the centre simply increased the sharply rising death toll. At first *Stavka* insisted on defending every metre of ground to the end but on 10 May Ivanov, at first equally jingoistic, granted permission for Third Army to fall back to the San River. Despite this crisis Ninth Army, to the south, pressed ahead with its attack and had almost succeeded in driving the Austrians from the Bukovina by the middle of May.

Although Third Army achieved some success against Austrian First Army late in May and Italy joined the allies on 25 May, these events did nothing to blunt the Central Powers' drive. According to Russian statistics SW Front lost over 400,000 men during May and Third Army was reduced to a "harmless mob." In part this was due to the reinforcing of Third and other armies with thousands of ill-trained, poorly equipped local *Opolchenie* who were thrown into battle with little or no preparation and who had little if any enthusiasm for sacrificing themselves in what they perceived as a lost cause.

But reaching the San River granted Third Army (General L. V. Lesh from 16 June) little respite. Having gained two bridgeheads Mackensen's Austro-German force was to begin the process all over again and on 3 June Przemysl was recaptured without a struggle.

Third Army's Chief of Staff, supported by his corps commanders, placed much of the blame for the army's collapse on the surrender of thousands

A remarkable image for the period. The wire entanglements on the Eastern Front were always less well developed than those in the west, but nonetheless effective. Unlike the Western Front, no-man's land could extend up to one or two kilometres, with peasant families living between the opposing trench lines.

of reservists and *Opolchenie*. It is also pertinent to note the attitude of many artillery officers who, anxious to conserve limited supplies of shell, would not provide fire support for second line units, the men of which were frequently referred to as "cattle". In a remarkable precursor of Stalinist behaviour, General V. V. Smirnov went so far as to threaten to court martial prisoners of war on their return to Russia. *Stavka*, itself concerned by reports of mass surrender, issued a directive to officers that, "there should be no hesitation before the harshest punishment in order that discipline be restored."

During these weeks the NW Front also found itself under German pressure but in a milder form, although a major gas attack had caused almost 8000 casualties. Hindenburg, under orders to prevent the transfer of reserves from NW to SW Front, had launched a mainly cavalry force across the Niemen River into Russia's province of Courland (Lithuania) in mid-April. Although Alexeyev recognised it for what it was, *Stavka* insisted he rush troops to the area in support of the few cavalry squadrons, Frontier Guard, and *Opolchenie* battalions that defended the river line from Kovno fortress to the Baltic Sea. Kovno's defences were regarded as a sufficient

Съ театра войны. Автомобиль—прожекторъ.

Searchlights were a popular asset with many European armies during WW1. Initially intended to illuminate the battlefields at night and interdict any reconnaissance or night attacks they were cumbersome and easily located. Each of the 39 Sapper battalions included a searchlight section.

deterrent to any major incursion in this region that had seen little if any fighting. The Russian navy had a small base at Libau but a much larger one at Riga and it was felt that these must be protected from a land attack. Over the next two months both sides increased their forces in this barren flatland. However, Libau was taken and the Russians were defeated at Shavle roughly half way between Riga and Kovno.

The retreat from Poland

To address the problems appearing everywhere along the 1700km (1056 miles) front the Grand Duke called a conference at Cholm on 17 June. Both Alexeyev and Ivanov counselled a retreat to shorten the line and create a reserve. *Stavka* felt this would provoke a German offensive in Poland which was daily becoming more exposed by the worsening situation on the flanks. However, it was decided to give up Galicia and retire slowly to the border but to defend Poland utilising the fortress system. In effect the Russian Army would be defending its own territory and rebuilding its

A rifle repair workshop of the 99th *Ivangorodsky* Infantry Regiment. Such was the shortage of rifles that special collection details were organised and a reward offered to those men who recovered weapons from the battlefield.

strength in much the same way as had been outlined in the pre-war plans for the early war period prior to going over to the offensive. The decision to hold the Polish salient was a matter of pragmatism, politics and prestige. In the first place a withdrawal from Poland risked being cut off from the north by a German incursion and the fortresses at least provided some stability. Furthermore Ossoviets and Ivangorod had held fast during previous offensives and would probably do so again. Finally the fortresses were a symbol of Russian power in Poland: what would be the effect on the Poles and on Russian public opinion should they be abandoned?

Another problem was that the fortresses were full of guns and ammunition and their evacuation would place an unbearable strain on the already over-taxed railway network. Would it not therefore be preferable, as Ivanov had said, "to hold our positions with the greatest tenacity in order to force the enemy to use up an enormous amount of ammunition"? If the Germans wanted an artillery duel why not give them one on more equal terms than those granted to Third Army? In some circles there was also the hope that Novo Georgievsk, the largest of the fortresses, would prove to be a Russian Przemysl and tie down an enemy army for months and thus go some way to restoring the glory of Russian arms. Unfortunately Russian prowess and prestige took another battering when Lemberg was recaptured by the Austrians on 22 June.

The Central Powers now began to mass their forces for a resumption of their offensives in three directions, one in Galicia, one in Poland and a third in Lithuania. These thrusts were aimed at Brest-Litovsk, Warsaw, and Riga respectively. Now that the Russians had lost the initiative completely and were in some disarray, the Central Powers, increasingly dominated by Germany, anticipated that they would be unable to use what reserves were available to any effect. All three attacks began in mid-July.

In Poland, now completely under NW Front's control, the Germans broke through the Russian lines due to a poorly timed insertion of reserves and the foolhardiness of the local commander who insisted that retreat was unacceptable and condemned his men to a pointless sacrifice. On 19 July Alexeyev was permitted to withdraw to the Vistula River and evacuate Warsaw "if necessary". For the next two weeks Alexeyev's forces retired in good order and on 4 August the Germans entered Warsaw. Ossoviets, the key to this operation, held out magnificently allowing the retreat to proceed with no danger of interruption from the north. However, its bigger brothers fell remarkably easily. The situation was much the same in Galicia, a steady retreat of several kilometres a day and then a defensive action. This process continued throughout the summer, Brest-Litovsk fortress falling on 26 August.

By 22 August the Polish salient was almost flattened out. Novo Georgievsk did not prove to be the Russian Przemysl, surrendering with scarcely a murmur on 20 August. Unfortunately almost an entire corps of reserves, 1,680 guns and a mountain of ammunition were lost.

However it was Riga that caused *Stavka's* alarm bells to ring furiously. Terrified by the prospect of a seaborne attack on Petrograd supported by cavalry dashing along the Baltic coastline, Alexeyev was categorically ordered to send considerable forces north. Sixth Army (General van der Flit) was in reality a shell, consisting of a motley collection of reservists, *Opolchenie* and local cavalry. Fear for Riga and the capital combined with Alexeyev's concentration on events to the south led to the creation of a separate Northern Front (N Front) that Ruzski was recalled to command. NW Front now, 17 August, became Western Front (W Front). This alteration was only part of the process of change that had begun earlier in the summer as a result of the disasters at the front. After a year of war there were many who believed that Russia needed a fundamental change in the way it was governed if survival, let alone victory, was to be achieved.

The Tsar presents St George crosses to men of the Guards Rifles at Novo Minsk railway station in Poland on 30 (17 old style) December 1914. In a letter to his wife the Tsar commented that he lunched with the regimental and brigade officers and was, "delighted with the Rifles."

Changes

From the beginning of the war there had been a confusion of priorities. The two main fronts had pursued operations that moved in different directions at the end of increasingly tenuous supply lines vaguely co-ordinated through *Stavka*. With the addition of the Silesian invasion force yet another factor entered an equation that was growing beyond the capacity of the system to balance.

By Christmas even the most convinced believers in the concept of a short war were having to reconsider their ideas as this was fast becoming a war without precedent. Nevertheless the Russian army in January 1915 held more territory than had been lost and had blunted their enemies' efforts to drive them out. However, the faults in the system were beginning to show and criticism of the regime was becoming increasingly vocal. Obviously something had to be done to improve matters, the question was what? One thing was clear above all else: no blame must attach itself to the Tsar. That was unthinkable, as he was the embodiment of the state.

From the war's beginning the Tsar had exercised power like a true autocrat. Under Article 87 of the Fundamental Laws he was empowered to act without recourse to the *Duma* due to, "extraordinary circumstances" which the war most certainly was. Legislation was merely discussed by the Council of Ministers, agreed by the Tsar and became law by dint of imperial *Ukase*: a remarkably simple process. The *Duma* called for a single day in August 1914 was closed until February 1915 when the Tsar summoned it to rubber stamp various economic measures. Many *Duma* members had thrown themselves into war work, devoting their efforts to relieving the condition of the wounded, refugees, and soldier's orphans and widows. However, the Provisional Committee of the *Duma* (PCD) acquired a political significance by acting as the guardian of the interests of the *Duma* and met, unofficially, at least twice a week. But as the situation at the front worsened, the discussions of the PCD began to range beyond its agenda of humanitarian work. In fact the Grand Duke Nicholas at *Stavka* and various senior officers had contacted members of the PCD when their efforts to improve the supply of munitions through the War Ministry had failed. This alliance of aristocratic military vested interest and political bourgeois presented a strange picture yet both recognised their mutual need for support in the peculiar circumstances of Tsarist Russia. On the one hand the soldiers, from the army commander down, were crying out for arms and ammunition; on the other hand the War Minister was claiming all was well and good. However, the condition of the army, as witnessed by *Duma* members and others, led to suspicions that all was not well at the front or the rear. The medical services had proved inadequate and had required a civilian initiative to improve them, winter clothing had proved inadequate and a similar initiative was addressing that problem. During the session of the *Duma*, which lasted from 9–11 February 1915, Sukhomlinov the War Minister spoke to the Committee for National Defence assuring its members that the army was adequately provided for. This assurance notwithstanding, special powers were granted by the Tsar to the Ministry of Transport to alleviate the problems facing the railways in distributing munitions and supplies for the armed forces and those enterprises supplying them.

As disaster heaped upon disaster in the spring of 1915 the search for scapegoats began. Tannenberg had been Samsonov's fault but he was dead, Zhilinski had been replaced and other failed generals had also been removed. Blame was scattered far and wide, ranging from the lack of weapons and munitions, the apparent eagerness of the men to surrender or run, Jews spying for the Central Powers to "unseen hands" in high places who sympathised with the Germans and sabotaged Russia's efforts.

Rumour and innuendo even began to include members of the royal family, particularly the German born Tsaritsa whose social aloofness had increased since the birth of her haemophiliac son in 1904 and who was distinctly unpopular with the aristocracy, not to mention the ordinary people. Refugees and wounded soldiers added, often creatively, to the tales of woe that circulated telling of German artillery – the like of which no one could imagine – as well as gas and other horrors of modern warfare. These stories had a profound impact on the minds of people for whom the next town was another world, let alone the firing line far away to the west.

Increasingly the fingers of accusation began to point at one man: the War Minister. Sukhomlinov, in post since 1909, had been implicated in a notorious (and rigged) espionage trial in 1915 and he had evidently lied to the Committee for National Defence in February. On 20 June a Special Council was created which took the general management of army supply from the War Minister. Its membership included industrialists and *Duma* members. On 26 June General A. A. Polivanov replaced Sukhomlinov. The Tsar, in a state of extreme concern over the situation, summoned the *Duma*. This was not an order he was ever happy to give and therefore a measure of his distress. Another tier of committees was formed including *Duma* members, which had the power to set food and commodity prices among other things. Although the Tsar retained the power of veto, the forces of parliamentary government viewed these events as massive progress towards liberalising the regime. In the *Duma* the cry went up for a, "government enjoying the confidence of the people."

This appeal coincided with a letter to the Tsar from his Council of Ministers imploring Nicholas to reconsider his decision to take over the role of Supreme Commander in Chief from his uncle, a decision to which very few were privy. Polivanov, who had been given the task of informing the Grand Duke of his removal, had revealed the secret to the Council. Several factions within the government, the military and the bureaucracy had been working away behind the scenes to engineer the Grand Duke's fall. Not least amongst them was the Tsaritsa who regarded him as a possible rival for the throne.

Alexandra, living a more and more isolated existence at Tsarskoe Selo had surrounded herself with a motley collection of mystics and sycophants including the notorious Rasputin. These characters were to feed her paranoid mind with a combination of pseudo religious and political advice, which was to have dire consequences for the monarchy during the next 18 months. Nor had his connections with industrialists and politicians improved the Grand Duke's position. With Russia's armies everywhere in retreat the fall of Kovno fortress in mid-August was the event that sealed the Grand Duke's fate.

The Tsar took up the post of Supreme Commander in Chief on 1 September 1915 and appointed Alexeyev as his Chief of Staff, General A. E. Evert replacing him at W Front. During the next fortnight Nicholas prorogued the *Duma* thus ending any hope for a "Ministry with Public

Confidence". The Grand Duke was promoted sideways to become the Viceroy of the Caucasus.

Change of command

As his ministers were well aware, Nicholas was no soldier – and certainly no strategist – and his characteristic indecision was often compounded by acting too late and with too little consideration of the matter in hand. One of them commented, "We are sitting on a powder keg…the Sovereign Emperor's assumption of the army's command is not just merely a spark but a whole candle thrown into a powder magazine." Nicholas' reasons for taking command are unclear. Possibly it was a mixture of his sense of duty and his firm belief in fate, along with the desire to sacrifice himself for the good of the empire. Or maybe he just wished to distance himself from the political stew of Petrograd. The French ambassador recorded a remark of the Tsar's in March 1916 referring to the matter. "Yes, that was a terrible moment for me. I thought God had deserted me, and a victim was necessary to save Russia." In practical terms it left the government of Russia without its ultimate arbiter immediately to hand. Now the decision making process would be carried out by telephone, telegram or letter or over the Hughes Apparatus (a teleprinter).

The *Stavka* where the Tsar, sometimes accompanied by his son, took up residence had relocated to the town of Moghilev on the Dnieper River: a picturesque situation allowing him to row and drive into the countryside. He later recalled the time he spent there as one of the happiest times of his life. This is understandable as he took to the role of figurehead with delight, reviewing parades, visiting hospitals and presenting medals in much the same way as his cousins King George V and Kaiser Wilhelm II. Unfortunately Nicholas was regarded by many of his superstitious subjects as unlucky and faith in his ability to lead the army was singularly lacking This widespread belief was based on the fact that Nicholas was born on Job the Sufferer's day, a negative association compounded by the deaths of hundreds of people during the celebrations for his coronation and his marriage which followed rapidly after the death of his father. Defeat at the hands of the Japanese and latterly the Central Powers only intensified the pessimism of his subjects. In fact Nicholas' arrival at *Stavka* coincided with the last efforts of the Central Powers and several Russian victories.

The operations of the Central Powers during late August and early September 1915 continued on the northern and southern flanks as in the centre they had reached the vast wetland known as the Pripyat Marshes which was an area where fighting was virtually impossible. To the north the main objective was Vilna. Ludendorff, against Falkenhayn's wishes

Men of the *Opolchenie*, the Imperial Militia, pose awkwardly for the camera before leaving for the front. The call-up of these formations could only be made by an express order from the Tsar himself. Their dress was the responsibility of the local government in the district from which they were recruited and was frequently of an obsolete style as shown here. The bronze cross on their caps denotes they are militia.

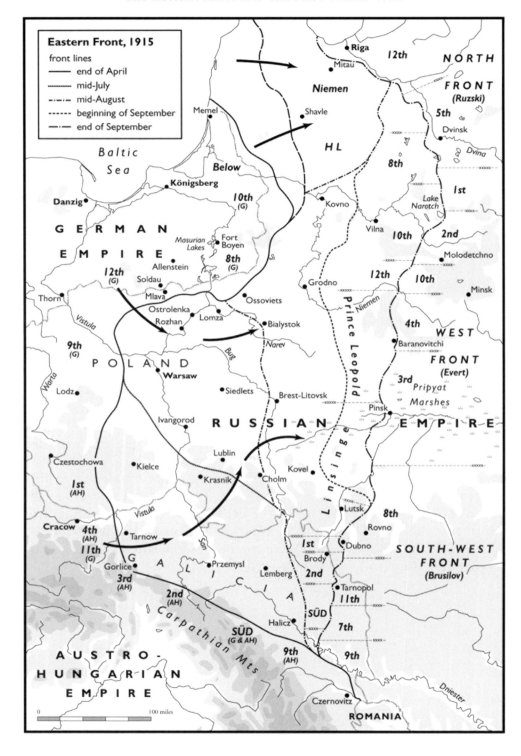

Eastern Front, 1915

front lines

— end of April

········· mid-July

—·—·— mid-August

------- beginning of September

—·—·— end of September

Baltic Sea

Riga
Mitau
12th
NORTH
FRONT
(Ruzski)
Niemen
Shavle
5th
Memel
HL
Dvinsk
Below
8th
Dvina
Königsberg
10th
(G)
Kovno
1st
Lake Narotch
Danzig
Vilna
10th
2nd
GERMAN
Masurian Lakes
Fort Boyen
Molodetchno
EMPIRE
8th
(G)
Allenstein
12th
10th
Minsk
12th
(G)
Soldau
Grodno
4th
WEST
Thorn
Mlava
Ostrolenka
Ossoviets
Baranovitchi
FRONT
Rozhan
Lomza
Bialystok
(Evert)
Vistula
Narev
3rd
Pripyat
9th
(G)
Bug
Marshes
POLAND
Warsaw
Pinsk
Warta
Lodz
Siedlets
Brest-Litovsk
RUSSIAN
EMPIRE
Ivangorod
Czestochowa
Kielce
Lublin
Kovel
Cholm
Krasnik
Lutsk
8th
1st
(AH)
Vistula
Rovno
Cracow
4th
(AH)
Tarnow
1st
Dubno
SOUTH-WEST
11th
(G)
San
Brody
FRONT
Gorlice
G
Przemysl
2nd
(Brusilov)
3rd
(AH)
Lemberg
Tarnopol
2nd
(AH)
11th
Carpathian Mts
Halicz
SÜD
AUSTRO-
SÜD
(G & AH)
7th
HUNGARIAN
9th
(AH)
9th
EMPIRE
Dniester
Czernovitz
0   100 miles
ROMANIA

Prince Leopold

Linsingen

opened a frontal attack on Vilna in early September. This effort failed but an outflanking movement to the north of the city succeeded in cutting the Vilna–Riga rail link and threatened to trap Tenth Army in and around the city. As Russian reserves were moved into the area the Germans launched a considerable force of cavalry towards the vital rail junction of Molodetchno, some 121kms (75 miles) behind Russian lines, while continuing to batter at the front of Vilna. Alexeyev assembled Second Army to the east of Vilna from where it struck at the advancing German cavalry. Unsupported by and separated from their infantry the German cavalry were defeated and driven back, suffering considerable losses in the process. Despite this success Vilna was abandoned, the Germans marching in on 18 September. Another Russian victory in the region of Pinsk and Falkenhayn's demand for more troops for the Western Front obliged Ludendorff to call a halt and, on 26 September, order his men to dig in.

Von Hotzendorf believed that it was possible to push into Ukraine and to this end launched the "Black-Yellow" Offensive named for the colours of the Hapsburgs. Although initially successful, by mid-September the Austrians were in trouble. Brusilov's Eighth Army, attacking the Austrian flank between Rovno and Lutsk, had recaptured Lutsk, another important rail junction, taken by the Austrians on 31 August. Austrian casualties, predominantly prisoners, amounted to over 70,000. Such was the scale of the disaster that German and Austrian forces *en route* to Serbia were diverted to prop up this sector. The Russians were driven from Lutsk but it was the Central Powers' last effort on the Eastern Front. By early October, following some jockeying for local tactical advantage, the fighting died down as both sides took stock.

With the Polish bulge ironed out the front now ran from the outskirts of Riga to the border of Romania in almost a straight line. Although the Russians had conceded vast swathes of territory the length of the front had fallen from almost 1,700kms (1,076 miles) to just over 1,000kms (621 miles), allowing for the creation of an almost continuous line with the opportunity to generate a substantial pool of reserves.

CHAPTER 4

Winter 1915–16

During September Polivanov had announced to the French that the Russian army would attack before the year's end. With the Central Powers' attention diverted to the Serbian campaign it seemed an opportune moment for SW Front to mount an offensive against the Austrians.

Seventh Army (General D. G. Shcherbachev), deployed on the Black Sea coastline, was to be used for the attack supported by Ninth Army (General P. A. Lechitski). *Stavka* issued its orders in late November, but it was another month before the attack began on 27 December. On paper the plan was good, replicating the German methods of the summer. As there were no flanks to turn, the attack would be frontal. The infantry would attack on a narrow front, little more than a kilometre, following a devastating bombardment by massed artillery including significant numbers of heavy guns amply supplied with shell. It was anticipated that the Austrian trenches would be flattened and the survivor's resistance negligible. To exploit the anticipated breakthrough two cavalry corps shivered behind the lines. But this was not the summer and the snow negated much of the thirty-six hour barrage's effect. Furthermore the Austrians had plenty of warning of the direction of the attack as the Russian infantry had to march several kilometres to take up their positions and made little effort to conceal their movements across the snow from prowling Austrian aircraft. When the first waves of infantry had gone in, the reserves had to be marched up to the front line as there were no convenient positions nearby where they could be assembled. Consequently all momentum was lost. The Austrian artillery had not been located and therefore was not able to offer powerful support against attacking infantry, reserves and Russian gun positions. Nor had the Austrian trench system been reconnoitred with any care and the problems that it would bring had been underestimated – at some points the attackers even had to cover over a kilometre of no man's land before reaching them. Yet despite all of this, the field regulations of 1912 which stated, "Offensive action is the best method of obtaining our object" was still closely followed.

So when the barrage lifted and the Russians left their positions they shouted "Urrah" in the time honoured fashion and surged forward led by their officers. At first the Austrian lines were silent but at 500m (547yards) red flashes followed by the hum of bullets and the screams of the wounded showed that the Russian artillery had not accomplished its purpose. Although the Austrian first line was taken, the Russians failed to hold it, and the narrowness of the attack zone allowed the Austrian artillery to enfilade the whole area. Several days of bitter attack and counter attack followed in what was termed by some as the "Polesie Quadrille" Polesie being an alternative name for the Pripyat region. At the cost of 50,000 casualties the Russians had learned the grim truth that more shells did not necessarily mean greater success nor had they the bitter consolation of reoccupying some land as they withdrew to roughly their original positions. The lesson was not taken to heart as three months later another equally costly one was to be delivered to N Front at Lake Narotch.

The London Times observed laconically at the end of these operations, "The losses on both sides were considerable, and probably more or less even. Their sum total was not far from 150,000." From the newspaper that much of the world regarded as almost the official voice of Britain it was a somewhat dismissive report.

As 1915 drew to a close everywhere, with the exception of a part of SW Front, the Russian army was fighting on its own soil. The "Great Retreat" had ended and trench warfare had finally begun. With the Central Powers occupied, the Germans with preparations for the Verdun operation and the Austrians with Italy, the Russians were granted a welcome respite.

Allied mistrust

Throughout the summer, from *Stavka* down the chain of command, the feeling had been growing that Russia was bearing the lion's share of the fighting and the Western Allies were not pulling their weight either in terms of fulfilling their munitions contracts or by attacking Germany to relieve the pressure in the east. Therefore at the inter-allied conference held near Paris during December Zhilinski, the Russian representative, was at pains to secure an agreement that mutually supportive offensives should be mounted to prevent the Central Powers from concentrating their efforts on one ally alone. To reinforce Zhilinski's argument Alexeyev had provided him with figures that noted Russia's weakness quoting front line strength of 1,693,000 men of which only 1,243,000 were armed. Although the French initially rejected the idea of mutual suport they finally agreed although they did not wish to undertake any major operations until the summer of 1916

General M. V. Alexeyev (centre), the Tsar's Chief of Staff and effective commander of the Russian army from September 1915. Alexeyev was one of the new generation of officers who had risen from humble beginnings to hold high office purely on merit. Alexeyev was determined to continue the war against the Central Powers and raised the Volunteer Army in late 1917 specifically to do this. Following the Treaty of Brest Litovsk Alexeyev's efforts were turned against the Bolsheviks. He died in late 1918.

Refugees

The Great Retreat (as the withdrawal from Poland was known) had generated problems beyond the purely military. The front commanders had, from the outbreak of the war, enjoyed powers that virtually allowed them to control areas from the trenches deep into the rear. Indeed on NW Front during early 1915 the army had taken to requisitioning food and foraging locally when its supply chain was in difficulties and as a consequence the civilian population suffered. Inevitably such actions brought the military into conflict with the civil authorities, a problem exacerbated by the army's often high-handed attitude. However, it was the forced evacuation of the population that lived in areas directly threatened by the Central Powers during their advance that caused the worst problems to arise.

The Grand Duke, in an effort to invoke the spirit of 1812, had permitted a scorched earth policy to deny the Austrians and Germans anything from recruits or accommodation to the very crops in the fields. This policy was successful and the invaders entered a devastated, depopulated region the crossing of which only increased their supply troubles. But for the people concerned the effects were dire. Nearly 2,000,000 refugees moved east. Not as the Tsar believed, "Because nobody wishes to be left in the hands of the Germans or Austrians" but rather because the army had ordered them to do so, often at the point of a gun or at the flick of a Cossack whip. Much of the evacuated territory was comprised of the Pale, the settlement area for Russia's Jewish population. It was here that the soldiers, carrying on the age-old Russian tradition of anti-Semitism, carried out the scorched earth policy with a will. In this they were encouraged by Yanushkevitch's exhortation regarding, "The dangerous attitudes [to the Russians] of the Jewish population of Poland, Galicia and the Bukovina." It was true that some Jews had acted against Russia but it was also true that considerable numbers fought in her army despite widespread prejudice. As the French ambassador wrote, "It is always necessary to have a scapegoat in reserve."

Naturally the army took priority on the railways so the refugees walked or if lucky rode east. There was little in the way of organisation and families became separated as the human tide gathered momentum. Thousands starved or died of exhaustion in the summer's heat but the majority plodded on until they had gone beyond the threatened regions and were able to obtain a place on a train and travel to a registration point from whence they travelled to the major cities and beyond. It was a tribute to the work of the various committees set up by the *Zemstvos* and others that there was not a major epidemic during that period such was the wretched condition of so many of their charges.

Aside from the exodus of people, factories were also relocated and remarkably many of them resumed production within a year. Indeed the efforts of industrialists, committeemen and *Duma* members were at last bearing fruit and munitions production began to rise. Field gun-shell output rose from 350,000 to over 1,500,000 per month during the period January to November 1915. The arrival at the front of supplies of rifles both from abroad and as a result of increased domestic production also began to have a noticeable effect on the troop's morale.

The men's training was beginning to improve: no longer were green battalions of *Opolchenie* expected to perform miracles against younger, fitter opponents. At the Cholm conference in the early summer it had been decided to spread the reserve/training depots beyond Moscow, Petrograd and Kiev as concerns had been expressed regarding these men being exposed to revolutionary propaganda. However, it was the lack of much to do at the depots that sapped the conscripts' morale more than a handful of agitators. The training depots were too few to cope with the hundreds of thousands of new recruits and consequently they did nothing more taxing than parade-ground drill. Furthermore these depots were officered by men often brought out of retirement with little or no relevant experience. Now replacements were to spend less time in the depots but would be sent to their units where they would be initiated into the realities of modern warfare before combat proper. To replace the heavy losses of NCOs short courses were made available for men deemed suitable for such responsibility at schools close to the frontline. Similar establishments to produce junior wartime officers had been set up earlier. These measures, designed to improve the efficiency and fighting capacity of the army, were to have a positive effect on the morale of the ordinary soldier. Those in authority at last appeared to be doing something to restore the troops' battered confidence in Russia's ability to defeat the apparently invincible Germans.

Innovations

With the advent of trench warfare and a more settled period along most of the front the higher commands were anxious that their men did not slip into torpor and lose the will to fight. One senior officer had even proposed that soldiers should be encouraged to fight by the offer of land at the end of the war. His suggestion was rejected.

In XXV Corps (General Y. N. Danilov) a part of Third Army (General L. V. Lesh) on the W Front began in October to train what were termed "Grenadier Platoons". These experimental units were created with the dual purpose of encouraging the martial spirit and utilising other weapons when rifles were in short supply. That the idea came from Danilov is unsurprising as he had been promoted sideways from the post of Quartermaster General and wished to prove himself still capable of creative thought. The grenadier platoons were to be the fourth in every company and would consist of "brave and energetic men". Each man would be armed with 10 grenades and equipped with a shovel, an axe and wire cutters. Later orders specified "shovels, revolvers, carbines, broadswords or short lances". Sample weapons, presumably the broadswords and lances, were created by XXV Corps' sapper battalion. With the training of the model platoons completed by January 1916, a top-secret order was sent out to all front commanders to form such platoons in their infantry regiments. However, the extent to which this order was acted upon is debatable. The Grenadier's remit included trench raiding, capturing prisoners for interrogation and leading attacks when they were to co-operate with the sappers by clearing wire

One of the army's new recruits, the so-called *Polivantsy*, men recruited during Polivanov's tenure as War Minister. The equipment worn by this man is made of canvas as leather was in short supply much having been lost when Lithuania was overrun. Across his chest is a bandoleer without cartridge clips.

and, by using special grenades, to demolish bunkers and other obstacles. Several armies and corps set up schools for grenadier training and these continued to provide instructors and graduates until 1917. To reinforce their elite status the officers and men wore a special badge on their left sleeves.

It was the cavalry who found themselves particularly under-utilised with the spread of positional warfare. So that their time would not be wasted, Ivanov, commanding SW Front, decided to detach individual squadrons and Cossack *sotnia* (one hundred men) to infiltrate enemy lines and do as much harm as they could. In his memoirs Brusilov is rather dismissive of these partisan formations implying, that they were out of control when behind Russian lines and that they rarely ventured behind enemy lines. Nevertheless the Grand Duke Boris Vladimirovitch did not share his jaundiced view and, in his capacity as *Ataman* (leader) of Cossack troops, ordered that all Cossack regiments on every front form a partisan detachment. Such *sotnia* operated individually or in groups and were very much a law unto themselves.

National formations

Nationalist sentiment was not encouraged in the Russian Empire nor was much effort made to undermine the multi-ethnic Austrian army for fear that such quasi-revolutionary ideas would backfire. Therefore, during the summer of 1914, when Czech settlers in Russia and Poles made representations to form national units, the response was circumspect agreement. A token force of each was to be created.

In October 1914 the Poles were permitted to raise an infantry battalion and, as a sop to their military heritage, two squadrons of lancers. At the same time the Czechs recruited a rifle battalion which expanded during 1915 with the inclusion of POWs who were deemed unfit for more productive work in industry or on the land. Both formations were then marginalised until 1917.

However, a six regiment cavalry division was formed from the Moslem peoples of the Caucasus soon after the war began. Each regiment was composed of volunteers from a particular group such as the Chechens or the Tartars (Moslems were not allowed to serve in the armed forces) and officered by a mix of Russians or native nobility. The official title for this division was the Caucasian Native Cavalry Division but it was more popularly known as the Savage or Wild division, the nicknames reflecting both a tribute to its fighting qualities as well as the attitude of the Russians to Caucasians generally. It was commanded until 1916 by the Tsar's estranged brother the Grand Duke Michael. This appointment caused a degree of

In late 1915 the Belgian government sent an armoured car unit to Russia. Known, as the *Corps des Autos-Canons-Mitrailleuses Russie,* the unit was equipped with 10 armoured vehicles. They were attached to the SW Front where they fought with distinction until the summer of 1917. Here the Tsar inspects the Belgians at Tsarskoe Selo.

marital conflict between the Grand Duke and his wife. The Savage Division fought throughout the war on the SW or Romanian fronts.

On the Caucasian Front Georgian, Armenian and Azerbaijani volunteer rifle battalions were accepted into the army during 1915 but only to serve on that front.

In terms of numbers the largest national unit at his stage of the war was the Latvian Rifles. During the retreat of NW Front across Lithuania and Courland the *Opolchenie* battalions from Latvia performed very well. Consequently on 1 August permission was granted to raise eight battalions of volunteers to create the Latvian Rifle Battalions. Many volunteers transferred from the regular army and some even returned from emigration to serve. The Latvian riflemen were to fight only in defence of their region and, like all the other national formations, they were not permitted artillery unless under Russian control.

Human exports and imports

To offset the cost of munitions the French government requested that the Russians supply men to fight in France. Alexeyev was opposed to the idea but the Tsar decided in favour of it. The first request in this unseemly auction was for 300,000 but this number was reduced to a strong brigade. Known as the First Russian Special Brigade it arrived in Marseilles late in April. A second Special Brigade served at Salonika. Both brigades were to serve with distinction until the revolutions of 1917 caused them to become preoccupied with events in Russia and they were disbanded although a small group of loyalists formed the Legion Russe, maintaining Russia's presence on the Western Front until the Armistice.

The Western allies contributed two armoured car formations, one from Belgium the other from Britain. The Belgians arrived in Petrograd in December 1915 and were sent to the SW Front. When the British arrived in January they were sent to the Caucasian Front and later to Romania. These units augmented the large number of armoured cars already in service.

Lake Narotch

Alexeyev could, at the beginning of 1916, look forward to a time of further expansion in terms of men and equipment. Polivanov, the War Minister, in early January 1916 acknowledged the munitions shortages of the previous year and commented on the improvements that had been made. He added, "Thanks to the great mass of men ordered some months ago and the doubling of the number of our depots, we now have a permanent reserve of 1,500,000 young recruits, which will permit us to feed the various units without sending to the front men with insufficient training."

However, such optimism did not prevent Bezobrazov, the commander of the Guards Army, from noting in his diary that, "One third of the men were without rifles", after a parade of Guards reserve battalions in the presence of the Tsar. Happily, he continued, "Their appearance and marching was very good."

Although Alexeyev had anticipated a German attack he had not foreseen the cloud looming over France and the strain it would place on his steadily recovering army. Within days of the start of the German offensive at Verdun on 21 February Joffre, the French Commander in Chief, was demanding that *Stavka* honour the agreement made less than three months before to relieve the pressure on other fronts.

The possibility of an offensive earlier than the promised summer operation had been under discussion before the request for intervention from the French. Now as the Tsar wrote to his wife (22 March), "it has been decided to take the initiative into our own hands, taking advantage of the situation at Verdun." The area under consideration was north of the Pripyat Marshes and the objective was to push the Germans back towards East Prussia. Therefore when the Tsar summoned his front commanders to a conference to be held at *Stavka* on 24 February, three days after the Verdun fighting had begun, part of the planning was in hand. The letters he wrote, in English, to his wife are interesting as they shed light on Nicholas' attitude to his role at Moghilev. Nicholas describes the conference to her in his letter of 25 February thus. It began, "at 6 [1800 hours]...dragged on till 8 [2000 hours], and was continued after dinner till close at 12.30 [0030 hours]". Despite Nicholas' injunction to, "speak out plainly...truth is of the utmost importance..." there was little choice. The Russians were bound by the promise made to support their allies. Joffre's implication that the Russians had frequently requested French help in similar circumstances doubtless rankled, as they had increasingly felt isolated and unsupported throughout 1915. Finally the Tsar was obviously in favour of an offensive as he expressed himself to the Tsaritsa to be, "quite satisfied with the results of our long conference. They disputed much among themselves." Two days later the Supreme Commander in Chief of Russia's Armed Forces in another letter to Alexandra wrote of the conference as, "a lot of bother...which lasted for 6 hours." In the same missive the weather was, "unfavourable for long walks." The "bother" had set in motion preparations for an attack by several hundreds of thousands of his men. If the weather was bad for "walking" how would it be for hauling guns or fighting? Not once is there an expression of feeling for what his men were enduring, even to his closest confidante. On 28 February, as preparations went ahead, Alexeyev spoke to the Tsar and, as Nicholas put it, "told me to go home." Clearly Alexeyev wanted his torpid master well away from *Stavka* and Nicholas, having waited to receive a delegation that promoted him to Field Marshal in the British army, left for Tsarskoe Selo on 2 March for ten days leave. Given the relish with which the Tsar reviewed his men the feeling that remains is one of someone playing with toy soldiers.

The fronts chosen to carry out the offensive were Northern and Western. Nicholas had replaced the ailing Pleve with Kuropatkin (of Russo-Japanese War fame) at the head of N Front on 19 February with the comment to the Tsaritsa, "He will be a good Commander in Chief. He will be directly under the *Stavka*, and in this way he will not have on his shoulders the same responsibility which he had in Manchuria." Furthermore, "the armies under his command will welcome the appointment." That the troops would "welcome" being placed in the hands of man who had so conspicuously failed a decade before seems a trifle optimistic. Kuropatkin, always a cautious leader, would prove even more so in the near future, seemingly more concerned about not appearing to do anything that hinted of independent thought than defeating the enemy. Not a great choice for such an important position but Nicholas' lack of faith in his senior officer pool is summed up in his fatalistic aside to his wife, "what can one do when there are so few good men?" He also noted that this appointment would, "provoke many rumours and criticisms…." If Nicholas realised that such would reflect on himself he seems to have kept that worry hidden.

The Russian recovery of the autumn and winter had generated a superiority of men. This was to reach approximately four to one in the areas chosen for the attack. During late February and early March men and guns moved into place particularly in Western Front's Second Army zone of 97kms (60 miles) where the main effort was to be made. Eventually over 350,000 men and nearly 1,000 guns would be massed there. However, of this frontage 27kms (17 miles) were lakes and marshland. Second Army was divided into three groups of which the two flanking groups would attack to the north-west to link up with elements of N Front's Fifth Army (General V. I. Gurko) in a pincer movement. First and Twelfth armies were to make a series of demonstrations intended to confuse the German placement of reserves.

On 27 February a band of Russian partisans attempting to sabotage German communications were caught red-handed. Aerial reconnaissance reported significant troop movements in the same and adjacent areas and radio intercepts indicated that an attack was likely in the immediate future. Consequently the Germans were on the alert and strengthened their already substantial defences.

Although the preparation time had been longer than anticipated by 17 March almost everything was ready. Unfortunately the Second Army's Commander General V. V. Smirnov was taken ill and replaced by General A. F. Ragoza who was unfamiliar with the area. This notwithstanding, with plenty of guns, (including many heavy pieces removed from the fortresses of Kovno and Grodno) ammunition, and infantry backed up with masses of cavalry to exploit the anticipated breakthrough, the Russians felt reasonably confident. Then, on the night before the first attacks were to take place, the weather changed. The ice and snow began to melt, the lakes and marshes over which the men were to advance were rapidly covered with water up to 0.45m (18 inches) deep. Behind the line wheels, hooves and boots converted the roads to glutinous mud and reduced movement to a snail's pace within hours. Spring had arrived, or more properly the *rasputitsa*, the muddy season.

At 0800 hours on 18 March the barrage began, the offensive was underway. The infantry attacks began at 1020 hours and the men, wave

An interesting group of men wearing a strange mix of clothing, including a German tunic. The original information suggests that they were members of a Partisan group, which operated behind enemy lines at various points along the line. Raised during the period of the retreat from Poland Partisan bands enjoyed a brief period of popularity. However, most were disbanded during 1916.

Russian corpses in the churned up ground near the shores of Lake Narotch in March 1916. As can be seen from this image the terrain was the stuff of machine gunner's dreams, open and flat. Although the wiring is unsophisticated by Western Front standards it is more than enough to cause men to bunch up if only for a brief time and providing the enemy with even simpler target practice.

after wave of them, were cut down in their hundreds as they attempted to advance across an increasingly grisly slough only 2kms (1.2 miles) wide. Incredibly both flanks of Second Army made some headway during the course of the next three days. But inevitably, the losses were completely out of proportion with the gains: a penetration of 1.8kms (1.1 miles) by 0.4kms (0.2 miles) wide scrap of land. Four thousand died on the first day, a tally that increased with hideous speed as the mud swallowed up the wounded while stretcher-bearers struggled valiantly to evacuate them as water filled their boots. At night the frost returned adding to the suffering of the *frontoviki* – the men of the front – as they huddled in the remains of the German lines. Such an achievement, as the Russians were swift to point out, would have been hailed on the Western Front as a tremendous victory. The first month's progress on the Somme during the summer was scarcely 4.8kms (3 miles) for the application of a considerably greater tonnage of shell and larger casualties. The Germans took advantage

Another shot from the Lake Narotch operation this time near the hamlet of Blizniki. Here Russian troops are occupying German trenches. Alongside the array of stick grenades is a rifle grenade and a spring powered bomb thrower. The shallowness of the trench is a result of the local water table.

The Tsar attends a demonstration of an experimental flame-thrower in early May 1916. The audience includes Alexeyev, the Inspector of Artillery and Albert Thomas (wearing a bowler hat) the French Socialist Minister of Munitions who was visiting Russia. The flame-thrower is a modified Austrian type known as the *Tovornitsky* that was adopted for use by the Russians. The Chemical Battalion trained several flame-thrower units during 1916 for front line deployment in 1917. Further details are unknown.

of a cold snap to counterattack regaining several positions and then it rained.

To the north Fifth Army had achieved a similar degree of "success" in equally vile conditions. The diversionary attacks had all been contained with little difficulty. Near Riga the Latvian Rifles went into action but as one of their historians wrote later, "the adjacent Siberian Rifle regiments... confined their assault to a lot of firing over the parapet." To what extent this lack of effort on the Siberian's part was due to orders or refusal to obey orders is not noted. However, the Latvians felt let down and this feeling of being expendable was to grow.

As March ended rising temperatures caused dense fog, restricting visibility and adding a surreal, even nightmarish quality to the near impassable marshes. The rotation of men in the front line was yet to be established on the Eastern Front and the famed passivity of the Russian peasant soldier must have been tried to the limit as he squatted in the filth.

There were several more small attacks at different points but by the beginning of April W Front's heavy artillery had been withdrawn to the

Three gunners of 2nd Siberian Artillery Brigade who died during a German gas attack in May 1915. At this time there were few gas masks available. The effects of this attack were reported to have been felt as far as 30km (19 miles) behind the lines.

rear and the offensive was called off. The entire Lake Narotch episode was rightly described, during the Soviet era, as "nightmarishly unsuccessful." However it had gained a week's respite for the French as the Germans considered the need to send troops east. 100,000 Russian casualties had bought a sliver of mud and cost the Germans 20,000 men. The ground was retaken a few weeks later.

Analysis

The official enquiry into the whole ghastly affair identified several areas of major concern. There had been poor co-ordination between the infantry and the artillery with imprecise target acquisition and fire planning.

An extemporised anti aircraft mounting for an M1910 Maxim machine gun. This photo was taken inside one of the Russian fortifications in the Pripyat Marshes. In this region it was impossible to dig trenches so both sides relied upon a series of "island fortresses" on the higher, dry ground.

Reconnaissance was weak or non-existent and staff work had been inadequate. There was a lack of trust in the higher command, training had been irrelevant and the reserves had been lodged too far in the rear. Colonel Knox, the British military attaché, noted, "So wrote the experts after the event. They naturally did not touch on the greatest folly of all, the launching of an offensive at such a season."

The enquiry also missed something else – tactical methodology. Flesh and shells had been thrown against a narrow front thus creating a wonderful killing zone for the German artillery. Lines of men had been swept away attempting to cut the often-negligible wire when the guns had failed to do so. What the alternative to explosives was seems not to have been within the enquiry's remit; senior officers were left to fathom that out for themselves. One man to whom the matter was now purely academic was the War Minister Polivanov as on 28 March he was dismissed by the Tsar for being too close to the *Duma* and the various war committees. Knox described his going as a "disaster". The French Ambassador's summation probably came closest to the truth when he said, "he appeared to be one of the regime's last defenders, a man capable of defending it both against the follies of absolutism and the excesses of revolution." Neither the Tsar nor his wife, increasingly the voice to whom Nicholas listened on all matters, liked him. Alexandra had described Polivanov as, "simply a revolutionist" and Nicholas had written to him, "The activities of the war committees do not inspire me with confidence, and I find your supervision of them insufficiently assertive." Knox visited Polivanov a month after his dismissal when, although depressed, he felt he had achieved the task he had set himself, namely the improvement of the supply of men, rifles and shell and the improvement of training facilities. The new War Minister, the son of a former army private, was General D. S. Shuvaev. Shuvaev was described by Nicholas to Alexandra as, "honest, absolutely loyal, is not at all afraid of the *Duma* and knows all the faults and shortcomings of these committees."

The replacement of Polivanov was only one of a series of personnel changes the Tsar was to make in an effort to sustain the regime from what he regarded as the malign influences of the *Duma* and the war committees. In doing this he installed a succession of increasingly reactionary but also less able men and set the course of his dynasty on the path to revolution. Yet in April 1916, as the summer campaigning season was about to begin in European Russia and considerable success had been achieved far away on the Caucasian Front, this was still not an inevitable outcome.

CHAPTER 5

The Caucasian Front

Background

Since time immemorial the Caucasus has seen armies march to and fro through its mountainous passes and across its rolling pastures between the Black and Caspian seas. Russia began displacing the Persians and the Ottoman Turks who had traditionally dominated the region during the mid-eighteenth century, but the process of conquest was difficult as the Moslem Caucasians resisted vigorously. However, by 1879 the border was established and ran from the Black Sea coast just south of Batum through the mountains of Armenia veering south towards Lake Van and then southeast to the Caspian Sea at Enzeli. The ancient Christian state of Armenia had been absorbed into the Ottoman Empire centuries before and it was across this region that much of the fighting during 1914–16 would range.

The terrain on both sides of the border was some of the most inhospitable in the Middle East. Sparsely populated by Armenians and nomadic, Moslem Kurds, it was mountainous and lacked roads and railways. As a result of Russian pressure in the years before 1914 the Ottoman rail system had hardly moved beyond Ankara in central Anatolia while the Russians had developed their own network slowly. In the valleys farming was well developed but centuries of grazing had denuded the hills of topsoil and erosion had left vast tracts of barren rock. Consequently troops would lack firewood, shelter and even the soil in which to entrench.

The high ground, varying between 1,500–3,000m (4,921–9,843 feet), ran in a series of wave-like ridges cut by narrow rivers, which differed in depth according to the season. With few valley to valley roads travel was limited to a handful of roads, goat tracks often providing the only route from one to another. Travelling for large bodies of men, animals, wagons and artillery was, in theory, limited to the roads between the major towns, which were few and far between. In Russian Armenia the major towns were Kars and Sarikamish, the HQ of the Army of the Caucasus was at Tiblisi (Tiflis) in

By the time hostilities broke out many units of the Caucasian Army had been transferred to the west. Men like these Frontier Guards were drafted in to supplement the infantry. What they lacked in sartorial elegance was more than compensated for by their local knowledge and enterprise.

This method of casualty evacuation was common in regions where the roads and railways were few and far between. The barren nature of the terrain is clear and the wounded soldier would have had shelter during his bumpy ride.

Georgia. Sarikamish was the most forward point that the Russian railway had reached some 32km (20 miles) from the border. On the Caspian Sea Baku was the centre of the Russian oil industry and the largest oil field in the world. Batum, a small, fortified port, was the main Russian outpost on the Black Sea coast and served the inland mining villages but was not capable of supporting deep-water shipping such as large warships.

In Turkish Armenia the base of the Third Army was the heavily fortified city of Erzurum, other major centres of population were Van, Mush and the Black Sea port of Trebizond (Trabzon). So poor was the quality of the roads that it was easier and quicker for the Turks to move supplies and reinforcements from their western bases by sea. However, this link ran the gauntlet of Russian warships. Despite the best efforts of German engineers there was still a gap of 332km (200 miles) between Erzurum and the nearest railhead. With few motor vehicles the Turks would still have to march great distances to reach the combat zone.

As well as the inhospitable terrain the climate was extreme. During the winter, which lasted roughly from November to April the temperature fell far below zero. In the summer it was frequently over 100 degrees Fahrenheit (38 degrees Celsius). Therefore the campaigning season was limited unless one was prepared for and capable of supporting a huge

A Russian artillery position somewhere on the plains of Anatolia. The gun is the standard Putilov 76.2mm Model 1902. In such isolated areas the gunners were particularly careful to keep their weapons well maintained, as the lack of replacement parts was often acute. Note the cases from discharged rounds lining the rear of the emplacement.

exercise in logistics. Both sides were to make extensive use of the local population as guides, labourers and informers.

Russia also shared a border with Persia (modern Iran) but it was not as important militarily as the Turkish frontier. Following the agreement of 1907 Britain and Russia divided Persia into two zones of influence the north under Russia the south Britain. With an almost non-existent government presided over by a weak, young Shah, Persia was theoretically neutral and destined to become an extension of the battlefield particularly Persian Azerbaijan.

In August 1914 the Ottoman Turks declared themselves neutral but began the lengthy process of mobilisation. The power of the Ottoman Empire lay in its stranglehold over access to the Black Sea and the Russian ports of the Crimea and Odessa. Other than Vladivostok on the Pacific these ports were the only significant warm water access to Russia that Britain and France could use should it become necessary to ship munitions to Russia.

Although Turkey was still an empire ruled by the Sultan and his ministers their power was negligible, effective control lay in the hands of the Young Turk movement. The Young Turks were a group of army officers who wished to revive the fortunes of the empire by military means. Under the leadership of the War Minister, Enver Pasha, the Young Turks harboured ambitions far beyond the capabilities of the forces at their disposal. These ambitions included the re-conquest of the Caucasus, expansion into Russian Turkestan and the re-conquest of Egypt. On 2 August, a secret agreement was reached with the Central Powers whereby Turkey would enter into the war as their partner when the time was ripe.

In the event of a European war Russia's strategy in the Caucasus was mainly defensive. The only possibility of offensive action was the occupation of the Eleskirt valley. The root of this strategy was an adherence to the theory that the only road to victory lay through Berlin. Indeed troops were to be transferred to the western fronts from the Caucasus during the period of mobilisation and the shortfall in men was to be made up from local levies.

By October 1914 transfers had reduced the Army of the Caucasus to three major formations: II Turkestan, I Caucasian corps, and the 66th Infantry Division. The II Turkestan Corps was made up of 4th and 5th Turkestan Rifle brigades plus the Siberian and Transcaspian Cossack brigades. I Caucasian Corps consisted of the 20th and 39th Infantry Divisions, the 2nd Caucasian Rifle Brigade, and the 1st Kuban *Plastun* (Cossack infantry) Brigade. In addition there were the 2nd and 3rd Kuban *Plastun* brigades, the 2nd and 4th Caucasian Cossack brigades and two other Cossack regiments. Four Sapper battalions and five Frontier Guard battalions completed the order of battle. The Frontier Guards were picked for their intelligence and local knowledge and were to prove their worth on many occasions. In total the Russians had 100,000 infantry, 15,000 cavalry and 256 guns including specialist mountain artillery, but were lacking guns over 76.2mm (3 inches). 150,000 local reservists were in the process of training as were six volunteer battalions: four of Armenians and two of Georgians. Although the raising of such national formations was not unprecedented, these monoethnic battalions were very much against the regime's practice of allowing its subjects to have anything approaching an armed force.

The Viceroy of the Caucasus and titular commander of the Army of the Caucasus was Count Vorontsov-Dashkov, a highly regarded administrator but short on military experience. His deputy and military commander in chief, General A. Z. Myshlayevski, was an historian and theoretical soldier ill-suited for his role. Happily the chief of staff was the excellent General N. N. Yudenitch who knew his men and the area very well.

Expecting to be outnumbered the Russians had formed five groups to cover the five principal routes across the frontier with a reserve at Tiflis. The bulk of their force faced the Turkish border.

Following the declaration of mobilisation, the Chief of the Austrian General Staff, von Hotzendorf, raised the possibility of landing 50,000 Turkish troops near Odessa in Bessarabia to create a diversion behind Russian lines and raise a nationalist rebellion in the Ukraine. Austria had

An interesting shot of a regimental priest addressing his flock. The reverend gentleman seems to be wielding something more aggressive than a cross.

been encouraging Ukrainian separatists for some years and hoped they would gather supporters for such a venture. A similar proposition, this time targeting the Kuban, in the northern Caucasus, was tabled some weeks later. Neither scheme was feasible, as the Ottoman navy was incapable of mounting such an operation.

Turkish mobilisation was completed by the beginning of October. However, with German plans for a rapid conclusion to the war in the west so much waste paper and Austria reeling from her defeats in Galicia and Serbia eyes turned to Turkey with 400,000 men and over 1,000 guns.

At the end of October German warships, nominally in Turkish service, along with ships of the Ottoman navy bombarded Odessa and other Russian ports sinking some small naval craft. This action provoked Russia into declaring war on 2 November 1914.

First steps

The Turkish Third Army in eastern Anatolia was based on Erzurum and consisted of IX, X, XI corps and the 2nd Cavalry Division. The regular

Hundreds of thousands of camel and donkeys were bought or requisitioned by the armies in the Caucasus and throughout the year vast convoys were to be seen plodding the roads. Escort duty along the supply lines was a risky business as the lack of a distinct front line led to the proliferation of bandits robbing any unwary group. Large parties of Kurdish tribesmen would lie in ambush in the hills strike any opportune target and disappear almost without trace.

cavalry was to be supplemented by local irregulars – Kurds who enjoyed a reputation for ferocity and cruelty far beyond their military value.

The Russians knew the Turks had concentrated IX and XI corps in the Erzurum region and were moving more men eastwards. On 2 November Russian troops crossed the border at several points to occupy strategic locations just inside Turkey. Overcoming the Turks locally proved less difficult than anticipated; consequently the Russian field commander in the centre overstepped his orders and marched in pursuit. The Turks were also advancing. The Russian centre was driven back, losing 7,000 troops in two weeks. On the Black Sea coast Turkish irregulars defeated a Russian force of 2,000 forcing their right flank to retire on Batum. Only on the left did the Russians achieve any success. General N. N. Baratov's force in Persia took the Kotur Pass, thus gaining the initiative in Persian Azerbaijan. When Turkish ships shelled Batum, the Russian commander reported that his guns were inadequate to deal with a serious attack. It was an inauspicious start for the Russians and it convinced Enver Pasha that an immediate all-out offensive was likely to pave the way for the re-conquest of the Caucasus. It was for this reason that he set out for Erzurum to direct operations personally.

The Turkish invasion of the Caucasus

Enver's plan was to outflank the Russians, capture Oltu and Ardahan, advance on Kars, invade Georgia and raise an uprising amongst the Moslems of the Caucasus. By reaching Kars, roughly half of the Russian Army of the Caucasus would be cut off from its main bases and isolated on the border.

Demonstration attacks would pin the Russian centre and left on the Persian border. Detailed planning was delegated to a group of German staff officers. Because of the nature of the terrain route planning was difficult and to ensure a good road to Kars it was vital that the Turks capture Sarikamish.

The Sarikamish Campaign

The reinforced Third Army numbered some 120,000 men with roughly 300 guns commanded by Hasan Izzet Pasha who promptly resigned in disgust when told the plan. The commanders of IX and XI corps were also replaced for lack of faith in a winter offensive. Turkish troops began to move towards their start points during the early days of December. Despite heavy snow falling on the 20 December, the invasion still began on 22 December.

The Turkish left included the 17th, 28th and 29th divisions (IX Corps led by Ihsan Pasha) with a complement of irregulars and several mountain guns. The plateau along which they were to advance was almost treeless and they had no winter kit. Indeed it is believed that Ihsan Pasha ordered his men to leave their greatcoats and knapsacks behind to speed up the march. One of their objectives was Oltu.

The Turkish right comprised the 28th and 31st divisions. Elements of X Corps (Hafik Hakki Pasha), 30th, 31st and 32nd divisions, whose arrival was unknown to the Russians, were to march on Ardahan. The Russians did not anticipate a Turkish attack as winter was fast setting in. However on 22 December, reports began to arrive at Tiflis of Turkish movements near Oltu. The Turkish attacks on the Russian centre were also noted and on 22 December the Viceroy sent Myshlayevski and Yudenitch to the field HQ at Mecinkirt on the border to meet with the field commander General Bergmann. The next day Oltu fell but the Turks were too exhausted to follow up having spent the previous two nights exposed to the elements with no shelter and little food. Elsewhere the Turks were beginning to feel the effects of the weather and began to fall behind schedule as the snow deepened. The 17th Division began to disintegrate in a blizzard with forty per cent of its men becoming stragglers. Enver, learning from a Russian POW that Sarikamish was unoccupied, decided to push ahead with only the 29th Division; the 17th was to follow as best it could.

Meanwhile Bergmann and his visitors were at loggerheads. Despite the pleas of his staff Myshlayevski refused to take over command. As the situation reports became more serious reserves were moved and Bergmann's plans for occupying the Eleskirt valley cancelled. Indeed while motoring from Sarikamish to Mecinkirt Myshlayevski's car had been fired on by an enemy patrol and he decided to order a retreat to the north-east. The Russian centre was to be withdrawn starting on 25 December.

Yudenitch, now commanding II Turkestan Corps, was told to fight his way though to Sarikamish where defences were being prepared. In Sarikamish were 2,000 *Opolchenie* armed with old Berdan rifles from 1877, two companies of Frontier Guards with a couple of machine guns, roughly 1,000 railway men and two field guns. The town commander posted the *Opolchenie* at strategic points around the town and the artillery in the main square, the Frontier Guards and railwaymen were sent to cover the Bardiz Pass 8kms (5 miles) away.

On the same day Turkish 29th Division moved out of Bardiz. The Turkish maps put Sarikamish nearer than it was and the march through the pass took longer than anticipated. Units of 17th Division began to arrive and the Turkish column plodded on through deep snow. At midday its leading elements reached the end and ran straight into the Frontier Guards and railwaymen. Unaware of the Russian's weakness the Turks deployed with caution. Only at 1600 hours did the Russians fall back on Sarikamish. With darkness falling the Turks did not follow up, thus condemning themselves to a night in the open exposed to 20 degrees of frost.

Sarikamish was the most advanced point for the railway in the Caucasus and also stood astride the metalled road that ran to the border. The Turks were approaching the town from the north-east, heading into the valley where it lay. The heights from which they were descending were wooded, reaching up to 2,600m (8,530 feet). The Russian garrison had been reinforced by eight machine guns, 300 regular infantry and 100 newly commissioned officers. A battalion of Turkestani riflemen arrived on the 26 December. During the night hundreds of *Askers* (Turkish infantry) had frozen to death and the 29th Division, 8,000 strong less than a week before, was reduced to 4,000 effectives. Enver, sure that the Russians had no artillery, deployed four of his eight mountain guns in an exposed position overlooking the town. To his horror the Russian gunners immediately knocked out three. Consequently it was decided to postpone the infantry attack until the 17th Division arrived. By midday only one regiment had struggled up but nonetheless the attack was launched. Despite being cut to ribbons by the Russian machine guns the Turkish infantry kept going and overran the western suburbs of the town. Exhausted, the Turks once more bivouacked in the snow for the night as more Russian troops including cavalry and more artillery arrived. Enver slept that night anticipating the arrival of reinforcements from the left wing.

X Corps, having taken Oltu, had strayed from their original orders by following the retreating Russians. When word reached them to march on Sarikamish they changed direction. Once again deluded by abysmal maps the Turks undertook a punishing nineteen hour march (which should, in theory, have taken five) that cost them 7,000 men, one third of their strength. The attacks on Sarikamish continued throughout the 27 December but all were beaten off.

The Russians were unaware of the parlous condition of their enemies and three events occurred which caused Myshlayevski to despair. The initial concern was raised when a Turkish cavalry unit blew up the railway between Kars and Sarikamish. Then news arrived that told of the fall of Ardahan. Finally a Cossack patrol captured a Turkish staff officer carrying a complete set of plans. Myshlayevski, now aware of the XI Corps facing his left and the strength of the Turks on his right, decided to order a withdrawal along the whole of the frontier. Appalled, Yudenitch counselled against such precipitate action and a postponement was granted until the situation at Sarikamish became clearer. Having ordered two more brigades into Sarikamish, Myshlayevski left for Tiflis. On the way he ordered the commanders of the troops on the Persian border to retreat, disregarding the fact that they were in no danger. In Tiflis Myshlayevski, convinced that the Turks were victorious, announced this 'fact' causing an immediate panic. Christian civilians crowded into the station to escape the anticipated Moslem uprising.

The truth was somewhat different. The Turkish left flank, X Corps, rested on the railway from Sarikamish to Kars, connected with IX Corps in the heights overlooking the town where it held a line that curved to the Akardahar River west of Sarikamish. Only a rough goat track connected Sarikamish with the outside world but fresh Russian troops continued to arrive by this difficult route.

Turkish numbers had fallen to 18,000 men and twenty guns whilst reinforcements had increased Russian numbers to over 14,000 men with thirty-four guns commanded by General M. A. Przevalski.

Throughout 29 December several fierce Turkish attacks were held as was a Russian counterattack. Enver concluded that desperate measures were called for and launched a night attack at 2200 hours. Once more the Turks penetrated into Sarikamish itself, Przevalski threw in his last reserve and forced the Turks to retreat. Having gained the initiative the Russians began to move out of Sarikamish outflanking the Turks towards the Bardiz Pass and Enver's advance supply base.

Around Sarikamish silence reigned as reality dawned for Enver and his staff. IX Corps was reduced to 1,000 effectives and fourteen guns with thousands suffering from exposure and frostbite. X Corps was in a slightly better condition. Accompanied by a small staff, Enver re-crossed the frontier on 3 January heading for XI Corps, his last hope of snatching something from the chaos that was fast consuming his army.

XI Corps, on the offensive since 31 December, attempted, during the course of the following week, to break through to Sarikamish but failed. By 5 January both IX and X Corps were in ruins. On 7 January Enver abandoned his men and departed for Erzurum. Ardahan was recaptured as, on 12 January, was Oltu.

Yudenitch was appointed field commander on 6 January (Myshlayevski was dismissed in March) and immediately ordered an outflanking move against the rear of XI Corps. The Russian force allotted this thankless task, waded through waist-high snow and, out of touch for five days, appeared in the rear of XI Corps, which promptly retreated back across the border.

The Turks had lost some 75,000 men and most of their artillery. Of the reminder only 18,000, mainly XI Corps formations, maintained some semblance of organisation. Russian losses were 16,000 killed and wounded and 12,000 sick, the majority with frostbite.

Reorganisation

During January 1915 the British invited Russian participation in an offensive to clear the route into the Black Sea. On 19 February Admiral A. A. Eberhardt, commander of the Black Sea Fleet, was informed that an expeditionary force was to be formed and his ships were to support it. Orders were issued to the effect that Seventh Army, slowly being formed in the Crimea and Odessa, was to become the Army of Descent. However, as the Russians clearly indicated to their allies, this was to be merely a demonstration. The newly formed V Caucasian Corps was sent to the Crimea and Odessa. On both sides of the frontier re-organisation was carried on apace. Enver replaced Third Army's casualties and sent troops to occupy Tabriz in Persian Azerbaijan abandoned so precipitately in December.

Yudenitch's losses were also replaced with many new recruits drawn from the local non-Russian population including many Armenians who nursed a bitter, long-standing hatred of the Turks. The transport system behind the lines was upgraded, road and rail links were established and an extensive telephone network installed. Thousands of mules, oxen and camels were gathered to provide the transport where no wagons could go and to provide food on the hoof. During the following months Russian infantry strength increased to 130,000 but the cavalry doubled in numbers to 35,000 by the return of the Caucasian Cavalry Division (General Charpentier) of three dragoon and one Cossack regiments. The artillery received another forty guns.

Turkish Armenia

Attention at both Russian and Turkish headquarters now turned to the Persian-Turkish border. The Turks struck first with the 36th Division. Accompanied by several thousand Kurdish irregular cavalry, they crossed the border and occupied Dilman. The Russians concentrated their forces and struck back, driving the Turks back across the border. However, Kurdish anti-Christian pogroms had provoked the Armenian population of Van to revolt in mid-April. The Turks were forced out but promptly blockaded Van with reinforcements rushed up from Bitlis. Yudenitch determined to exploit this situation and sent the extreme left column of the newly-formed IV Caucasian Corps (Oganovski) to raise the siege whilst other units of this corps purged the region of Kurdish marauders. The Caucasian Cavalry Division and the 3rd Transbaikal Cossack Brigade were sent by rail to Tabriz with the intention of overawing the Kurds with a display of cavalry power. This huge cavalry force rode to Dilman re-establishing Russian prestige across Persian Azerbaijan and moved into Turkish territory.

By the end of May the siege of Van was lifted and Russian columns marched along the shores of Lake Van to north and south, Armenian volunteers providing a useful infantry supplement. The Turkish Third Army had, by the end of May, refilled its ranks with IX Corps on the left and X Corps in the centre. On the right XI Corps was moved to Hinis to complete its training and observe the movements of IV Caucasian Corps north of Lake Van.

Having weathered the first shock of the Gallipoli landings in April 1915 Enver prepared to mount a powerful offensive in the region of Lake Van. A special group of Third Army was formed under Abdul Kerim Pasha with the German Major Guse as his Chief of Staff. This force included 36th, 37th, 52nd, 51st, 17th, 28th and 29th infantry divisions, 2nd Cavalry Division and supporting arms plus innumerable irregulars. Russian intelligence failed to discover the size of the group assembling, believing only four divisions (of which two were incomplete) opposed them. In fact, a group of 70,000 Turks were gathering. West of Lake Van the Russians occupied Tutak, Malazgirt and Adilcevaz. The Turks held the Cossack-Armenian force south of the lake during the last week of June.

The Caucasian Cavalry Division was ordered to proceed along the lake towards Ahlat where it was to anchor the line whilst the infantry stormed the

Turkish positions along the Belican Hills 24km (15 miles) west of Malazgirt. Oganovski launched his attack on 12 July but, despite support from the Caucasian Cavalry Division, no ground was taken. On 16 July part of the Belican line was taken. Two dragoon regiments were ordered to continue the lakeside advance and link up with the Cossack-Armenians, which they did in July. However, such detachments weakened Oganovski's force. It was at this moment that the Turks attacked the western-bound Russians from the front and both flanks. Early in the morning of 23 July Don Cossack *plastuni* broke and Oganovski's right flank collapsed. The Russian troops began to fall back on Malazgirt where they were joined by other retreating units. The Cossack-Armenian group, south of Lake Van, fell back on Van, which was evacuated on 4 August as they retired towards Persia.

With his left flank gone and his right mauled, Oganovski's situation was grim. In Malazgirt the Russians had 10,000 infantry and some 5,000 cavalry with which to confront 35,000 Turks. Malazgirt was evacuated on 26 July and, accompanied by thousands of Armenian refugees, the remains of IV Caucasian Corps began a full-scale retreat north-eastwards as the Turks advanced on a wide front. Elated with this success, Enver pressed Abdul Kerim to forge ahead and invade Russia. The Turks followed up and established bases at Eleskirt and Karakilise but did not pursue Oganvski who retreated across the Eleskisk Plain. However, Yudenitch had prepared well and assembled a force of just less than 18,000 infantry and 4000 cavalry with 36 guns under Baratov, north-west of the advancing Turks' left flank. The dispersed parts of IV Caucasian Corps (now commanded by Charpentier) that had retreated into Persia were ordered to threaten the Turks' right flank. Yudenitch intended to use Baratov's men to cut the Turk's line of retreat.

Luckily for the Turks their slow advance and Adbul Kerim's assessment of the situation saved them. A weak Turkish attack gained Abdul Kerim twenty-four hours to organise the retreat from Karakilise. However, it was a far from orderly withdrawal and the Turks lost some 6,000 prisoners, the greater part of their artillery and nearly 10,000 casualties. Only the slowness of the Russian flank movements saved the Turks from utter disaster but once again IX Corps had been shattered. IV Caucasian Corps had been seriously weakened but was able to reoccupy Van and move to the south-eastern tip of Lake Van in September. Yudenitch did not intend to try again in this region.

Caucasian Front's successes had gone someway to offset news of the retreat from Poland but Russian losses there meant that no troops could be spared for Yudenitch who was compelled to draft in older, local men to fill the ranks.

On 24 September the Grand Duke Nicholas arrived in Tiflis to take up the post of Viceroy. One of the new Viceroy's orders concerned the formation of a special expeditionary force for Persia. The force commanded by Baratov was mainly cavalry including the Caucasian Cavalry Division, 1st Caucasian Cossack Division and two Kuban Cossack regiments. Two regiments of Frontier Guards and two battalions of *Opolchenie* brought the numbers up to 6,000 infantry and 8,000 cavalry. Sixteen field guns, twelve mountain guns and two 122mm (4.8 inch) howitzers made up the artillery. The arrival of the Grand Duke raised the profile of the Caucasian Front and his presence guaranteed an improvement in the flow of supplies.

The Erzurum campaign: the battle of Koprukoy

Considerations other than the Persian expedition occupied Yudenitch during November 1915. The Allied operation at Gallipoli was obviously drawing to an end and shortly Serbia was to be overrun by the Central Powers. These factors would allow the release of experienced Turkish troops for deployment elsewhere and open up supply lines from Germany and Austria to upgrade the Ottoman forces – particularly its heavy artillery. Enver Pasha was equally aware of the advantages but was slower to make use of them. Yudenitch, on the other hand, planned to go over to the offensive during the Orthodox Christmas period of 7–14 January.

Turkish Third Army held a strongly fortified position, the Koprukoy Line, roughly 120kms (75 miles) long covering the approaches to Erzurum, the northern flank was covered by the Pontic Alps rising to almost 3,000m (9,843 feet) and to the south by Bingol Dag of similar height the terrain was brutal. As a wide outflanking move during the Anatolian winter was out of the question, Yudenitch's plan avoided a frontal attack on the Turks' main line preferring an advance aimed at the junction of XI and X corps on the left.

Surprise and secrecy were essential ingredients of the plan. Consequently no Russian officer below the level of divisional commander was party to it. The deception, a classic Russian *Maskirovka* (deception/masking), was scrupulous in its detail. The rumour was spread of a Russian offensive in Persia, troop trains moved in that direction only to return during the night. Officers and men were sent on leave and Christmas preparations went on apace. Reinforcements were brought into the line under cover of darkness. Although preparations were extensive, particularly equipping the men for the brutal weather and winter conditions, such efforts were viewed as part of Yudenitch's proclivity for taking care of his men.

However, the Grand Duke was not fully convinced that the offensive should go ahead. It was not until Alexeyev telegraphed from *Stavka* intimating that units from the Caucasus would be transferred to Galicia that the Grand Duke confirmed Yudenitch's plans. On 9 January Yudenitch announced that II Turkestan Corps would attack the next day and I Caucasian Corps three days later. These attacks were diversionary, intended to draw off Turkish reserves. On the fifth day the breakthrough attack would go in, spearheaded by 4th Caucasian Rifle Division.

The Turks did not anticipate an attack and had not been reinforced by units released from the Gallipoli Front. Their order of battle, excluding the force on the Black Sea Coast numbered 70–75,000 men with 120 guns. From left to right it consisted of X Corps, three divisions; XI Corps, five divisions; XI Corps, three divisions; twenty battalions of Gendarmerie and Frontier Guards and 2nd Cavalry Division. The irregular formations consisted of several thousand Kurdish cavalry. The cavalry, regular and irregular, and the 37th Division were based around Mus near Lake Van. The three corps held a line of roughly 118kms (73 miles) with 17th Division in reserve. However, the defences did not form a continuous line due to the nature of the terrain. Detachments held fortified hilltops protected by barbed wire. Blasted out of the rock with dynamite machine gun nests and artillery positions were well sited to cover lines of approach. But in places communications were poor and the reserve of 6,000 men would be unable to move rapidly.

Yudenitch's first attack went in as planned on 10 January but failed to draw in the Turkish reserves. The second Russian attack sustained heavy casualties but on 13 January, the Turks moved their reserves to this sector to support a counterattack. Now it was time for the main attack. In bright sunshine, units of the 4th Caucasian Rifle Division, supported by thirty-four guns, struck and breached the Turkish defences. Next day columns of Russian infantry began to push ahead and reached the Turks' second line. Although resistance was slight, the 4th Caucasian Rifle Division was battling with narrow tracks waist-deep in snow.

Elsewhere Yudenitch's good fortune continued and all along the line the Turks began to fall back as the situation became clear. A crack at the junction of X Corps and the south was growing wider by the hour. During the night of 16–17 January the Turkish commander ordered a retreat on Erzurum. Generally the Turks withdrew in reasonable order but XI Corps lost seventy per cent of its men and thirty guns. In all 40,000 Turks reached Erzurum but exposure and desertion cost them dearly. The Russians lost upwards of 11,000 men of which twenty per cent were frost-bitten.

Flushed with success Yudenitch proposed to the Grand Duke that they should storm Erzurum. Again the Grand Duke wavered but, with the encouragement of Alexeyev, consented on 23 January. No extra troops were forthcoming therefore more local reservists and *Opolchenie* were summoned to fill the ranks. Road improvements were carried out and a light railway from Sarikamish pushed forward. Orders were issued to General Lyakhov's forces on the Black Sea coast and Chernozubov in Azerbaijan to begin offensive operations.

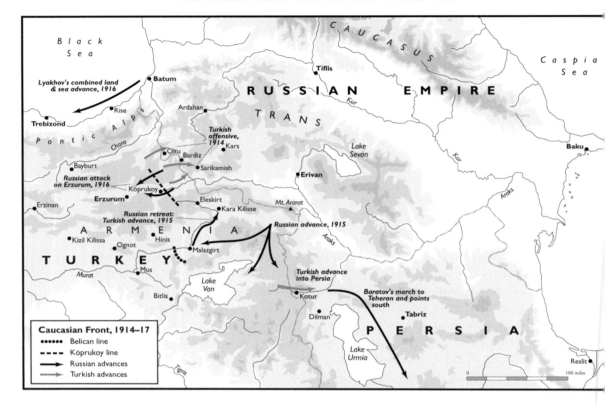

Within days IV Caucasian Corps (Chernozubov) had secured Yudenitch's left by taking Malazgirt and Hinis and Lyakhov's force had opened communications with II Caucasian Corps and was preparing to act as its flank guard on the coast. On the main front the lines were pushed forward to the outlying forts of Erzurum and heavy guns were transported from Kars to be deployed as a siege train. Enver was moving seven divisions from the west to the Caucasian Front. But to reach their destination these troops would have to march almost 805kms (500 miles) from the railhead at Ankara and were not expected until April. However, the Turks were confident that Erzurum would hold out.

Erzurum's defences

The fortified perimeter of Erzurum consisted of a central group of eleven forts and batteries and two flank groups each of two forts. Behind and overlooking these works was another line of four forts. A third line of six forts completed the major defences. Trench lines and wire had been prepared where possible. There were also areas that were considered impassable – always a dangerous assumption. However, to man the defences strongly required upwards of 75,000 men and the Turks had fewer than 50,000. On paper the fortress had 1,000 guns, though in reality there were less than 400 and of these fewer than 150 could be regarded as modern. Nevertheless Enver anticipated a long siege, confident in the Turkish infantry's splendid reputation for defensive fighting and his belief that the Russians lacked heavy artillery.

Russian plans

Yudenitch had no desire, nor the material, to undertake a siege. Erzurum was to be treated as an extended, albeit heavily fortified position. The Russian plan was essentially a repeat of the previous operation: a series of diversionary attacks to be followed up with the main thrust at a thinly defended, theoretically impassable section of the line. This time men of Przevalski's II Turkestan Corps would break through to the plain of the Kara Su River. Occupying this position would put the Russians behind the Turkish main lines and force them to withdraw from Erzurum.

On 8 February Yudenitch informed his senior officers that the attack would commence within three days. At 1400 hours on 11 February the Russian artillery opened fire on two of the Turkish forts and several batteries. Under cover of darkness the Russians took Fort Dalan-goz. Elsewhere results were not as positive but Przevalski's men made good progress. In five columns with strong supporting artillery the riflemen crossed heights averaging 2,000 metres (6,562 feet) and took Fort Kara Gobek. Again the Turks had been misled by a diversionary attack and committed their reserves uselessly.

As Przevalski battered X Corps, Fort Tafet was taken and supporting troops moved in rapidly. By the end of 14 February the Russians were beginning to descend onto the Kara Su plain. Sufficient pressure was maintained on the entire Turkish line to prevent them moving troops to seal the breach.

On the morning of 15 February aerial reconnaissance reported such activity in Erzurum that Yudenitch signalled Przevalski thus, "Turks retreating...March on Erzurum and capture it from the north." By that afternoon the Russians had occupied the outer ring of forts. Throughout the night of 15–16 February the Turkish rearguard fought an increasingly difficult battle to hold the Russians. At 0700 hours Terek Cossacks rode into Erzurum. Initial Turkish losses were put at 5,000 prisoners and 10,000 casualties. Over 300 guns were captured. Russian casualties were 8,000 wounded and frost-bitten and 1,000 dead, a remarkably low figure for the scale of the victory. Fresh Cossack cavalry was sent in pursuit along the road to Erzinan as far as Mamahatun, 81kms (50 miles) west of Erzurum. A Russian column set off towards Bayburt.

The IV Caucasian Corps took Mus on 16 February but the region had been so devastated by the summer campaign of 1915 that it was impossible to buy food or forage and supply columns were under continual attack from the locals and Kurdish irregulars. Consequently the operation was halted.

Combined operations

Lyakhov's forces on the Black Sea coast had to contend with sheer cliffs, ravines and dense forests as well as good Turkish defence lines along the Arhavi River. However, the navy had provided a battleship, the *Rotislav*, and several smaller ships to provide enfilading fire. On 5 February the naval bombardment levelled the Turkish defences and forced them to retreat. This performance was repeated ten days later and 32kms (20 miles) further west at Vice.

The Turks retired along the coast to Atina where their position was much stronger. Lyakhov accepted the navy's suggestion of landing infantry behind the Turkish trenches and using special Black Sea cattle transport vessels known as *elpidiphores* such an operation was mounted.

Two Kuban *Plastun* battalions were landed at Atina just before dawn on 5 March. The Turks were caught napping and their front line troops fled into the hills. Lyakhov had achieved a bloodless victory. Within less than a week his men had reached Rise within 48kms (30 miles) of Trebizond where they halted. They had advanced of over 80kms (50 miles) for less than 300 casualties.

The Russian victories of January to March had not passed Enver Pasha by and he now created a plan to strike a decisive blow against his enemies now re-organising themselves in Erzurum. Third Army (Vehip Pasha) reinforced by V Corps was to engage the Russians between the Kara Su River and the Black Sea. Second Army (Izzet Pasha) was to operate in the Mus–Bitliss area and outflank Yudenitch at Erzurum. This fantasy disregarded the difficulties of the terrain and the lack of railways, and it did not consider the condition of the men or the fact that the Russians had ideas of their own. Enver Pasha was nothing if optimistic but in March 1916, the Ottoman Empire required more than optimism to stop the Russians.

Yudenitch had neither the desire nor the resources to exploit his success on a grand scale; consolidation was uppermost in his mind. Furthermore Alexeyev had again ruled out the possibility of more troops. But a limited combined operation with the navy to capture Trebizond was well within the realms of possibility. On 20 March Yudenitch met with Admiral A.

A. Eberhardt at Batum. Both commanders agreed to co-operate sooner rather than later as Lyakhov feared a strong Turkish counter attack was imminent. Two Kuban *Plastun* brigades (10,000 men with 18 guns) were to be transported from Novorossisk to Rise, the first substantial port west of Batum, The *elpidiphores* and other transports left Novorossisk on 5 April escorted by sea plane carriers and warships. Yudenitch requested that the *Plastuni* disembarked nearer the front line but the navy, fearful of submarines, refused. However, half the brigade was shipped on, escorted by an armed steam-yacht, on Yudenitch's authority. On 14 April, supported by naval gunfire from the two battleships the *Rotislav* and *Panteleymon* (formerly the infamous *Potemkin*), Lyakhov attacked. After heavy fighting the Turkish positions covering Trebizond were overrun and the city evacuated. On 19 April the Russians marched into Trebizond and Lyakhov ordered the occupation of Platana which the navy planned to organise as a base for future operations. Reinforcements were shipped to Trebizond in early June to support Yudenitch's advance.

By now Enver's preparations were complete. The Turks attacked Mamahatun on the Erzurum-Erivan road capturing the town on 29 May. Vehip Pasha had chosen the moment when Yudenitch was re-arranging his units in preparation for the Russian offensive. The divisions of Third Army, including V Corps, had been brought up to some 80,000 men. Unfortunately for Vehip Pasha, Enver had received news of the Russian reinforcements landing at Trebizond and ordered him to move in that direction with 60,000 men.

At first the Turkish attack went well but they were too weak to exploit their achievements and on 2 July Yudenitch ordered Lyakhov's newly constituted V Caucasian and II Turkestan corps onto the offensive. The latter were to mount an attack directed at Bayburt whilst the troops screening Erzurum were to demonstrate vigorously. On the left Yudenitch committed his reserve that worked its way behind Bayburt, which fell on 13 July. The Turks attacking towards the coast were held and when news of the fall of Bayburt reached them they began to withdraw encouraged by a series of Russian night attacks. To the south Mamahatun was reoccupied. Vehip Pasha's Third Army had lost thirty per cent of its strength in six weeks of fighting and confusion was growing as poor communications led to a loss of control. Meanwhile Lyakhov's troops were moving steadily down the valleys toward Erzinan, which was occupied, on 25 July, by Russians moving west. Two days later Yudenitch called a halt, as reinforcements were needed further south where the Turkish Second Army was preparing to attack. With the Turkish Third Army reduced to less then 30,000 men (and desertion cutting this total daily) and fewer than 100 guns it was out of the reckoning.

On 2 August Second Army (commanded by Ahmet Izzet) attacked the Russian lines at Mus and Bitlis. The Russian commander, General

Nazarbekov, fearing an outflanking move abandoned Bitlis four days later. On the same day the Turks recaptured Mus. Less successful was the Turkish attack on Ognot to the northwest where lacklustre generalship provided the Russians with the opportunity to re-align their forces. Furthermore a *Plastun* Brigade was marching to reinforce the Ognot line. From 18–25 August fierce fighting raged around Ognot. The Russians lost heavily on both flanks but in the end their heavier weight of artillery proved too powerful and the Turks were forced to retreat. Ahmet Izzet ordered a withdrawal along the whole line. Desultory fighting continued throughout September. Winter came early that year, the first snow falling on 26 September, and the two sides decided to call a halt to the battle. The Turks evacuated Mus with a total loss of 30,000 men out of an initial strength of 100,000. Details of Russian casualties are unavailable but sources indicate a figure of twenty per cent with typhus a major killer. The Turkish Second Army wintered in areas that had been ethnically cleansed of Armenians during 1915 (a ghastly operation, the scale of which continues to be the subject of much debate). Hundreds of thousands of Armenians were purposely killed by the Kurds and Turks, died of starvation or sought refuge with the Russians. The result was to turn this once fertile region into semi-desert. Consequently rations fell to very low levels. The position of Third Army was somewhat better. Both forces were to undergo a complete re-organisation but it was a slow process as they were in a very poor condition and Turkey was facing a manpower crisis. Following previous defeats and retreats, Turkish deserters usually returned to their units, as rations were fairly regular. However, during the winter of 1916–17 this was not the case. In the words of the Austrian military representative in Turkey, "It may be considered as certain that both Turkish armies were, by the end of the winter, in such a state that they would not have been able to resist any serious Russian attack." Luckily for the Turks such an attack never came.

1917

The revolution of March 1917 put an end to operations on the Caucasian Front almost immediately. When the Grand Duke Nicholas left for *Stavka*, Yudenitch took his place. Revolutionary committees were established in the Russian units but they do not appear to have been particularly extreme in their outlook. The very isolation of the area proved to be a major factor in saving it from the worst excesses. It was also spared a visit from Kerensky. Nationalist tendencies were beginning to surface in Georgia, Russian Armenia and Azerbaijan. A Transcaucasian Council was formed which soon began to espouse separatism in all three regions. During the time of the Provisional Government no units were disbanded nor did many

The stony ground that covered much of the region made trench digging a difficult task. Here a group of Russian infantrymen rest behind their loop-holed parapet.

serious incidents with officers occur, but the formation of national units was encouraged and they were given recognition as such. Several Georgian rifle battalions were raised with their own officers and distinctive uniforms. The Armenian units already in existence were formally recognised as such, amalgamated into higher formations and recruitment encouraged. However, the Russians retained control of the artillery. From May an unofficial cease-fire existed and during the next few months Russians units gradually withdrew from the frontline. Mus was evacuated during the early summer and Erzinan and Bayburt were handed over to the Armenians. Yudenitch resigned in June, blaming the interference of committees and politicians from Tiflis and Petrograd. Przevalski succeeded him.

By the time of the Bolshevik coup in November 1917 the Georgian battalions were in the process of organisation and the Armenians held much of the line. Huge dumps of equipment were available for their use but numerically they were weak. When the armistice was signed in December the Russian troops simply packed up and began the trek north to their homes. However, many would fall victim to increasingly militant, anti-Russian groups along the way. Now the moment that Enver had been

Britain's Royal Naval Armoured Car Division (Commander Locker Lampson MP) had made the journey to the Caucasian Front from Murmansk arriving in the summer of 1916. Here one of the Lanchester armoured cars crosses a ditch. The unit was later transferred to the Romanian Front.

waiting for seemed to have arrived and his dreams of Caucasian conquest resurfaced with a vengeance: Turkey intended to fill the power vacuum left by Russia.

The Turkish revival

The Turkish Second Army was disbanded and many of its men were used to bolster the Third Army. By January 1918 this force had recruited some 45,000 men and 160 guns. In mid-February the Turks re-occupied Trebizond. The 20,000 strong Armenian Corps, spread across eastern Anatolia could do little but wait on events. With the signing of the Treaty of Brest-Litovsk in March, Turkey's former borders were restored. The Transcaucasian Federation rejected this and the Turks advanced driving the Armenians before them. The scene was now set for over three years of horror as Bolshevik, British, anti-Bolshevik, Turkish and German troops, plus numerous bands of brigands and religious fanatics waged war in this unhappy place.

Generals Evert and Kuropatkin at *Stavka* in 1916. Neither man wished to risk his reputation with an offensive that year.

context of 1916 it seemed a reasonable plan, the artillery was to shred the wire, flatten the enemy's defences and thus allow the infantry to take the position. Hopefully the weather would be better than in March and there would be more shell. But Evert was not happy; intellectually he was already beaten. As Langois, one of the French observers succinctly put it, "From the point of view of morale [the Russian Army] has but a single fault, and that is the lack of confidence that reigns in the High Command..." However, one member of the High Command was not steeped in the general aura of pessimism – the newcomer Brusilov.

To the astonishment of Evert and Kuropatkin, Brusilov declared that he would attack in the summer with no additional forces. Brusilov had proposed this to the Tsar during an inspection of Eighth Army earlier in April. Naturally the Tsar had been non-committal. Later that day the conference ended after it was decided that all three fronts would contribute to the offensive but that the main effort would be that of W Front supported by N Front while SW Front would confine itself to diversionary attacks. With varying degrees of confidence the front commanders returned to their HQs to prepare for the summer's operations. The Tsar returned to his library of sentimental novels.

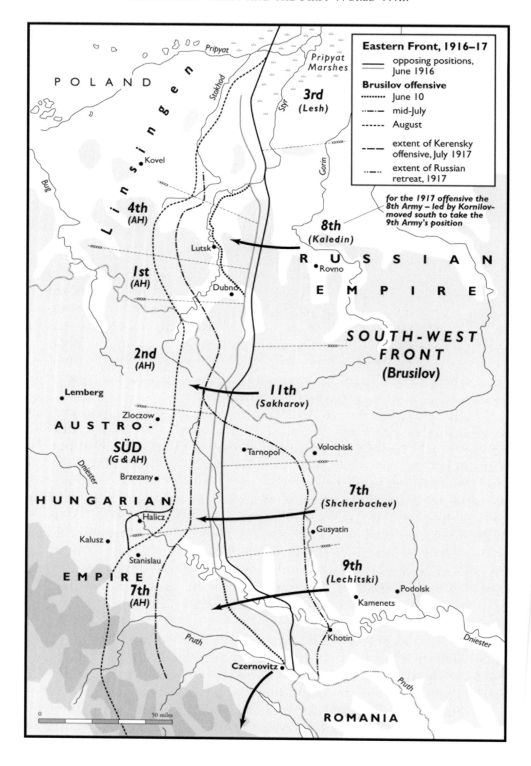

Eastern Front, 1916–17
 ―――― opposing positions, June 1916
 ――――
Brusilov offensive
 ·········· June 10
 ·―·―· mid-July
 ------ August
 ――― extent of Kerensky offensive, July 1917
 ·――·― extent of Russian retreat, 1917

for the 1917 offensive the 8th Army – led by Kornilov – moved south to take the 9th Army's position

POLAND

Pripyat

Pripyat Marshes

3rd
(Lesh)

Kovel

L i n s i n g e n

Stokhod

Styr

Gorin

Bug

4th
(AH)

Lutsk

8th
(Kaledin)

R . U S S I A N

1st
(AH)

Rovno

Dubno

E M P I R E

2nd
(AH)

SOUTH-WEST
FRONT
(Brusilov)

Lemberg

11th
(Sakharov)

Zloczow

AUSTRO-

SÜD
(G & AH)

Dniester

Brzezany

Tarnopol

Volochisk

HUNGARIAN

7th
(Shcherbachev)

Halicz

Gusyatin

Kalusz

Stanislau

9th
(Lechitski)

Podolsk

EMPIRE

Kamenets

7th
(AH)

Pruth

Khotin

Dniester

Czernovitz

Pruth

0   50 miles

ROMANIA

SW Front prepares

On SW Front Brusilov summoned his army commanders to his Berdichev HQ. If they had anticipated a discussion they were wrong and if they anticipated a repeat of the winter offensive they were also wrong. Their new commander intended to wage war in a far more organised but untried manner. Gone were the demands for mountains of shell and even more artillery: thought and preparation were now the order of the day. Brusilov and his staff at Eighth Army had analysed the mistakes of 1915 and 1916 and reached some novel conclusions that were to be incorporated into the front's preparations.

To address the problem of how to catch the opposition unawares each army would prepare for a simultaneous attack by several of their corps. Now there would be no obvious single concentration point. This would lead to confusion on the Austrian side as to where to place their reserves. In reality the Eighth Army (General A. M. Kaledin) was to launch the main attack towards Lutsk. Should Eighth Army's efforts fall short of expectations then the direction of the attack would be switched to another army where success could be reinforced. The four army commanders were given until 23 May to complete their preparations.

With the exception of two divisions the Germans had withdrawn their forces from this region and SW Front faced an almost exclusively Austrian force. Several divisions had been transferred to the Italian Front but the reduction of manpower (in the minds of the Austrian High Command) was more than compensated for by the strength of their defences, which was the result of six months hard work during a relatively quiet period. Three belts of three trenches ran almost continuously from the Pripyat Marshes to the Romanian border. Barbed wire, often with attached fougasse mines and sometimes electrified, had transformed no man's land from the green pastures of 1915 into a deadly killing zone. The trenches themselves were provided with dormitory style bunkers for the infantry and concrete machine gun nests were positioned for maximum destructive effect. Well might the Austrians feel complacent.

To break through this formidable defensive system in the conventional French, British or German fashion would require incalculable amounts of shell and a crassly stupid defending general. Neither condition applied. Therefore for SW Front's diversionary attacks to succeed, tactical innovation was vital.

SW Front's staff obtained aerial photographs of the Austrian lines and from these maps were drawn and issued to officers of all ranks to familiarise themselves with their opponent's positions. Replica Austrian trench systems were built so that the Russian infantry could familiarise themselves with

In many places Brusilov's troops tunnelled under the Austrian wire to shorten the distance that the advance was exposed to fire. The entrance to such a tunnel is shown here. The work was carried out during the night so that the soil could be removed under cover of darkness.

them, avoid disorientation and practice defensive techniques. Brusilov's artillery was to adhere to a strict firing plan and co-ordinate its work with the infantry by extensive use of the telephone. Immense camouflaged dugouts were constructed to house the reserves immediately behind the front line to avoid the time, energy and men lost during previous operations when the troops had to march, often over open ground, for up to two or three kilometres. The front line trenches would be sapped forward, often to within 75m (82 yards) of the Austrians and camouflaged. Wherever possible tunnels were to be driven under the wire to minimise the exposure time in no man's land. Finally artillery registration was to be conducted several days prior to the main barrage and the guns moved closer to the front to allow for deeper support during the later phases of the attack.

To ensure that his orders were carried out Brusilov and members of his staff made frequent visits to the front lines. While the SW Front team worked rapidly and efficiently little work was carried out on the other two fronts where the tried and trusted methods of slaughter were to be applied again.

Italy appeals

However, from 20 May onwards a series of increasingly desperate appeals arrived at *Stavka* from Italy where the Austrian offensive was proving very successful. Although Alexeyev had no wish to begin the offensive prematurely the pressure on him to adhere to the inter-allied promise of support increased. Finally the Tsar, in response to a personal request from the King of Italy, prevailed upon Alexeyev to canvass the front commanders to see if they could do something. Evert declared the impossibility of attacking before 14 June. Brusilov, overriding the concerns of his subordinates, declared that his front was ready. After some prevarication the SW Front's diversionary attack was scheduled to begin on 4 June and the appropriate orders were therefore issued.

Diversionary attack

A particular touch of good sense during the Russian barrage was a series of pauses to allow scouts to assess the effects and report back to the gunners. A knock on effect from this was to confuse the defenders who would clamber out of their dugouts, man the parapets and peer through the dust, smoke and gloom to find there was no attack underway. Then the guns would start again and the Austrians would scurry back underground. This pattern repeated itself at intervals for 36 hours so that the Austrians became more and more reluctant to leave their shelters.

When the Russian infantry finally stormed out of their saps and tunnels they speedily overran what was left of the first Austrian line. Hundreds were captured in their dugouts. Others who refused to surrender were bombed out by the Grenadier platoons. As the Austrians had committed the bulk of their men to the first defence belt, their casualties were enormous. Russian reserves were speedily despatched to sustain the attack's momentum and in a short space of time Austrian Fourth Army (commanded by Archduke Joseph Ferdinand) was pulling back towards Lutsk.

Russian Eighth Army had attacked on a 37km (30 miles) front with three corps. By the end of 5 June the three Austrian positions had been breached and the following day Lutsk fell. Austrian Fourth Army had been reduced from 150,000 to 27,000 men, most of who were retreating as fast as possible to the Stokhod River.

Below Eighth Army, from north to south, the other armies of SW Front were advancing. Eleventh Army (General V. V. Sakharov) had broken out from its bridgehead, defeated the Austrians at Sopanow and captured

The cost of victory: Russian corpses await burial in the last line of Austrian trenches. The contrast in the conditions between Eastern and Western fronts is marked, simple chevaux-de-frise, undamaged trees and ground testify to the more fluid conditions in the east.

Dubno. This event led the Austrian High Command to commit its reserves to this sector.

Seventh Army (General D. G. Shcherbachev) using a more traditional narrow front attack suffered greater casualties but advanced nonetheless. Ninth Army (General P. A. Lechitski), with only forty-seven heavy guns (most of which were obsolete models from the 1880s from the Odessa harbour batteries) broke through near the town of Okna on 5 June. Its opponents were Seventh Army. The Dniester River divided the Austrian defences in this region and their commander switched his reserves to south of the river. On 7 June the Russians broke through to the north of the river and forced the Austrians to withdraw to the south-west to cover the Bukovina region which they believed to be the Russian objective. However, Falkenhayn, via the Austrian High Command, ordered the retreat to be directed to the west. In the ensuing confusion Seventh Army began to lose its cohesion by moving in two different directions and its commander calculated its losses at roughly 100,000 men in ten days.

As early as 6 June German troops began to move south. Two days later Falkenhayn insisted that von Hotzendorf abandon the Italian offensive. On 12 June the Russian returns for Austrian POWs and captured weapons were as follows:

Army	Officers	Men	Guns	Machine Guns	Minenwerfer
8th	437	76,000	87	276	90
11th	594	25,000	16	91	64
7th	716	34,000	47	106	9
9th	1245	55,000	66	172	32
Total	2992	190,000	216	645	196

In many places the Austrian line was on the point of collapse and Russian cavalry had raided west as far as Vladimir Volyinsk, Fourth Army's HQ, approximately 32kms (25 miles) behind the front. However, by this time SW Front was reaching the limits of its resources, particularly artillery ammunition. Infantry were also in short supply despite the fact that most of the cavalry, with the exception of the Cossacks, had been dismounted. Furthermore Brusilov was concerned about the possibility of an attack into the northern flank of Eighth Army should it move nearer to Kovel as had happened the previous year. Kaledin was therefore ordered to stop.

The Central Powers were moving reserves east, three Austrian divisions had left Italy and sixteen German divisions including four from Verdun were also on their way. Falkenhayn, utilising the remnants of Fourth Army and nine newly arrived German divisions, planned a counterattack against the north face of the Kovel salient. The other reinforcements were scattered piecemeal to prop up other areas of the front. Although some ground was taken along the marshy banks of the Stokhod River, an attempt against the salient's south face cost 40,000 men and achieved nothing. Meanwhile Lechitski was advancing into the Bukovina but the speed of his army's movement was retarded by the near impossibility of regular, adequate supplies due to the primitive infrastructure. The start of the bombardment on the Somme on 24 June precluded any further movements from the west until the seriousness of British intentions became apparent.

June 1916 was something of a curate's egg for *Stavka*. Brusilov's diversionary attacks had succeeded beyond belief. But Evert had postponed his offensive until 17 June and caused further problems by shifting the focus of that offensive to a different point on his front. Another postponement,

Motor cycle dispatch riders pose by their machines on 7 June 1916 at *Stavka*. The Russians imported various models of motor cycle and motor cycle combinations. A particular favourite was the American made Indian which was robust enough to withstand the primitive roads of Eastern Europe.

this time until the end of the month, followed. Sporadic attacks were made but they amounted to very little. Support for Brusilov would be confined, as Evert put it to Alexeyev, to, "frontal blows, promising only very slow progress with the greatest of difficulty".

A major component of the force allotted to Evert was the Guards Army (General V. M. Bezobrazov) which was transferred from N Front to W Front in late May. Only on 4 June did Evert show Bezobrazov the, "points where it was planned to break through enemy defences, and the action of the cavalry for developing our success". Two of Bezobrazov's diary entries for the next week deal with planning the cavalry exploitation phase of the offensive but there is no mention of the infantry. On 10 June the Guards received orders from Evert outlining their part in the upcoming attack.

On 20 June Bezobrazov ordered one of his staff to resign due to his heavy drinking. Yet four days later he wrote to Alexeyev requesting the drunkard be, "given command of a brigade"! Equally indicative of the casual approach that pervaded Evert's command was the fact that the commander of the Guards artillery, General the Duke Mikhail of Mecklenburg-Strelitz

German POWs await transport to the rear during August 1916. Many would be transported to Turkestan or Siberia where food was reasonably easy to obtain and escape well nigh impossible. However, an investigation into conditions in the camps in Turkestan during late 1916 led to several being closed due to the bad conditions. Some POWs were retained as agricultural labourers west of the Ural Mountains.

(a member of the Russian royal family and the German aristocracy), only in post since 16 May, spent at least 13–15 June at the St George's Council discussing the issue of medals. As Evert's men shuffled from place to place Kuropatkin remained almost entirely passive. All this prevarication was carried out with the permission of the Supreme Commander in Chief, the Tsar himself. Alexeyev had ordered both N and W fronts to provide reinforcements for SW Front and these had been willingly given, possibly to avoid any attacks by those fronts thus weakened.

July

The first two weeks of July were critical for the Central Powers. A reinforced Eighth Army had struck against the new positions east of Kovel and driven the Austro-Germans back to the Stokhod River. Lechitski's Ninth Army was advancing through the Bukovina threatening the southern flank of the Austrian lines.

On 2 July W Front had finally attacked. For several days 1,000 guns had pounded the German defences but achieved relatively little simply because the preparation had been appalling. Artillery registration was late, little or no reconnaissance had been done and the officers in charge were unfamiliar with the ground. For six days the infantry valiantly pressed home attack after attack but the offensive petered out for the loss of some 80,000 men and negligible gains. Kuropatkin made a feeble effort at Riga but achieved nothing more than heavy losses, particularly amongst the Latvian Rifles.

In France the long awaited British offensive on the Somme was providing little in the way of success. The Tsar's faith in Evert was wavering. Nicholas wrote to his wife (5 July), "The offensive at Baranovitchi is developing slowly – for the same old reason – that many of our commanding generals are silly idiots, who, even after two years of warfare, have not been able to learn the first and simplest ABC of the military art. I cannot tell you how angry I am with them but I shall get my own way and learn the truth." Alexeyev took advantage of his master's attitude and transferred Third Army which connected SW and W fronts to SW Front's control and, with Nicholas' approval, provided Brusilov with the Guards Army the elite of Russia's armed forces. Brusilov intended to do nothing less than take Kovel and thus turn the flank of the German line from there to the Baltic coast. SW Front was in dire need of fresh troops as the trained men the so-called "*Polivanovtsy*" were beginning to run out.

The Guards Army

The Guards were described by Britain's military attaché Colonel Knox as, "physically the finest human animals in Europe and all of the best military age". As it was provided with the pick of the empire's manpower this was a reasonable comment. Having suffered very heavy casualties during the first three months of the war the Guards were taken out of the line on 19 December 1914 and placed under the direct authority of the Supreme Commander in Chief. For the next 18 months they saw very little action. However, Bezobrazov, by a combination of incompetence, arrogant insubordination and tactlessness was removed from his post at the same time as the Tsar took command at *Stavka*. Reinstated by Nicholas some months later Bezobrazov was instructed to oversee a reorganisation of the Guards into the Guards Army that would involve its consolidation into one large, all arms formation.

By 1916 the Guards had been restructured into two infantry and a cavalry corps with trench, field and heavy artillery (part of which was motorised) and two units of aircraft. Behind the lines the men underwent

The Tsaritsa and her daughters, Maria, Anastasia, Olga and Tatiana leave *Stavka* at Moghilev during August 1916. Nicholas described the weather as, "rotten cold and damp" which is evident from the photo. The Tsaritsa was not popular with many of the senior army officers due to her alleged pro-German sympathies.

training based on pre-war concepts as though their combat experience was meaningless. Officer casualties had been so high in 1914 that many of the replacements were volunteers from the Guards cavalry who were keener to show the "correct spirit" than to learn about realities. Others still were the products of accelerated officer's courses. Bravery in battle was still regarded as the greatest of military virtues, a more valuable commodity than an eye for terrain or the ability to throw a grenade accurately. Unfortunately it was commanded by a selection of the aristocracy that had little or no idea of modern warfare. Appointments to the Guard were the prerogative of the Tsar who took a close and protective interest in its doings. General G. O. Rauch, who from late 1914 to the summer of 1916 had successively commanded the Guards cavalry, I Guards and II Guards corps, was described in December 1915 as having, "a reputation for cowardice under fire..." although, "I [Bezobrazov] personally appreciate him as a clever person and good military commander." A fine body of men with gallant officers they may have been but they were not well-schooled in modern warfare and Kovel in 1916 was no place for amateurs.

The Guards Army received orders to entrain for SW Front on 9 July. To increase its already formidable strength the I and XXX corps were added to it. Transporting over 100,000 men, more than 25,000 horses and 200 guns plus the other equipment that made up the Guards Army was in itself a mammoth undertaking. The assembly of forces caused the attack to be postponed for several days during which time the weather improved. With the Guards and other reinforcements in place Eighth Army numbered over 250,000 men. Facing them were 115,000 weary Austro-Germans.

As Brusilov explained to Knox, the Third Army was to attack Kovel to the west, the Guards to the north-west, and the Eighth Army was to move west on Vladimir Volyinsk. Eleventh Army was to wheel on Lemberg. Seventh Army would follow the Austrians retreating from Brody and Ninth Army would, "get its turn when Romania joins in".

Bezobrazov's order of the day for 27 July exhorted his men to, "open by fire and bayonet a road to Kovel and thus liberate the, since immemorial times, Russian soil from an invasion of aliens…. Forward for the Tsar and Motherland." After these stirring words and under the watchful eyes of Italian and Japanese observers on 28 July the slaughter began.

The Guards infantry advanced and drove the Germans back towards the Stokhod River. But the marshlands in that area funnelled the attack lanes to narrow tracks. As a consequence the Russians were cut to ribbons. Attempting to fan out, men waded chest deep into the water presenting themselves as even simpler targets yet despite everything positions were taken and progress made. Interestingly Knox mentions that the attack waves were, "preceded by grenadiers and sappers to clear such of the wire as may have escaped the artillery." The casualty lists began to grow with horrific speed and by the end of the first week in August the Guards alone had lost 30,000 men.

Such was their frustration with their seniors that Guards officers began to criticise them openly even to the foreigner Knox who recorded some of their comments. It was a "pity that we spared our guns so much", the artillery could have "destroyed Vitonej [a particularly well defended village] but no one told them to fire at it." The Guards Rifle Division had lost almost an entire brigade assaulting that point. As the attacks floundered on Bezobrazov was ordered to replace infantrymen with cavalry in the quieter trenches, though he refused, still clinging to the hope of launching them across open ground in pursuit of a broken enemy.

On 8 August Bezobrazov confided his thoughts on a subordinate to his diary, "Grand Duke Pavel Alexandrovich does not understand anything." Not only was this the uncle of the Tsar, but he was also commander of I Guards Corps and therefore a dangerous person to express criticisms to as

Bezobrazov did only days later. On the same day, 12 August, Bezobrazov wrote to the Tsar explaining the situation. Brusilov and Rodzianko (the President of the *Duma* who was visiting the SW Front and whose son was a Guards officer) wrote to Alexeyev. Brusilov and Rodzianko expressed the "rage and discontent" of the Guards who felt that the senior officers were, "incapable of handling it in such critical times and felt very bitterly the number of useless casualties." A young officer said to Rodzianko, "We are willing to give our lives for Russia, for our Motherland but not for the whims of generals."

The Tsar replied to Bezobrazov, on 20 August, stating that he had "full confidence in him". However, by now Bezobrazov was convinced that both the Tsaritsa and the Grand Duke Pavel were plotting against him. On 28 August Bezobrazov received a telegram informing him of his replacement by General V. I. Gurko and the renaming of the Guards Army which became the Special Army. Seemingly it was the attacks of mid-August that had sealed Bezobrazov's fate. Nevertheless, a couple of days later, Nicholas promised, "I will return the Guard to you".

Third and Special armies reverted to the control of Evert's W Front and the battering of Kovel continued to no effect and increasing casualties. N Front, quiescent for most of the summer, also had a new commander, General N. V. Ruzski, who replaced Kuropatkin in early August. Kuropatkin had been sent east to deal with the uprising in Turkestan.

Uprising in Central Asia

The Russian Empire had expanded into central Asia during the latter part of the nineteenth century. When the borders with Afghanistan, Persia (Iran) and China were settled, Russian migrants began to move into the area which became known as Turkestan. The immigrants (mainly peasants from western Russia) marginalised the native Moslem Khirgiz and Kazak population. In many respects the movement east and conditions paralleled the American west, with small garrison towns and settlers bent on a new prosperous life. Following the 1905 revolution the flow eastwards increased markedly to over 100,000 per year. Moslems were exempt from conscription although a small unit of volunteer cavalry was raised – the Turkmen Horse, a two-squadron half-regiment recruited from the Tekin tribe.

However, as Russia's manpower problems increased it was decided to conscript Turkestanis into labour battalions to release ethnic Slavs for combat. To this end the Tsar, on 25 June 1916, signed an *Ukase* calling for the drafting of 250,000 Moslems from Turkestan.

Before the Tsar's order could be acted upon mass protests broke out and spread across Turkestan as a result of misunderstandings and a simple

Building the Murmansk railway line involved thousands of workers. However, the refusal of local people to work in the severe conditions led the Russian government to import Chinese labourers and use POWs. The number of those who died has not been established but 20,000 has been suggested.

unwillingness to go. Demonstrations in Tashkent resulted in thirty-six executions and the protest movement threatened to develop into a full scale uprising against Russian rule. As he had prior experience of the area Kuropatkin was sent to the region as Military Governor in August. More Russian troops were deployed to support the garrisons and martial law was declared in Turkestan and the Caucasus which also had a large Moslem population.

Local negotiations resulted in a lowering of the initial quota of 250,000 and the first transports west were postponed until the harvest had been gathered. For some Turkestanis this was not enough and sporadic fighting continued. Punitive detachments of Cossacks, regular troops and groups of armed settlers roamed the steppe often acting brutally to bring the situation under control. At this time there were over 150,000 POWs in Turkestan and it is claimed that some were armed by the Russians and took part in such expeditions. By a combination of carrot and stick the situation improved for the Russians and on 18 September the first transport of conscripts left Tashkent. Towards the end of

1916 most of Turkestan was under control but as a Russian communications officer recalled even in January 1917 travelling was unsafe without, "several hundred Cossacks...hussars and...artillery." At the same time a journalist recalled seeing a column of Uzbeks "shuffling through Moscow to build an Arctic railway and to die." The railway was part of the solution to the problem of transporting imported supplies from the north.

The supply problem

The munitions shortage began in 1914 and the short-term solution, as had been the case in earlier wars, was to import the necessary shells and weapons. Although orders were placed abroad, a major difficulty lay in how to get them into Russia when they were finally produced. The Black and Baltic seas were closed which left only Vladivostok on the Pacific Ocean and the ports of Archangel and Murmansk on the White Sea and the Arctic Ocean respectively.

The problems were that only Murmansk and Vladivostok were ice free all year round, Archangel was closed from October to May and transportation from all three ports was problematic. Vladivostok lay at the end of the Trans-Siberian Railway 9,300kms (5,770 miles) from Moscow. Much of the line was single track and its capacity was limited as Siberia's food and mineral resources took up most of the available freight capacity.

Archangel was connected to the main rail network at Vologda by a poorly built, single track, narrow gauge line which meandered for 560km (350 miles) across ground which was a swamp when not frozen solid. It was decided to convert the track to broad gauge and by early 1916 this had been accomplished. However, capacity was limited to 5,000 tons per day.

Murmansk had no rail link with Petrograd. The nearest railhead was at Petrozavodsk over 1,138kms (707 miles) to the south. To put this distance in context it is roughly the same as the distance between London and the north of Scotland. There the similarity ended: this was a wilderness. The terrain was incredibly difficult with over a quarter of the projected route lying across marshland and neither men nor building supplies were easily obtainable. Work began on a line to connect Murmansk to Petrozavodsk in late 1914. However, many of the original labourers refused to renew their contracts due to the conditions and by 1916 indentured labourers had been recruited from China. They, along with POWs and convicts, made up the great bulk of the workforce. The mortality rate was high, as malaria was rampant and conditions harsh. The line was opened for traffic in November 1916 but again capacity was low. Other methods were used whilst the line was under construction such as horse and reindeer convoys however, these moved but a tithe of what was required.

At all three ports supplies piled up and were often left to the mercy of the elements as warehousing was scarce with the consequence that material began to corrode or sink into the ground under its own weight. The entry of Romania would also increase the pressure on Russia's rail network.

Autumn 1916

With the transfer of the Special and Third armies back to Evert's W Front what became known as Brusilov's Offensive came to an end. However, there was to be no let up in the fighting around Kovel that now fell into Evert's area of responsibility. Unfortunately nothing had been learned from Brusilov's tactical methods. Wave after wave of Russian infantry bogged down in the Stokhod marshes achieving little more than dents in the Central Power's front and longer and longer casualty lists.

Although SW Front continued to make progress reaching the foothills of the Carpathians once again it had, by mid-September, reached the limits of its strength and with the supply lines stretched to the limit and denied reinforcements the advance came to an end. On 4 October the Tsar ordered Brusilov to call a halt only to yield to a request for an extension a day or so later. When Nicholas informed the Tsaritsa she immediately telegraphed him saying, "He [Rasputin] approved of your original plan to stop [the offensive] and begin in another place. Now you write otherwise. May God help us". Nicholas justified his actions to Alexandra, and thus to Rasputin, on 6 October and implored her to keep the military details to herself. The Tsar also added, "You will really help me a great deal by speaking to the Ministers and watching them." During his year at *Stavka* Nicholas had become increasingly dependent on his wife's opinion of ministers and their worth while she had fallen back more and more on the advice of Rasputin.

Now SW Front began the complex process of realigning itself with the Romanians. However, military operations did not end completely, corps commanders were ordered to choose a part of their front within 100m (109 yards) of the enemy and, as Gourko recalled, "from time to time provoke close fighting in trenches, especially using trench mortars instead of artillery, hand grenades instead of bayonets. These districts had to be also a fighting school for the divisions of the corps." Evidently SW Front at least intended to use the winter months to train its replacements in modern warfare.

The results of Brusilov's diversionary offensive were, on paper at least, spectacular. The Austrian army had lost roughly 25,000 square kilometres (9,653 square miles) of territory – an area almost the same as Belgium. As a result the Germans had taken control of the entire Eastern Front inserting

Described only as "French mortars" these two weapons are in the front line to give close support to the first assault waves. By 1916 such technology was becoming more common in the Russian Army. These men are part of the 73rd *Krimsky* Infantry Regiment with XII Corps. Note the lack of revetments in the trench.

German officers and units throughout the Austrian line to act, as some have described it, as "corset staves". Italy had been "saved" and troops drawn off from France. But it had also drawn in Romania whose army was to prove more of a liability than an asset certainly until it too absorbed the lessons of conducting a modern war. The advances made by SW Front had finally tipped the balance in Romania and on 27 August it joined the allies.

Alexeyev was firmly against Romanian intervention as were many other Russian senior officers. Indeed he had argued against encouraging their participation during the winter of 1915–16. Romania was even less prepared for a long war than Russia had been and it lacked any accessible harbours. Consequently, as part of their intervention package Romania had negotiated a list of munitions to be supplied by France, Britain and Russia that would tax the transport system almost to breaking point.

CHAPTER 7

Romanian Winter 1916–17

Despite being a member of the Triple Alliance, in August 1914 Romania had repudiated her commitments to the Central Powers. Under the terms of the treaty of October 1883 Romania had agreed to fight if Hapsburg territory adjacent to Romania was invaded. In return Austria-Hungary and Germany guaranteed to defend her: an arrangement intended to deter Russian aggression. During the late nineteenth century Bucharest was heavily fortified, as were strategic locations in the path of any Russian invasion. With a royal family that was related to the Kaiser and certainly sympathetic towards Germany and a government that was trusting of neither Russia nor Germany but keen to include Austrian Transylvania and Russian Bessarabia within its borders, it is unsurprising that Romania came down on the side of neutrality as she had more to gain from exacting a high price for her intervention at a favourable time than the demands of honour.

Romania was shaped like an inverted T and consisted of two regions, Moldavia sandwiched between Russia and Austria-Hungary and Wallachia surrounded by Russia, Bulgaria, Serbia and Austria-Hungary. Its capital was Bukarest and its major port Constanza on the Black Sea. It was a fertile country with a mainly rural population whose condition was described as "feudal" by Knox, Britain's military attaché to Russia.

Fearful that Romania would honour her treaty obligations and concerned for the security of Russia's left flank, Sazanov, Russia's foreign minister, promised in October 1914 that Romania would receive Transylvania in return for "benevolent neutrality." It was not only Romania's geographical location that gained her such a promise. At Ploesti lay the biggest European oil field now accessible to the Central Powers. It was essential to German and Austrian industry that Romanian oil kept flowing and, having reneged on her treaty obligations, she remained unaligned. Furthermore, the agricultural produce was there for the Central Powers to buy, albeit at inflated rates. Consequently Romania settled down to comfortable and profitable neutrality.

However, geography made Romania indefensible. The border with Austria-Hungary followed the line of the Carpathian Mountains but these were riddled with passes. To the south the Danube River defined part of the border with Bulgaria. The former Bulgarian province of the Dobrudja, taken by Romania in 1913, had advanced the border beyond the Danube River but to no natural boundary. The Romanian defences in their region relied on the Turtukai complex of thirteen fortresses and the miles of marshy riverbank. There was a ferry crossing at Turtukai, a pontoon bridge at Silistria and a railway bridge much further north. As each bridgehead was in Romanian hands the Danube River appeared impassable, and the Romanian's belief that the Bulgarians were preoccupied with defending their southern flank against the Allied forces in Salonika.

Railways and roads in Romania were poorly developed. Those running towards Russia had been purposely left in such a condition for strategic reasons. Indeed there was a 32km (20 miles) gap between the Russian railhead at Reni and Galatz inside Romania. The Pruth River defined the border with Russia. Another rail line crossed the Pruth River at Jassy with the change of gauge at the junction.

The Romanian Army

The Romanian army was very much influenced by the Central Powers in dress and weaponry. The infantry rifle was Austrian and the field gun the German 75mm Krupp M1903. Between 1914 and 1916 the army expanded to twenty infantry and two cavalry divisions, in August 1916 numbering 833,601 officers and men equipped with 800 machine guns and a veritable artillery museum of 1,300 guns. If the militia was armed with weapons from the 1870s there were just enough rifles to go around. The artillery formations for infantry divisions 10–20 were mainly equipped with 57mm light guns dismounted from the Bukarest fortress system mounted on extemporised chassis with part of their cupola as a shield. The howitzers were a mix of 127mm (5 inch) M1896 Vickers and French and German pieces.

Ammunition re-supply was clearly a nightmare, the rifles alone having four different calibres but, with reserves of only 1,000 rounds per man, it was to be short-lived. Lacking an armaments industry Romania depended on munitions that were either captured or imported but the government was clearly anticipating a short victorious war. The airforce was equipped with a ramshackle collection of pre-war French machines.

The army was divided into five corps, the first fifteen divisions had full artillery and machine gun complements, the 16th some and the remainder none. The infantry were a mixture of regular, reserves, territorials, and

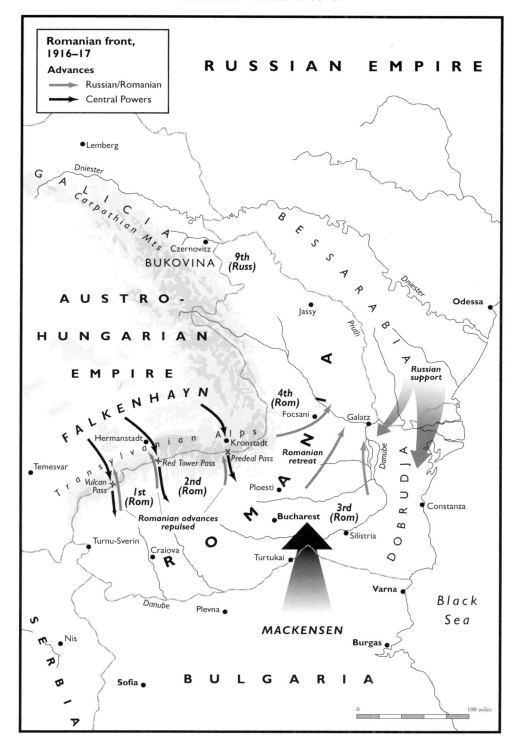

militia. Naturally the regulars were issued with the best weapons and equipment and the militia with the most aged.

Terms of alignment

When the Romanian government agreed to join the entente it did so under the following provisos: Romania was to receive Transylvania, the Banat and Bukovina in addition to,

A.   Energetic action by the Russians, particularly in the Bukovina against the Austrians
B.   Co-operation by the Russian Fleet in the Black Sea
C.   Two Russian infantry divisions and one cavalry division to be sent on the first day of mobilisation to the Dobrudja to be increased as and when necessary
D.   A minimum of 300 tons of munitions to reach Romania daily
E.   An Allied offensive on the Salonika Front to be initiated practically simultaneously with Romanian entry into the war

With territorial rewards and military support in place it only remained for the Romanians to formulate their plan. As Bulgaria was not expected to fight (particularly against the Russian troops assigned to the Dobrudja), Transylvania was to be the objective. The first Romanian Army (General Culcer) was placed at the extreme west of the Carpathian Mountains, the Second Army (General Averescu) from the west to the point where the Carpathians turn north and the Fourth Army (General Presan) would face west into the Carpathians with Ninth Russian Army across the border on its right. In total there were approximately 500,000 men with 800 guns.

Third Army (General Aslan) consisted of 17th Infantry Division at Turtukai, 9th Infantry Division based on Silistria covering the land border of the Dobrudja with 19th Infantry Division at Constanza. The 16th, 18th and 20th infantry divisions were spread out along the Danube River. Their combined strength was less than 150,000 men with fewer than a hundred guns and a hundred machine guns. Finally, with men and agreements in place, the Romanians declared war on Austria on 27 August 1916 and their men began to move into the mountain passes. Within four days Germany and Bulgaria had declared war on Romania.

Alexeyev had only agreed to provide minimal forces and did so sending the 61st Infantry Division, the Serbian Division and 3rd Cavalry Division under the command of General A. M. Zaionchkovski towards the Dobrudja. However, the Russian force was not able to cross the Danube River until 10 September when the pontoon bridge near Galatz was completed.

Russian line cavalry enter Romania preceded by their regimental band. The bandsmen, all mounted on fine greys, appear to be riding hands free.

The Carpathian Front

Three Romanian armies had marched through the passes and into Transylvania on 28 August. The First Army 1st, 11th and 13th infantry divisions with the 2nd, 12th and 23rd infantry divisions in reserve numbered 134,403 men while the Second Army 3rd, 4th, 5th and 6th infantry divisions, 1st Cavalry Division, 21st and 22nd infantry divisions in reserve totalled 126,800 men. The presence of the Fourth Army 8th, 7th, and 14th infantry divisions and 2nd Cavalry Division with two infantry and a cavalry brigade in reserve was an additional 108,000 men strong.

The timing of the Romanian advance had taken the Central Powers by surprise as they had expected the Romanians to wait until after the harvest in mid-September. Five Austrian divisions covered the border, none of which was particularly well provided with men or equipment. The Austrians fell back offering only a token resistance but demolishing anything that would hinder the advancing Romanians. By 9 September the Romanians had established a strong presence in Transylvania and Second Army had occupied Kronstadt. However, the plodding speed of the advance, due more to inexperience and the difficulty of moving large bodies of men, horses and equipment along roads not designed for such masses, had given the Central Powers time to move in reserves using the excellent railway system at their disposal. To add to the Romanians' difficulties their forces were now isolated from one another and lacked the necessary communications equipment to co-ordinate their operations.

With the Romanians appearing at points along a line over 320km (200 miles) long it was not feasible, with the forces at their disposal, for the Austro-Germans to act defensively. It was necessary to attack and at some point to take the initiative. Luckily for Falkenhayn, who had just taken command of the Transylvanian Front, the Romanians did not appear to want to proceed any further. With German and Austrian troops arriving daily, the forces available to Falkenhayn were increasing. Amongst them were the Alpine Corps, Austrian 51st Infantry Division, 187th, 76th, 89th German infantry divisions plus Austrian and German cavalry with strong artillery support. From the outset the Central Powers enjoyed air superiority. Falkenhayn's group was to become Ninth Army and they were to make their first move against the anticipated junction point of Romania's First and Second Armies at Hermanstadt. The plan was to use the Alpine Corps to cut the 16km (10 miles) long Red Tower Pass through which elements of First Army were advancing and threaten its line of retreat. The operation began on 25 September.

The empires strike back

The task of holding off Second Army devolved on the Austro-German cavalry while three infantry divisions attacked the Romanian centre. For three days the fighting raged, the Alpine Corps initially cut the pass and the cavalry maintained its front. However, the Romanians rushed troops into the pass and re-opened the road. Throughout the next two days the First Army held its position but was unable to link up with Second Army. During the night of 28–29 September First Army withdrew into Romania. Falkenhayn had not achieved a "Tannenberg in the mountains" but he had grasped the initiative as both First and Second Armies were ordered to go over to the defensive. The hopes of the Romanians were now pinned on Fourth Army, which was still moving slowly forward but with its left flank exposed.

Falkenhayn sent a small force to monitor the Romanian retreat through the Red Tower Pass and switched the bulk of his troops to face Second Army outside Kronstadt. This time the plan was to cut the Romanians off by sealing the Predeal Pass to their rear. On 5 October the Central Powers drove back the invaders who lost forty-three guns. However, reinforcements arrived and the line held as did the tenuous connection with Fourth Army on their right.

The battle of Brasov began on 7 October with a bombardment that shattered the Romanian's left flank. German mountain troops took control of the Bran Pass but were rapidly driven out. During the night of 8–9 October Second and Fourth Romanian armies began a timely withdrawal. Although Transylvania had been cleared Falkenhayn now had to fight his way through the mountains. The Romanians, fearful for Bukarest, now appealed to the Russians for more help. Alexeyev's reply was blunt. He proposed that they withdraw from the west and defend a line running from Constanza, through Bukarest to the Predeal Pass. The idea of abandoning western Wallachia was unacceptable to the Romanians and the plan was shelved. Beyond the mountains the Central Powers had assembled three armies: the Ninth, First, and Seventh armies. Nominally under Archduke Charles of Austria, they enjoyed a unity of command that the Romanians were, as yet, not inclined to accept.

The Austro-Germans now disposed of a large force of specialist mountain warfare units, the German Alpine Corps and two brigades of Austrian mountain troops. These formations were sent by a series of paths over the heights towards Campulung. However, the operation achieved very little in the face of strong resistance and the first snows of winter. But a more conventional attack through the Vulcan and Szurduk passes against First Army was launched on 23 October. Followed by an entire cavalry corps (von Schmettow) the Austro-German infantry broke through and onto the Wallachian plains. However, a well-managed Romanian attack stopped the advance in its tracks but failed to recapture the exits from the passes.

To the north the Romanian Fourth Army had taken up positions awaiting Russian support which was now delayed by the inadequacy of the railways. The Russian Ninth Army (commanded by Lechitski) to their right was to launch an attack in mid-November timed to coincide with an offensive in the Dobrudja.

Mackensen had surprised the Russo-Romanian forces in the Dobrudja, virtually annihilating the Serbian Division and taking the port of Constanza, almost intact, off the march. The fall of Constanza was a disaster, huge stocks of cereals and oil fell into the hands of the Central Powers and Romania lost its major seaport and railhead. General V. V. Sakharov replaced Zaionchkovski but Russo-Rumanian relations were deteriorating as Alexeyev's shortened defensive line was rapidly being forced on the Romanians by events that were slipping from their grasp. The line from the coast to the Danube River stabilised with the arrival of Russian troops just north of Constanza and the Romanians evacuated the railway bridgehead over the Danube River at Cernavoda. Leaving a screen of five divisions to contain Sakharov, Mackensen moved south to cross the Danube River,

A Cossack on patrol in Romania during the winter of 1916–17. Cossacks always slung their rifles over the right shoulder whereas other cavalry used the left. The sword, *shashka*, was in the case of the Cossacks issued without a guard as can be seen here.

utilising the specialist Austrian Danube Bridging Section. The Central Powers intended to advance on Bukarest from the south and the west.

Falkenhayn's forces were gathering strength. Eight infantry and two German cavalry divisions and several Austrian infantry and cavalry divisions arrived with powerful artillery support. Along the Carpathian Front casualties forced the Romanians to combine several infantry divisions: such as the 9th and 19th and the 2nd and 5th. The 20th had been destroyed and ominously in the 4th cholera had appeared. The Romanian's hope lay in the weather holding up their enemies, but unfortunately nature was not on their side. Choosing the Vulcan Pass as the point of entry, the Central Powers, blessed by good weather and a full moon by night, pushed 60,000 men along the 32km (20 miles) track. Between 10–17 November infantry and cavalry streamed into Romania, opposed by the equivalent of one Romanian division. Though the Romanian infantry fought gallantly, by the night of 16 November they had been driven back. A last desperate counter-attack to close the pass failed and on 17 November the Austro-German cavalry was sent on a wide flank march. Craiova fell four days later cutting off the Romanian 1st Infantry Division at Orsova where it held out until late December.

With western Wallachia all but lost, Bukarest was the next objective. To the north Lechitski's Ninth Army, weakened by detachments sent to

Romania and bad weather, was unable to go over to the offensive until the end of November. Alexeyev ordered Russian troops to take over the line as far as the Predeal Pass releasing Romanians to take up position on the Olt River, the only viable defensive line west of Bukarest. The Olt line was roughly 161km (100 miles) long and to man it the Romanians disposed of some eight infantry divisions along with two cavalry divisions, most of which were tired and under-strength.

Stavka expressed its opinion of the situation thus:

> The Romanians are now being forced back to positions which they should long ago have occupied and fortified. This line is well adapted to defence, and, in spite of training, equipment etc…the Romanians may be able to stand there till the Russians are ready to move and relieve pressure.

The fall of Bukarest

To add to the Romanian's problems, on 23 November Mackensen's troops began to cross the Danube River at Sistovo and advance northeast towards Bucharest. News of this move prompted the Romanian government to begin an evacuation of essential personnel to the Moldavian city of Jassy near the Russian border. On the same day German troops captured an intact bridge across the Olt River and the cavalry corps of General Count von Schmettow crossed to the eastern bank.

The Romanian high command was now assisted by a French military mission under General Berthelot and it was under his influence that the Romanians prepared to defend their capital. The First Army (14th, 8th, 1st/7th and 13th infantry divisions) was to fall back west of Bukarest. To the north of the capital Second Army was to cover the oil fields at Ploesti 48km (30 miles) from Bukarest. Mackensen's Army of the Danube was to be held by 18th Infantry Division and some smaller units. Behind these screens a "mass of manoeuvre" including 9th/19th, 21st and 2nd/5th infantry divisions to be joined by 7th and 10th infantry divisions and two Russian infantry divisions was to be built up for a counter attack. The Romanians were to attack Mackensen's left flank and the Russians his right. During the time that these groups took to assemble the Danube Army had not been idle. The Romanian attack began on 30 November but confusion reigned almost from the outset as conflicting orders and exhausted men marched hither and thither squeezing themselves into a position that allowed their opponents to encircle them. However, the Germans were lucky enough to capture Romanian orders, which disclosed much of their plan. The Russians and Romanians achieved some success but all came to nought when German cavalry and infantry appeared in the rear of 2nd/5th and

9th/19th infantry divisions which collapsed on 3 December. The Russians retired in good order but to the north of Bukarest Second Army was driven out of Ploesti and First Army to the west withdrew as rapidly as possible to escape envelopment from the north and south. As one British commentator put it, "The amputation of a limb of the German Armies was a delicate surgical operation requiring a sharper instrument than the Romanian Army."

Little now remained in front of Bukarest but the tattered remains of several infantry divisions that lacked artillery and ammunition. The Russian Ninth Army's offensive had little or no effect on events in Romania and on 7 December Mackensen entered Bucharest. To the north the Ploesti oilfields burned having been set ablaze by a British saboteur Colonel Norton Griffiths MP, the only speck of light in an otherwise black period.

The Romanian Army was a shattered hulk reduced to 70,000 effectives. A Russian officer described a Romanian infantry regiment in the following terms, "Company after company of utterly dejected men tramped by. Rifles carelessly slung back, collars of greatcoats unbuttoned the haunted look of the beaten soldier in their eyes. I noticed that there was not one machine gun in the whole outfit."

1917

These tattered remnants accompanied by hundreds of thousand of refugees marched through the snow and ice until they found refuge beyond the Seret River. The Royal Family and the government established itself at Jassy and took a long sober look at the condition of their forces. With the Russians now providing a screen the Romanians would have to rebuild their armed forces and learn from their hard-won experiences. A political arrangement was made whereby the Romanian King was given a token position of authority. To all intents and purposes the Romanian Army had become a tiny cog in the Russian war machine and the responsibility for rebuilding it fell to the French Military Mission. During early 1917 fifteen infantry divisions and two cavalry divisions were organised into the First and Second armies with 2nd, 4th and 11th infantry divisions in reserve. Various French specialists travelled to Romania bringing with them promises of artillery of all calibres, small arms, ammunition, aircraft but particularly machine guns.

On the theme of machine guns a British officer noted that in November 1916:

…The 2nd/5th Infantry Division, a day or two before it marched south, had been issued with new French machine guns, which the men did not

Lorries, possibly FIATs, of the RNACD evacuate Russian wounded in the spring of 1917. Although the RNACD saw some action in Romania conditions were not ideal for mobile warfare until the ground firmed up.

understand and for which ammunition was lacking. They were thrown away early in the battle.

If it underlines nothing else, this episode demonstrates the logistical nightmare facing the Russians and Romanians – doubtless the French ammunition had arrived elsewhere or was held up on the border.

At *Stavka* Alexeyev grudgingly authorised further injections of men. But an unforeseen difficulty, again connected with the railway system, slowed down the Russian troop movements. Rolling stock had been evacuated into Moldavia by the Romanian authorities and very quickly thousands of passenger coaches and freight wagons simply clogged the lines and movement came to a virtual standstill.

As cholera, typhus and starvation ravaged its army and the huge numbers of refugees Romania faced the New Year of 1917 with little but promises and hopes to sustain them. Defeated and humiliated the Romanians were regarded with a mixture of pity and scorn and the Russians generally perceived their army as a leaderless rabble. As Dukhonin, the Quartermaster General of S W Front, commented, "After all, the Romanian Armies are only semi-detached advanced outposts, and the right of the Army of the Danube is almost in communication with the left of the Ninth Army." However, General A. I. Denikin formed a better opinion of the Romanian soldier having two Romanian army corps under his command during the winter of 1916–1917:

> In the beginning of the campaign the Romanian Army showed complete disregard of the experience of the World War. In matters of equipment and ammunition their levity was almost criminal. There were several capable Generals, the officers were effeminate and inefficient, and the men were splendid. The artillery was adequate, but the infantry was untrained. These are the main characteristics of the Romanian Army, which soon afterwards acquired better organisation and improved in training and equipment. A separate Romanian Front was created in January 1917 with the Russians holding the left and right flanks and the Romanians roughly 30 km (19 miles) in the centre.

Relations between the actual Russian Commander-in-Chief, who was designated as the Assistant Commander in Chief, and the King of Romania, who was nominally in overall command, were fairly cordial. Although the Russian troops began to commit excesses, which had a bad effect upon the attitude of the Romanians, the condition of the Front did not, however cause serious apprehension. Brusilov agreed with Denikin's comments about the men, noting acidly to the Romanian officers, "one idea was to go on leave to Bukarest."

Gourko at *Stavka*

The Russians had provided the Romanians with captured Austrian equipment including 60,000 rifles and ammunition that went someway to alleviating their problems. While Romania had been almost hammered out of existence events were underway at *Stavka* which were to have far reaching consequences. Alexeyev was gravely ill and it was decided that he should be sent on sick leave and replaced by General V. I. Gourko. On the way to his new post Gourko called in on Brusilov to discuss support for Romania and meet with the Grand Duke Nicholas who was returning to the Caucasus. The Grand Duke advised Gourko to be, "fully frank with the Tsar and not hide the reality with an idea of sparing him the grief."

During the course of the next few days Gourko became very aware of the range of his duties commenting, "I understood why the gradual and imperceptible illness finally broke down his [Alexeyev's] health." Before 1916 was over Gourko had appointed General V. N. Klembovski to be his Assistant Chief of Staff. Klembovski took over many of the more routine duties that Alexeyev had carried out himself.

German and Russian troops fraternise at Christmas 1916. Such events were frowned upon by the high commands of both sides but were so common that a blind eye was usually turned. Easter generated another round of such celebrations being the most important festival of the Orthodox calendar.

Over the next few weeks Gourko came into frequent contact with the War Minister, General Shouvaiev, but more frequently with the Agriculture Minister, Count Alexsei Bobrinsky, as the question of supplying food not only to the army but also to the cities, especially Petrograd, was becoming increasingly problematic. Militarily, Gourko's first problem was to oversee the establishment of the Romanian Front and the movement of large numbers of Russian troops into the region. This was accomplished despite the season (it was the worst winter in almost forty years) and the fact that the Russians had to march hundreds of kilometres to reach their places in the line.

On 29 December a conference of front commanders was held to discuss the operations for 1917. The Russians were party to the discussions held in France where it had been agreed in principle that Russia would undertake an offensive in the spring. What the British and French had overlooked was the collapse of Romania, the consequent extension of Russia's front and the fact that troop movements took an exceedingly long time. Therefore in the event of an Allied attack in the west during January or February the supporting efforts of the Russian Army would be limited.

Russian infantry prepare to move into the line in early 1917. This is an interesting image, as the men appear to have packs that were only issued to Guardsmen or engineers.

The Russian contribution to the allied effort of 1917 was to be an offensive in April, with the main effort being made by SW Front. When the front commanders returned to their headquarters Brusilov outlined the part SW Front was to play to the army commanders:

> The principal blow was this time to be entrusted to the Seventh Army, the shock troops moving north-west towards Lemberg; the Eleventh Army was to thrust due west, and likewise against Lemberg; the Special Army and Third Army were to continue their previous operations with a view to the capture of Vladimir Volyinsk and Kovel. The shock troops of the Eighth Army, which was in the Carpathians, were to play a purely auxiliary part, and their attack was designed to assist the right wing of the Romanian Army when the latter made its forward movement. This time my front was given relatively considerable resources for use in the offensive.

Brusilov's reference to shock troops simply meant those who were to be involved in the attack, it did not denote any elite status.

The Russian Army ran on copious amounts of highly sweetened black tea as being brewed here. Daily rations were plain but nutritious, 0 .9kg (2lbs) of bread, 0.45kg (1lb) of meat and 0.25kg (9oz) of sugar. Unfortunately in Romania supply problems led to looting and consequently bad relations with the local population.

Army reform

To cope with the extension of the front Gourko decided to undertake a re-organisation of the structure of the army. (The concept was simple in theory but difficult to carry out.) The idea was to increase the number of infantry divisions by reducing the battalions in the existing ones. Thus sixteen-battalion divisions would be reduced to twelve with the four left over being combined with eight others found in a similar fashion to create a new division. In theory, the firepower, with rifles supplemented by machine-guns and increased weight of artillery, of a new-style division would be at least the equivalent to that of the old-style division. In round figures this would create sixty new infantry divisions. But raising the officers and staffs to lead these divisions was difficult and the allocation of artillery even more so. To alleviate the staff problem the new divisions were bolted on to existing army corps so that each now contained three infantry divisions instead of two. Artillery was not such a simple matter, although the solution seemed obvious. 'Quiet' areas of the front were to be stripped of modern

Russia's most common mountain gun, the Schneider-Danglis 76mm M1909. Licence built by the Putilov company it was an extremely reliable weapon. It broke down into six pack animal loads and was widely used in the Carpathian Mountains and on the Caucasian Front.

field guns, which would be replaced with less-mobile, obsolete guns from the rear. The batteries thus released would be allotted to the new divisions. At Brusilov's instigation the cavalry was also to be re-organised with the single rifle battalion attached in early 1916 to each division being increased to a three-battalion regiment. The riflemen were actually dismounted cavalrymen. The horses thus released were transferred to the artillery. Each cavalry division was to receive eight 114mm (4.5 inch) howitzers from Britain. Cossack *sotnia* previously attached to corps headquarters were to be organised into divisions and sent to the Caucasian Front to increase Baratov's force in Persia.

The reorganisation was put into operation immediately. However, it was a system that was open to abuse, as officers would not transfer experienced troops from their commands. Consequently the third divisions, as they became known, became dumping grounds for the older, less physically able soldiers. The problem of the "over 40s" was one that had been generated during 1915 when several classes of reservists and *Opolchenie* had been called to the colours by Imperial *Ukase*. Their conscription was a cause of

An interesting image of a Russian officer with a woman in uniform. Women served in the armed forces and some became the "field wives" of officers. Similar relationships developed with refugees particularly during the retreat from Poland. It was not uncommon for soldiers to adopt orphans many of whom were pictured in army dress. Such images were used as "evidence of Russia's lack of manpower" when they were more often than not simple acts of kindness.

much resentment as many families were left without a male breadwinner. Furthermore the artillery quota was rarely, if ever, filled. Although it would have enhanced the flexibility of command in peacetime it was a risky move during a war. Alexeyev was not in favour of this restructuring and on his return to *Stavka* did not encourage its fulfilment.

Militarily, the weather was the major enemy of all sides on all fronts. Only on the N Front was there any activity where Twelfth Army had carried out a surprise attack, details of which were kept from *Stavka* and known only to the staff of Twelfth Army and VI Siberian Corps. It was as much a surprise to *Stavka* as it was to the Germans. The operation took place along the coast of the Baltic Sea towards the port of Mitau.

During the autumn of 1916 the eight Latvian battalions were expanded to eight regiments divided into two brigades, one with the II Siberian Corps and the other with the VI Siberian Corps. With roughly 30,000 Latvians concentrated thus a plan was hatched with the ambitious aim of liberating Courland, the German occupied half of Latvia.

The Christmas battle

Under the cover of darkness what became known as "The Christmas Battle", with both Latvian brigades united in the VI Siberian Corps, began on 5 January 1917. With the snow falling, advance parties in white camouflage coats began to cut the German wire. At 0500 hours the attack began, the wire was bridged with mats or blown up with gun-cotton charges and very rapidly the German positions were overrun. The dominant feature of the area, Machine-Gun Hill, was taken on the third day. However, the attacks cost the Latvians heavily and support from the Siberians was almost non-existent. The 3rd Siberian Infantry Division on the Latvian right failed in its attack and another one of the divisions had refused to leave its trenches.

The Christmas Battle passed into legend and, due to the large number of dead, it became known in Latvian folklore as the "Blizzard of the Souls." Latvian loyalty to the empire was badly shaken by what was perceived as Russian antipathy to the operation and lack of support. An alleged comment by Grand Duke Nicholas, who was reported to have remarked, "I spit upon your Courland ", did nothing to improve relations.

However, elsewhere, practical considerations fostered discontentment at the front. Transport difficulties on the South Western and Romanian Fronts had led to all manner of shortages. Food, winter clothing and boots were becoming difficult to find and the complaints of the men thus affected grew louder. "We'll hold the front, but we won't attack." "Give us boots and warm clothing." "Take us and have us shot, but we aren't going to fight any more." All these cries were heard during December 1916 when rioting broke out in a dozen or so regiments. Such shortages had occurred before giving rise to a resurgence of the regimental economies of the past where soldiers would spend their time producing boots, clothing and other necessaries. But towards the end of 1916 the men's patience was wearing thin.

Political manoeuvring

In the cities and in the countryside there was growing unrest. The number of strikes had increased as inflation destroyed the value of wages. Peasants hoarded food in the hope of increased prices or distilled into bootleg vodka the production of which had been banned at the outbreak of war. 1916 had seen a bewildering variety of changes at ministerial level as the Tsar fell more and more under the influence of his wife. She saw threats to her son's inheritance everywhere and consequently pressed Nicholas to appoint men who were totally unsuited for their positions but apparently devoted to the autocracy. A loose, cross-party coalition of *Duma* members, known as the Progressive Bloc, had assembled during 1915 with the ambition of liberalising Russia's government at the end of the war. However as the Tsar appointed more and more reactionaries to the Council of Ministers during 1916, the Progressive Bloc faced the problem of supporting men whose policies they abhorred or gathering popular support and risking a revolution. The military were also becoming increasingly involved in politics. In late June 1916 Alexeyev had proposed to the Tsar that, "one single plenipotentiary" should assume responsibility for the "internal provinces of the empire" (those areas outside the control of the army) and "direct by his will alone the activities of all ministries and all government and civic organisations that function outside the theatre of military action". In effect Alexeyev was suggesting a form of dictatorship responsible to the Tsar. Although only a confidential discussion, documents and rumours began to circulate regarding the Tsar's intention to reduce the power of the *Duma* by such methods.

Rodzianko, the *Duma* President, met with the Tsar in the summer to discuss matters pertaining to the government's activities. Rodzianko claimed that he suggested that the Tsar, "grant a responsible ministry" to which the Tsar replied that he would "think it over." Nicholas had no intention of doing any such thing. In fact he appointed B.V. Sturmer to be the President of the Council of Ministers with the intention of creating Alexeyev's "dictator". In reality Alexeyev loathed Sturmer who had a remarkable track record for incompetence and corruption. The appointment of A. D. Protopopov as Interior Minister in October did something to calm the *Duma's* growing anger and fear but he proved himself to be wedded

A Russian officer poses with a collection of weapons. The rifle is a Japanese *Arisaka* 1905 pattern. The Japanese sold almost 450,000 rifles to Russia during the course of the war. The collection of grenades on the table includes British types and the one in the man's hand is the domestically produced Russian type.

to reaction and autocracy much to the surprise of his many supporters. On 14 November the *Duma* reconvened and P. N. Miliukov, one of its senior members, made a speech. In it he damned the government, accusing it of having weakened Russia at home and undermined her relations with her allies so as to make victory impossible. Miliukov continued that, "While the *Duma* everlastingly insists that the rear must be organised for a successful struggle against the enemy the government persists in claiming that organising the country means organising a revolution." Nicholas, under pressure from Alexeyev and most of the Romanov clan, excluding his wife, dismissed Sturmer. But some members of the *Duma* were still not content. An extreme right winger V. Purishkevitch, who had the ear of the Tsar, went further and demanded the removal of Rasputin, "as the director of Russia's domestic and public affairs." The monk who had exercised so much influence over the royal couple and generated millions of smutty cartoons had not merely been alluded to but named in the *Duma*. The foundations of the monarchy were beginning to crumble.

It was during the front commanders' conference that news arrived from Petrograd announcing the murder of Rasputin. In Brusilov's words, the Tsar, who was presiding over the conference, "…was constantly yawning… was indifferent to us and our discussions… On hearing the news [he] hurriedly bade us farewell, and left us." He was not to return to *Stavka* until 7 March, spending the time comforting the Tsaritsa over the loss of her guru Rasputin and dealing with the stream of advice from all quarters about the condition of his empire and what should be done.

Although the upper echelons of the army, and society greeted news of the death of Rasputin with only partially concealed delight, the comment of one soldier may cast light on the thoughts and opinions of the ordinary people: "Yes, only one *muzhik* (peasant) has got through to the Tsar, and him the masters killed."

CHAPTER 8

1917: The Hopeful Revolution

Apart from the "Christmas Battle" January 1917 was a quiet month at the front while at Tsarskoe Selo Nicholas was fully engaged comforting his wife following the death of Rasputin.

At *Stavka* the work of implementing the army restructuring was underway but the length of time these changes would take made it necessary to delay the spring offensive until the summer. However, to support the British and French, diversionary attacks would be made by all fronts to prevent the withdrawal of men to the west.

In late January Gourko left *Stavka* to attend the Inter–Allied conference that was being held in Petrograd and to meet the new War Minister, General M. A. Beliaev, who was appointed on 17 January.

Inter-Allied conference

A major outcome of the Chantilly conference of November 1916 was that a further conference be held in Russia. The simple reason for this was that Russia's representatives abroad did not speak with the full authority of the Tsar; they were merely reporters of events. It was essential that a conference requiring firm Russian commitments be held where such commitments could be made. The Tsar agreed to hold the conference in Petrograd in early January 1917. However, the death of Rasputin and ministerial reshuffling led to a postponement so it was not until 29 January that the conference opened. The western delegations had travelled via Murmansk and several commented on the chaotic situation they witnessed there with stores of all kinds heaped up awaiting transport south.

Sir George Buchanan, Britain's ambassador to Russia, briefed the British delegation on its arrival. He informed them that the Tsar was hesitating between granting a more liberal constitution and the complete dissolution of the *Duma* and was veering towards the latter course. It was in this atmosphere of intrigue and uncertainty that the Inter-Allied committees

The Inter-Allied Conference of early 1917 in Petrograd was one of the last occasions on which the Tsar performed as head of state. Pictured here with members of court and his staff Nicholas' position was the subject of much behind-the-scenes discussion.

gathered to listen to Pokrovski's (Russia's Foreign Minister) opening address that set the tone for the conference. "We [the Allies] have got to distribute as usefully and intelligently as possible all our resources – men and materials – and thus assure from them the biggest return. That, gentlemen…is the principal object of our meetings." Aid to Russia was therefore placed squarely at the top of the agenda. Gourko, Russia's military representative, reiterated this point. The term 'Inter-Allied' was actually something of a misnomer as only British, French and Italian delegations had travelled to Petrograd. Portugal, Belgium, Serbia and Romania had not been invited.

Lord Milner, a member of the War Cabinet, with General Sir Henry Wilson as his military adviser, led the British delegation that included finance, munitions and transport experts. The French and Italian delegations were similarly high-powered. There were no representatives of the *Duma* included on the Russian side, which consisted exclusively of government ministers and civil servants.

As the civilians gathered to discuss the minutiae, the military representatives held three meetings and then left to visit the front. The

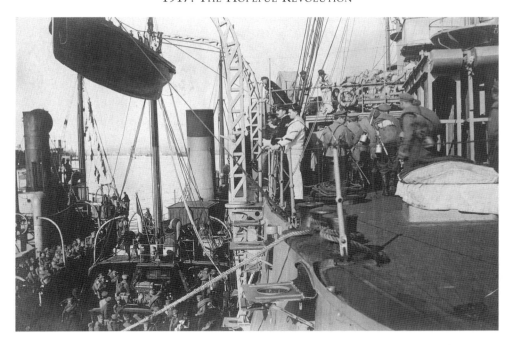

Four Russian infantry brigades were sent overseas in 1916, two to France and two to the Salonika Front. The impression that Russian troops were being bartered for munitions did nothing to enhance the government's popularity with many of the officer corps. Here men of the Third Brigade disembark in France. Shortly after the March Revolution these units were withdrawn from the trenches as being unreliable.

impressions gained by Wilson and Castelnau, his French opposite number, were discussed on their return to Petrograd. Wilson had visited N Front and reported glowingly of, "well-clothed, well-booted, well-cared for troops...the morale of the Russian Army is good." Castelnau's views were more pessimistic. Wilson noted, "He [Castelnau] was not impressed by their men, nor officers, nor staff...in short he did not think they were in a position to hold the Boche divisions in front of them."

However contradictory the soldiers' assessment of the situation in the army, there could be very little doubt regarding the political climate. Although not included in the official meetings there were a host of social events at which *Duma* members and politicians could express their views on the situation. These discussions proved a revelation to the westerners. Clerk, a member of the Foreign Office delegation, reported to Milner, "every member of the Mission heard from all sides, Russian and foreign, of the inevitability of something serious happening; the only question was whether the Emperor, the Empress or Protopopov would be removed or perhaps all three.... The open way in which people of all classes, including those nearest to the throne and officers holding high military commands, spoke against the Empress and her two blind tools – the Emperor and Protopopov – was, to one who knew anything at all of Russia, extraordinary."

Other delegates heard talk of assassinating the Tsar or Tsaritsa or their replacement by a regent. Exposure to this sort of treasonable discussion went unchallenged. To quote Lloyd George, "the Mission was kept in a sort of ring fence and prevented from hearing any defence or serious explanation of the Emperor's policy."

The French ambassador had given his delegates a somewhat blunter assessment of Russia's condition than Buchanan, "Russia was walking straight into the abyss…." Contact with the royal family was minimal but at an official dinner given by the Tsar the senior French delegate secured from the Tsar his agreement to the French post-war border being established along the Rhine River just in case there was a change of government and the Tsar was toppled.

Whatever the overall impression of conditions in Russia the delegates may have gained, no-one anticipated anything more cataclysmic than the removal of the current Tsar and his replacement by a constitutional monarchy or parliamentary government without a royal figurehead. Whatever transpired in Russia she would remain as an ally and the war would continue, therefore it was vital to improve the flow and more particularly the distribution of western supplies. As proof of their good faith the British agreed to supply on a monthly basis four batteries of 152mm (6 inches), two batteries of 203mm (8 inches) and one battery of 234mm (9.2 inch) howitzers plus all the requisite tractor vehicles necessary for such heavy weapons.

Strategically the conference reaffirmed the Chantilly resolution to begin major operations by 1 May. But should the Central Powers attack first then all Allied armies would respond with their maximum force within three weeks. Castelnau's attempts to persuade Gourko into supporting the French offensive, planned by General Nivelle and due to start in mid-April, were evaded by Gourko's riposte that the Russians would be unable to do much before mid-May.

In an attempt to overcome the bottlenecks at the northern ports, a British supply mission under General Poole was to be established. It was also agreed that the Western Allies would send technical missions including aviation and artillery specialists to enable the Russians to use their new weapons effectively. The Allied missions expressed their desire to stay for the reopening of the *Duma* but were informed that it was impossible and on 21 February they left Petrograd.

It was NCOs such as Sergeant Timofei Kirpichnikov, pictured here, who brought the soldiers onto the streets during the March Revolution. Kirpichnikov led the mutiny of the *Volynsky* Guards Regiment and enjoyed a degree of celebrity for several weeks.

The March Revolution

The speed with which the revolution of March 1917 overthrew the government of the Tsar was remarkable. Throughout the first two years of the war inflation had driven up the price of food and to an extent wage increases had kept pace. However, the money paid to farmers had little

A typical scene following the March Revolution troops holding a meeting. The culture of meetings, discussion and decision was new to the mass of Russians but was adopted with gusto. Here the regimental committee of the 490th *Rhzhevski* Infantry Regiment on the Caucasian Front listens to a speaker from the floor despite many of the onlookers being more interested in the camera.

value, as there was virtually nothing for them to buy. Much of Russia's industrial capacity both new and old had been taken up with fulfilling lucrative military contracts. Therefore the cereal suppliers began to cut back on the produce they were prepared to sell on. The bootlegging of spirits increased, as did the amount of grain hoarded in the hopes of a price rise at a later date. Consequently the army, which took priority in matters of food supply, asserted itself to take the greater part of those available supplies at the expense of non-grain producing areas such as Petrograd. Unfortunately supplies for the army began to dwindle in late 1916 reaching the point where the troops were complaining bitterly of the poor quality of their rations.

In Petrograd supplies (particularly of bread) had, by late 1916, become erratic. Queuing for such bread as was available had become a hugely time consuming way of life. Shortages of food combined with cold weather and a lack of firewood to create an ever-increasingly critical attitude toward the Tsar and his ministers. One *Okhrana* (the secret police) report predicted, "A

In a scene unimaginable only days before, civilians and revolutionary troops casually brew up outside the Admiralty building on Palace Square in Petrograd during the March Revolution. It would have been unwise for any officer to interfere with such an event.

revolution," explaining further, "if it takes place [it] will be spontaneous, quite likely a hunger riot."

The Tsar, quarantined from reality either at *Stavka* or Tsarskoe Selo, had been subjected to what amounted to a dressing down from the Buchanan in late 1916. "Your Majesty, if I may be permitted to say so, has but one safe course open to you, namely to break down the barrier that separates you from your people and to regain their confidence." Nicholas replied, "Do you mean that I am to regain the confidence of my people or that they are to regain my confidence?"

Members of the Romanov family had also used their positions to voice equally unwelcome opinions. Nevertheless Nicholas maintained his sublimely detached position. In January 1917 when Rodzianko submitted a report outlining the crisis in raw materials, transportation and food the Tsar told him to, "Hurry up and finish, I can't waste time on this."

On January 22 over 100,000 demonstrators crowded the streets of Petrograd to commemorate the anniversary of Bloody Sunday; this action was repeated across the empire. Throughout the next week a succession of strikes and demonstrations broke out with the demonstrators displaying increasingly militant, revolutionary attitudes. Although contained by the police who were supported by Cossacks the *Okhrana* noted, "There was an impression that the Cossacks were on the side of the workers." Sympathy for the people had cost 150 soldiers their lives when they had been called to support the police break up a strike in Petrograd the previous autumn. The troops had fired on the police and the Cossacks had to be used to control the mutineers. The military support, which had enabled Nicholas to crush the 1905 Revolution, was ebbing away.

The Tsar left for *Stavka* on 6 March and arrived the next day to be met by Alexeyev who had just returned from sick leave. Gourko resumed his position as commander of the Special Army. As the situation in Petrograd deteriorated Nicholas appears to have been oblivious to everything but his daughter's measles.

The abdication

In and around the Petrograd were over 150,000 soldiers in reserve Guards battalions, technical and armoured training units. But these formations lacked experienced officers and were, in the main, unlikely to respond enthusiastically if ordered to undertake crowd control duties. The troops were called out during the first week of March 1917 but this time the crowds did not disperse and soon gained the soldiers' support. The *Duma* did not co-operate with its own dissolution and, almost before anyone realised what was happening, the long-anticipated revolution was an accomplished fact. The Military Governor of Petrograd requested reinforcements but events moved too swiftly, indeed Alexeyev was in no apparent hurry to send troops. The revolution was almost bloodless although an unknown number of policemen, officers and civilians were killed.

The Provisional Government

A Provisional Government was established to oversee the course of events until elections could be held later in the year for a Constituent Assembly. But as no legislation existed to deal with such a state of affairs, a welter of laws and directives was issued from Petrograd in an attempt to bring order out of chaos.

At the same time as the cabinet of the Provisional Government was assembling another body was also establishing itself as the voice of the people and soldiers, the Council of Workers and Soldiers Deputies, better

Industrial production declined after the Tsar's abdication as the workers were otherwise engaged. Here a small firm is completing steel helmets that had been introduced during 1916. Until Russian manufacturers had geared up to produce them the French Adrian pattern was imported. These ladies are attaching the coat of arms to the front. However, following the March Revolution these royal symbols were swiftly removed.

known as the Soviet. Almost from day one of the revolution the Provisional Government and the Soviet vied with one another for authority. The members of the Provisional Government were drawn from politicians of a liberal-centrist background whereas those of the Soviet were more radically socialist in their views though by no means overwhelmingly Bolshevik. However, as both groups feared a counter-revolution they were forced into a marriage of convenience and were prepared to compromise in order to protect their achievements.

The Tsar had been intercepted travelling back to Petrograd from *Stavka* and signed the abdication document in a carriage on his train. He then returned to Moghilev. The front commanders were canvassed for their opinion and all, including the Grand Duke Nicholas, were in favour of abdication. As one

The wording of the new oath of loyalty caused some problems for the Provisional Government as there were similarities between the words used by the former regime that were difficult to overcome or avoid. Here the Turkoman Cavalry Regiment parades before swearing allegiance to the Provisional Government. They wore an exotic uniform, a yellow and orange striped kaftan with a large black fleece hat. This unit was later to become Kornilov's bodyguard when he was appointed Supreme Commander in Chief.

of his final acts the Tsar appointed the Grand Duke Nicholas as Supreme Commander in Chief and awaited his return at *Stavka*.

Nicholas II abdicated on 15 March not only for himself but also on behalf of his son and in favour of his brother, the Grand Duke Mikhail. When representatives of the Provisional Government approached the Grand Duke he declined the honour unless the people, via the Constituent Assembly, offered it to him later in the year. Thus the Russian Empire found itself without a Tsar. Remarkably there had been almost no one who lifted a finger, let alone a gun, to defend the royal family. Only two Generals, Count Keller and Khan Hussein Nakhitchevanski, commanding the 3rd Cavalry Division and the Guards Cavalry Corps respectively, offered their men to suppress the mutineers in Petrograd but their offers were declined. In the company of his mother, who had travelled up from Kiev to be with him, Nicholas cut a rather pathetic figure having even less to do than before. The former Tsar was taken to Petrograd and kept under house arrest with his wife and children until the summer of 1917 when they left for Siberia and eventual death at the hands of the Bolsheviks a year later.

On 22 March the USA recognised the Provisional Government. Within two days the British, French and Italian governments followed suit. The Provisional Government used this occasion to declare that it would continue fighting and honour the previous regime's obligations. At this time the Grand Duke Nicholas arrived at Moghilev, but when told that he was unacceptable to the new regime promptly left, his place being taken by Alexeyev with General A. I. Denikin as his Chief of Staff. One of Alexeyev's first duties was to agree to the creation of Soldier's Committees at all levels throughout the army in accordance with the terms of Order Number One.

Order Number One

On 14 March soldiers burst into the Petrograd Soviet and insisted that it immediately address their demands. Faced with an angry, armed mob the Soviet had little choice and the result of their deliberations was Order Number One that was addressed exclusively to the Petrograd garrison. The changes introduced were as follows:

1 Committees to be elected of representatives of the men in all companies, battalions, regiments, parks, batteries, squadrons and separate services of various military institutions, and on the ships of the fleet.
2 All military units not yet represented on the Soviet of Workmen's Delegates to elect one representative from each company. These representatives to provide themselves with written certificates and to report to the Duma at 10am on March 2 (15 new style).
3 In all its political activities the military unit is subordinate to the Soviet and its committees.
4 The orders of the Military Commission of the Duma (the War Ministry) are to be obeyed only when they are not in contradiction with the orders and decrees of the Soviet.
5 All arms – rifles, machine guns, armoured cars, etc – are to be at the disposal and under the control of company and battalion Committees, and should never be handed over to the officers even should they claim them.
6 On parade and on duty the soldiers must comply with strict military discipline; but off parade and off duty, in their political, social and private life, soldiers must suffer no restriction of the rights common to all citizens. In particular saluting when off duty is abolished.
7 Officers are no longer to be addressed as "Your Excellency," "Your Honour," etc. Instead, they should be addressed as "Mr General", "Mr Colonel", etc.

At the front groups of officers such as this simply waited on events. The majority of the officers who had enlisted during the war viewed the abdication of the Tsar with equanimity.

Finally, there was a paragraph which dealt with the manner in which the officers should address their men.

Following rapidly on the heels of Order Number One a committee of the Soviet was given the task of revising Russia's military regulations and producing a Declaration of Soldiers' Rights. One of its members was Polivanov the former War Minister. On 18 March A. I. Guchkov, the new War Minister, lifted a number of minor restrictions such as the time and place of smoking (a practice dear to the heart of the *Frontovik*) and card playing, but the right to join political clubs and organisations was also granted.

Order Number One was disseminated widely and rapidly across the army at the front as well as in the rear and throughout the fleets. Soldiers' Committees sprang up overnight with members whose political views were coloured from deepest red to palest pink but at this time there was very little Bolshevik representation. The reaction of the officers was, in many cases, despair: suddenly they were marginalised. What was their purpose now that their orders were subject to approval by committees? Clearly if they wished to remain in the army they would have to adopt new inter-personal skills to an undreamt of extent. On top of this came the new oath of allegiance in which the state replaced the Tsar as the subject of fealty. Swearing this oath under flags still bearing the symbols of the empire was a case for further confusion and soul-searching. In many instances these Tsarist decorations were tactfully covered in red cloth. In mid-April it was ordered that all regimental standards to were to be sent to Moscow for alteration but compliance was sporadic, such was the devotion of many of the rank and file to these emblems of former glory.

As part of the Provisional Government's manifesto of 18 March the troops, "who had participated in the Revolutionary Movement will not be disarmed, but will remain in Petrograd." Therefore these men would not be going to the front so discipline and training were suddenly rendered pointless and many took part-time jobs to earn some money.

At *Stavka* several messages arrived from France requesting support for the offensive planned for April. Alexeyev first used the inclement weather as an excuse but on 26 March he frankly admitted that the army would be in no condition to do anything until the summer, such were the effects of the revolution. Nevertheless Alexeyev informed Guchkov that, despite the revolution, an offensive must be undertaken towards the end of May, his reasoning being that the Central Powers would attack and that the Allies would cut off loans and supplies. At a conference in late March Alexeyev asked the front commanders when they would be able to undertake an offensive.

On the N Front Ruzski was pessimistic and expressed his concerns about the possibility of a German invasion of Finland. In the Riga area there had been several German attacks during the course of the past few weeks although they had made little headway. However, Gourko had been recently appointed to command W Front, and Brusilov had accepted the need for an offensive. Brusilov was very optimistic, claiming his men had been enthused by the revolution and were keen to prove themselves. It was decided to retain SW Front as the main theatre for the offensive but Ruzski was to be replaced by General A. M. Dragomirov. This new appointment was one of many made across the army's command structure as Guchkov conducted a "purge" of those officers who felt to be too reactionary, too old fashioned militarily or just plain incompetent. With Alexeyev's agreement over a hundred generals were removed from N and W fronts alone.

Although the revolution had grown out of food shortages these shortages had not disappeared with the Tsar. Indeed the situation was regarded as so critical that it was decided to cut the numbers of men in the army by about a million. On 18 April soldiers over forty years old not in front line units were given leave until the end of May. This order was followed on 23 April by the discharge of all men over forty-three. Naturally the men over forty in front line units decided they also wanted leave and began to demobilise

Kornilov's replacement as commander of the Petrograd Military District was General P. A. Polovtsov (centre in light Circassian uniform). Formerly a regimental commander with the Savage Division, Polovtsov was more politically astute than Kornilov and did much to keep the Petrograd garrison in hand particularly during the July Days.

themselves. Many gravitated to Petrograd where they established what the commander of the Petrograd Military District, General P. A. Polovtsov, described as a, "republic, which amounted to several thousands". Polovtsov had taken over this very difficult post when his predecessor General L. G. Kornilov resigned following a dispute with the Soviet.

Central Powers' response and the battle of the Stokhod bridgehead.

The Central Power's initial response to the revolution was cautious. Sporadic fighting had continued at various points along the front but there was nothing to indicate that the Russian Army was going to lay down its arms and go home. On 28 March the Germans announced that the improved weather had brought an end to any large scale operations. However, this did not stop General Linsingen (commanding the Austro-German troops on the Stokhod River) from carrying out an attack on a Russian bridgehead during the first week of April.

Following heavy artillery preparation, including a large number of gas shells, infantry attacks drove the Russians back across the river. The official German report listed over 10,000 Russian POWs. Embarrassingly *Stavka* was unable to establish accurate estimates due to the chaos in the area. However, concerned that the operation might rekindle the Russian soldiers' desire to fight, the Germans issued what amounted to an apology – via the neutral press! The causes of the defeat at the Stokhod bridgehead were the subject of debate and reflected the gradual polarisation of feelings towards the army. The Moscow Soviet blamed traitors in high places, others the laxity of discipline and some the incompetence of the generals. In part the reason was a combination of surprise, the extensive use of gas and the laxity that pervaded parts of the front in the wake of the revolution and the imminent Easter truce.

Aware of the Provisional Government's decision to remain at war, the Central Powers now determined that propaganda was their best means of continuing the war in the east. Their next move was the repatriation of V. I. Lenin who they hoped would cause even more trouble for the Provisional Government than its own internal squabbles.

On 15 April Easter Week began. As the most important festival in the Orthodox calendar it was a time of great celebration and 1917 was to be no exception. All along the front line unofficial truces were declared and the men of both sides fraternised in no man's land. Although this had happened from the first Easter of the war this time very few officers dared raise any serious objections. This was precisely the situation the Central Powers High Command had hoped for.

The journal of an RFC man attached to the British Mission in Russia named Ibbertson commented on this culture of peaceful co-existence when he described the indignant attitude of a German pilot shot down and captured near Tarnopol in late June. The German asked his Russian captor, "what he meant by firing on him, as they never fired on any Russians who came over their lines."

Petrograd politics

The changes in government brought about by the overthrow of the autocracy had, within a month, spread across the country. Every major city

The March Revolution generated wide support amongst the socialist parties of Western Europe. The civilians in the centre are the British Labour MPs James O'Grady and Will Thorne who joined a French deputation to express support for the Provisional Government.

had its own Soviet alongside the organs of the Provisional Government but Petrograd was where the real power lay and decisions were made.

Without going too deeply into the political machinations in Petrograd the dual power structure that existed was beginning to lose its fragile unity. The Soviet had begun to flex its muscles in March when it issued Order Number One and called for an end to the war. Furthermore its support of the workers' successful demands for an eight hour day in opposition to the Provisional Government had increased its strength. The Provisional Government struggled to maintain its authority but was already heading down the road to oblivion as in reality its strength relied upon distancing itself from the Tsarist regime and the pace with which it was doing that was too slow for many. Yet to others it was moving too quickly towards an unacceptably socialist destination. However, when Lenin reached Petrograd in mid-April neither the Soviet nor the Provisional Government felt that they could do without one another. On his arrival at Petrograd's Finland Station Lenin addressed a welcoming committee of Bolsheviks and called for an end to the war, the distribution of land to the peasants and the transfer of power to the Soviets across Russia in his so-called April Theses. As fast as possible the Bolshevik newspaper *Pravda* explained that such ideas were personal to Lenin and did not reflect the party's general view.

On 27 April the Provisional Government called a session of the members of all four *Dumas* (1906, 1907 twice and 1912–1917) believing that such an assembly would provide a better representation of national public opinion than simply those members elected in 1912 and the Petrograd Soviet which was only a local institution.

At the opening session of this "super *Duma*" the Foreign Minister, Miliukov, in a move calculated to reassure Russia's Allies of her continuing allegiance to the cause, spoke of the absurdity of claims that Russia was seeking a separate peace and declared that Russia was determined to, "bring the world war to a decisive victory." This declaration outraged the Soviet, which orchestrated demonstrations in Petrograd that led to Guchkov's resignation followed by that of Miliukov. The Provisional Government threatened to retaliate by following their example en bloc but at that point the Soviet furiously back-peddled as they lacked the confidence to take over. On 15 May the Soviet agreed to some of its members joining the Provisional Government. One of these was A. F. Kerensky who became War Minister in the new coalition. Kerensky was a man of ordinary appearance but blessed with remarkable charisma and an oratorical power that, according to a young British diplomat, "was more impressive in its emotional reactions than any speech of Hitler…." In the weeks following his appointment Kerensky came to dominate the Provisional Government. Almost in parallel Lenin's ideas became gradually more and more acceptable to his supporters although not the majority of the Soviet. Slowly but surely the two engines of government were moving onto a collision course.

Stavka and Petrograd

Fraternisation and defiance of authority by the soldiers at the front had grown out of the events following the March Revolution. The latter was naturally a matter of grave concern as it directly affected the willingness of the men to fight. Although there were instances of officers being murdered they were not as widespread as later alleged. However, throughout April disobedience increased as replacements, particularly from Petrograd, began to arrive at the front as officers in the rear sought to rid themselves of troublesome elements. These men were less well-trained and more truculent than their predecessors. Consequently when Alexeyev was informed by Guchkov that a government crisis was imminent and that the men were to be granted yet more freedom, he summoned the front commanders to Moghilev to consider the situation.

Dragomirov, Gourko, Brusilov and Shcherbachev (Romanian Front) all painted a picture of collapsing discipline, fraternisation on a massive scale and an army that would refuse to fight. Even Brusilov was losing his earlier enthusiasm for his revolutionary troops. When they learned of the proposed extension of the men's freedoms under the Declaration of Soldier's Rights they anticipated a further erosion of the martial spirit. Dragomirov's suggestion that they travel to Petrograd to confront the Soviet was unanimously agreed upon. On 18 May Russia's senior commanders arrived in Petrograd. However, it was not the Soviet that they met but the new coalition and this situation somewhat reduced their belligerence as they were anticipating dealing only with a rogue element and not a reshaped government. Kerensky assured the generals that he would do all in his power to restore the army. Alexeyev requested that the Soviet send representatives to repair the worst excesses of Order Number One. Other issues were addressed and the generals returned to their commands in a slightly more optimistic frame of mind. On the same day the government issued a statement announcing,

> In the conviction that a defeat of Russia and her Allies would be a great misfortune for all peoples, and would delay or make impossible a universal peace, the Provisional Government firmly believes that the revolutionary army will never permit German troops to destroy our Allies in the West and then turn on us with their full military might. The strengthening of the principles of democratising the Army, and the organisation and strengthening of its military capacity for both defensives and offensive operations, shall be the first priority of the Provisional Government.

Two days later the Foreign Minister reassured the French that Russia remained committed to the war and the following day Lenin pointed out that, "the essence of the new programme was offensive, offensive, offensive."

The Kerensky tour

Kerensky was concerned that the front commanders lacked faith in their men. He passionately believed the army had been truly inspired by the revolution and would, despite all appearances, fight. In order to demonstrate his faith and the men's enthusiasm he set out on a whistle stop tour of all the front committees beginning with SW Front. His method was simple but extremely effective and he repeated it wherever he went with little alteration in word, gesture or dramatic pose. He would harangue his audience, appeal to their patriotism, then lead them through a simple pattern of question and response. Finally, having worked himself up to a pitch of physical and emotional euphoria (a result of their positive feedback), he would swoon dramatically. Kerensky's rewards for such performances were promises of obedience to orders and a willingness to fight to the death. This remarkable talent for the theatrical worked very well and the committees on all fronts almost unanimously declared their support for the offensive.

However, away from the quasi-revivalist atmosphere of Kerensky's meetings when the committeemen attempted to pass on their enthusiasm for the offensive, not all their audiences were as willing to echo their fervour. In general most of the men were simply confused as to what they should do. Much of their negative behaviour since the revolution had been, so they believed, to prevent a counter-revolution and support the Soviet. But now that Soviet was part of the coalition and was calling for an offensive through Kerensky. Only a few Bolsheviks were able to argue coherently against the offensive and they were a tiny minority without a cohesive organisation to co-ordinate tangible opposition. Bolshevik propaganda spread by simple articles in their tabloid "Soldier's Truth" which was distributed by replacement companies from Petrograd and Moscow did much to generate support for their ideas. N Front was particularly susceptible to Bolshevik influences due to its proximity to Petrograd. A *Stavka* survey conducted in June noted that on N Front, "There is no possibility of insisting on the execution of orders, as a bitter agitational campaign is being waged against the offensive, emanating from the rear, chiefly Petrograd". On W Front, by mid-June, some formations were even recorded by Denikin as, "incapable of military operations". Here it was the urban influence of Minsk that played a significant role. SW and Romanian fronts were more isolated and felt Bolshevik influence least of all, yet it was Eleventh Army's morale that gave cause for concern.

Although there was a sense of foreboding amongst many senior officers in the weeks leading up to the offensive this was balanced by the hope that success would breed success and that the words and charisma of Kerensky would prove to be a sufficiently powerful motivational force.

In the ranks of the Bolsheviks unity of purpose was lacking. When representatives from the front travelled to a congress in Petrograd late in June they found it impossible to convince the Central Committee that the moment to grasp power had arrived. By a slim margin the congress voted not to oppose the offensive. Although there was growing support for Bolshevik ideas amongst the rank and file there was, as yet, no organisational support or focus for it.

Kerensky during one of his tour of the front mixes with officers and men in Riga. Although an inspirational and dramatic speaker the effect of his words lasted not much longer than his visits.

Men of the RNACD with their machine-gun in the front line on the first day of the summer offensive. Split into small groups it was hoped their example would encourage the Russian infantry to attack. This was not always the case as it interrupted the live and let live policy adopted by many Russian units. Interestingly one man is wearing a steel helmet, a practice which was not encouraged by Locker-Lampson.

solidarity was to prove of considerable value. The Czechs took several Austrian positions and encouraged the desertion of considerable numbers of their fellow-countrymen. However, an enlisted man (Air Mechanic First Class R. H. Ibbertson) with the RFC Mission commented on the French pilots' knack of smashing up British planes (eleven during the course of a week) and, on one occasion, shooting down a Russian artillery observation balloon.

Only on Eighth Army's sector, where a subsidiary attack was made on 6 July, was the assault sustained. The ten divisions of XII and XVI corps took advantage of the collapse of Austrian XXVI Corps to drive forward some 30kms (19 miles). Despite orders from Brusilov to incline the push to the north in an attempt to revitalise Seventh Army Kornilov pressed westwards towards Lemberg. Unfortunately for Eighth Army, the reserves they were sent, XXXIII Corps, were almost useless. One division broke under fire and its panic had to be contained by cavalry. As exhaustion spread Kornilov withdrew behind the Lomnitsa River.

A mark 1 Austin armoured car of the Fifth Armoured *Divizion* sent to provide
support for the Provisional Government during the Bolshevik sponsored unrest of
July. The armoured troops are fraternising with men of the Petrograd St George's
Battalion in Palace Square opposite the Winter Palace.

N and W fronts were scheduled to attack later in the month but N Front's
contribution was delayed by serious events in Petrograd.

The July days

On 15 July anarchists and the more militant Bolsheviks decided that
the time had come to, "overthrow the Provisional Government just as it
overthrew the Tsar." Led by men of the 1st Machine Gun Regiment, who
were refusing to leave for the front, huge crowds of workers, soldiers and
sailors from the heavily politicised Kronstadt naval base, demonstrated on
the streets of the capital. Trotsky and Lenin, swept along by events as they
struggled to influence their course, were unwilling to take the ultimate step

and topple the Provisional Government. Three critical days passed before troops loyal to the Provisional Government and the Soviet cleared the streets. The skilful use of propaganda aimed at the Bolshevik leadership "proved" that they were paid German agents. Trotsky was imprisoned and Lenin went into hiding. The apparent ease with which this spontaneous, disorganised coup attempt had been put down emboldened the more right wing elements of the Provisional Government. Kerensky became the head of a "Government to save the Revolution" having just returned from Ukraine where the mood for independence had been growing almost unchecked since the Tsar's abdication.

The expansion of nationalist formations

In the period of hope and idealism that followed the March Revolution much had been promised to the Finns and the Poles by way of self-government. Inevitably these discussions had their effect in other areas of the empire. Ukraine, Georgia, Latvia, Estonia, Armenia and the tribes of the north Caucasus all began to agitate for greater autonomy, if not complete independence.

Ukraine, lying directly behind SW and Romanian fronts had established its own *Rada* (council) that claimed to speak for its people. The influence of the *Rada* grew during the months following the revolution to the point where it claimed to be an alternative government. The Provisional Government had effectively ignored these developments. However, on 26 June matters took a serious turn when Ukraine declared virtual independence. The effect of such a move behind the lines can only be imagined and Kerensky travelled to Kiev on 11 July where he and his delegation spent two days appealing to various political groups for unity. However, the legendary stubbornness of the Ukrainians remained unshakeable and Kerensky was forced to concede the demand for all-Ukrainian units in the army before departing. In fact this apparent concession only sanctioned what was already going on. Indeed, in Petrograd the Military Governor Polovtsov had already agreed to allow the formation of all-Ukrainian companies in several regiments, and the formation of similar units along the front line composed almost entirely of Ukranians (including Seventh Army's XXXIV Corps, whose commander, General P. P. Skoropadsky, would later become ruler of Ukraine) can only be seen as further evidence of this.

Despite the agitation, declining discipline and attendance at meetings, maintenance of the defences was sometimes undertaken. Here a wiring party improves the condition of the defensive wire along the N Front. Both men with their backs to the camera have their gas mask cases close to hand.

Romania

The diversionary attacks by the Romanian Front were planned to begin on 19 July. The Romanian Front consisted of three Russian armies, Ninth (three infantry and one cavalry division), Fourth (nine infantry and six cavalry divisions) and Sixth (twenty infantry and three cavalry divisions). The Romanians held 24 km (15 miles) of the front within Ninth Army with fifteen infantry and two cavalry divisions. Although politicised, the Russian troops on this front were less radical due to the difficulties of communication, the distance from revolutionary urban areas and the personality of Shcherbachev who displayed a positive attitude towards the new order. The plan was a simple one: the Fourth Army and the Romanians were to attack the Austrian Ninth Army. Fourth Army was chosen, as it was believed to be the most reliable Russian force in this region.

On the 24 July, following a two-day bombardment, the Romanian 3rd Infantry Division stormed the village of Marashti, a very strong and important position. During the next three days the Romanians drove forward giving their enemies little respite and taking several thousand prisoners and over fifty guns. However, the SW Front's condition halted further development of the offensive. In early August Mackensen launched a counterattack on the vital railway junction at Marasheshti on the Sereth River, which had the potential to split the front. Mackensen believed he was only facing demoralised, demotivated Russians who would simply cave in. The fighting was vicious, more Germans were committed and, in the blazing heat, the battle for Marasheshti raged. The Romanians held their ground. From 11–14 August Russo-Romanian forces counterattacked but achieved little. Following powerful artillery preparation, the Central Powers launched a series of probing attacks and by 19 August had taken part of Marasheshti but were held by a counterattack. Finally, on 20 August Mackensen suspended operations. By mid-September the Romanian Front had lapsed into inactivity.

N and W Front's offensives

N. Front's artillery preparation began on 22 July and lasted for two days. By this time however the effective force on this front had been reduced to a single corps, XIV, which went over the top on 24 July. Within hours an initially successful attack had broken down due to the unwillingness of the support troops to participate. The operation was speedily cancelled.

W. Front's I Siberian Corps advanced after a three-day bombardment on 22 July. Within an hour three German trench lines had been taken. But again no reserves were willing to move up. Denikin was forced to cancel Tenth Army's attack on 24 July.

Although it was unsurprising that N. Front's operations ended so rapidly, W Front had, at least superficially, appeared to be in a relatively good condition. In both cases the men who had fought so well during the opening hours had often been members of the so-called Shock or Death battalions which had been organised in the weeks before the offensive.

Specialist formations

In parallel with the replacement of senior officers, Tsarist uniform insignia and the general democratisation of the army, Kerensky also sought to capitalise on the revolutionary spirit by raising a new type of formation. These units would be motivated to fight by a sense of liberty rather than coercion or the possibility of punishment. Recruits were drawn from front line units where the more aggressive soldiers felt isolated (if not in danger) from their fellows, from men serving in the rear areas who were genuinely enthused by revolutionary fervour or civilian volunteers who

One of the formations that sprang into being following the March Revolution parades in Moscow's Red Square. As their flag reads these men are part of, "The Union of Refugees and those returned from German captivity." Under the Tsar almost all former POWs were treated as potential subversives and sent to obscure garrisons or the Caucasus. The Provisional Government was somewhat more trusting.

felt the revolution was something worth fighting for. Although the idea was dismissed by Alexeyev, some senior officers, notably Brusilov, viewed it positively. Kerensky authorised recruiting groups to travel the empire to raise men who would, as Brusilov put it, "arouse the revolutionary spirit in the army…by giving [the soldiers] faith that the entire Russian people stand behind them" and to "carry along the wavering elements inspired by their example."

The volunteers were put through a short training course similar to that of the Grenadier companies and in order to mark their special status they wore a red over black chevron on their right sleeves and a death's head on their French-style steel helmets. Although recruits did come forward, their low numbers were disappointing. Therefore the committees were employed to persuade complete units to declare themselves Shock or Death formations. Some success was achieved by this method. What many ordinary soldiers found difficult was swearing to always obey orders, to be at the forefront of attacks, to never surrender and to abstain from alcohol. Two of the newly founded units stood out, in particular the 1st Women's Battalion of Death and the 1st Shock Detachment.

The 1st Women's Battalion of Death was the idea of a female infantry officer, Maria Botchkareva, who had served with distinction in a Siberian regiment from 1915. Several other female units were raised including the grimly named Black Hussars of Death. Although more of a propaganda exercise, "to shame the men into fighting" Botchkareva's battalion was sent to form part of the 172nd Division on the W Front. When the division went into action on 22 July it suffered eighty per cent casualties and was eventually withdrawn from the line.

The 1st Shock Detachment was raised in the Eighth Army on SW Front during June. The majority of its officers and men appear to have been experienced soldiers. Despite its description as a detachment, its numbers suggested that it was closer to a regiment, for it included 2,000 infantry, 600 machine gunners, specialist reconnaissance, and trench mortar commands.

On 23 June, Kornilov presented the detachment with its colour and they adopted him as their honorary commander, embroidering the letter K onto their grenade and death's head sleeve badge. A contemporary account of the unit marching to the front describes it thus,

> For the first time I saw an infantry battalion wearing steel helmets. The men all had a skull and cross bones sewn on their sleeves...I noticed that there was an unusual number of machine guns in that battalion. I saw several telescopic sights on the rifles. War materials seemed to be available in great quantities. The men were well-dressed, and the ordnance supplies were brand new.... Perhaps the example of several fighting units will fire the others?

The 1st Shock Detachment acquitted itself well during the offensive but, during the subsequent retreat it was used, along with many of the Shock and Death battalions, to carry out police actions against Russian troops during the Central Powers' counter offensive in late July.

Tarnopol

The Central Powers could hardly have failed to have been aware of the Russian preparations for the summer offensive. The massive troop and hardware movements along the length of the front, conversations

A volunteer in an unidentified Shock formation pictured during the summer of 1917. This man is wearing the unofficial black staff officer's uniform and a motorised soldier's cap. Of particular interest is the rifle that is the famous American manufactured Winchester, numbers of which were supplied to the Russian Army from 1916 onwards.

during periods of fraternisation and the testimony of POWs and deserters confirmed that despite all that had taken place, the Russians were going to attack. At the end of 1916 the Central Powers had decided to launch their own offensive in Galicia but it had been postponed until the extent of Russia's operations had become known. When the advance on SW Front broke down in apparent disarray the Austro-German High Command decided the moment had come to attack. Defending their line with mainly second line formations had allowed them to retain troops of higher quality for the offensive. Nine divisions were quietly moved into position north of Tarnopol along with over two hundred heavy guns. Their objectives were twofold: to regain the strategic initiative in the east and to reduce as far as possible the capacity of SW Front to defend Ukraine. An eventual advance into Ukraine was regarded as vital due to the food shortages in Austria and Germany that were sapping civilian morale and the will to continue the war. Supplies of food from occupied Romania had tided them through the previous winter but much, much more was required.

On 19 July, after a short but powerful bombardment, the Germans attacked, striking first at Eleventh Army (General I. I. Fedotov). At that time Brusilov was preparing to restart the offensive and was shuffling units to that end. The Russian High Command was so focussed on its own problems that it neglected to heed the few warnings they had received. As a result the weight of the German attack came as a complete shock. Eleventh Army's front collapsed and within two days a wedge 40kms (25 miles) wide and 24kms (15 miles) deep had been driven towards Tarnopol. Two Russian corps, V and XVII, had withdrawn rapidly but were not covered by XLIX Corps which refused to move. Such a speedy advance had put Seventh Army's rear in jeopardy. When Austrian Third Army attacked Third Army's front it too broke and General V. I. Selivachev, its commander, lost control of his men as they fell back some 40kms (25 miles) to the south. The effect on the Russians was like knocking down a row of dominoes with each retreating force bumping into the next. In an area that lacked good roads and railways and with command and control all but gone confusion was inevitable as units jostled for an escape route. Order was almost non-existent as men threw away their weapons and equipment to escape capture. The possibility of a repeat of Tannenberg or the mass surrenders of 1915 was distinct. In the confusion the repeated orders of Brusilov to hold Tarnopol at all costs fell on deaf ears as the command posts of Eleventh and Seventh army's were themselves falling back. Tarnopol, a vital rail and supply centre fell, after heavy German bombing, without much of a fight, on 24 July. Amidst scenes of rape and pillage disordered Russian troops were shot down by punitive detachments in a failed attempt to regain control. To add to this vision of hell, an immense ammunition dump on the outskirts of the town blew up. Ibbertson's journal records his impressions of the road from Tarnopol, "…you could see the Russian Soldiers with their transport wagons or carts, whichever they were, coming from the front seven & eight abreast…." The backdrop was, "…a grand sight at night the front was all in flames…" with, "…men women and children all running away some driving cattle, pigs, sheep, all sorts of things. It was a continual line of humanity…."

The replacement of Brusilov with Kornilov

Following the capture of Tarnopol, the Austro-German thrust turned south destroying what structure remained in Seventh Army. Eighth Army retired over 160kms (99 miles) in good order, fighting as it went. Faced with an increasingly determined Russian defence and with their supply lines stretched to the utmost, the Central Powers halted off their advance without calling into action Austrian Seventh Army.

Although they had driven the Russians back to the border they had achieved nothing like the success they had anticipated. There had been no mass surrenders nor had any sizeable formations been destroyed. Indeed on the Romanian Front the Russo-Romanian forces had scored several notable tactical victories. However, the loss of all the ground taken at such cost during the summer of 1916 had to be blamed on someone or something and it was thus that the myth of treacherous, panic-stricken Bolshevised troops began.

The Bolsheviks, already tarred with the brush of treachery and counter-revolution due to the "July Days" episode were blamed for corrupting the men's will to fight. Both *Stavka* and the Provisional Government built on this spurious claim and embroidered it to the best of their abilities. Specific units were blamed for the disaster, notably both Guards infantry corps, the 6th Grenadier Division and several line infantry regiments. All were accused of not fighting, running away, mutiny, desertion and supporting disruptive counter-revolutionary policies emanating from the rear. These "facts" were seized upon and widely broadcast not only in the army but amongst the population as a whole. When the hysteria of the retreat had died down and the line solidified, a more sober inquiry conducted by *Stavka* demonstrated that few of the allegations had any substance but by the time the report was published in late August it was old news and almost irrelevant, the "truth" had been established.

On 21 July Kornilov was promoted to the command of SW Front and in his first order stated, "The wilful withdrawal of units from their position I regard as tantamount to treason. I categorically demand that all commanding personnel apply artillery and machine gun fire against such traitors." Two days later, with the support of Brusilov, he demanded the reintroduction of the death penalty, the abolition of which was one of the sacred cows of the March Revolution. Such a suggestion was in line with the way in which Kerensky's thoughts had been moving since the failure of the offensive and the mutinies. On 25 July the cabinet of the Provisional Government, with the tacit approval of the Soviet, approved the reintroduction of the death penalty *in principle* but with special court martials to investigate each case. The death penalty was prescribed, *at the front*, for treason, rape and flight from the battlefield.

Ibbertson, as his RFC unit travelled across the Ukraine in late July, witnessed the change of mood,

> Cossacks would board the train and anyone they found travelling without a ticket were in for it. There were so many deserters that orders were given to the Cossacks, that all the men who were deserting were to be taken off the trains and every fifth man was to be shot…one chap thought he would be a bit obstinate… so Mr Cossack simply pulled out his revolver and shot the chap where he sat.

On 29 July Kerensky summoned all the front commanders to Moghilev to hear their opinions on, "measures necessary to restore the fighting capacity of the army." As well as Klembovski, Denikin, and Shcherbachev, those attending included the retired Alexeyev, Ruzski and Dragomirov. Kornilov was absent due to the situation on his front. Denikin led the charge criticising everything from Kerensky, the Soviet and the Provisional Government down to battalion committees. He cited their interference in decision-making and planning and stirring up the men against their superiors as the causes for the failure of the offensive. Denikin then went on to outline his proposals to save the army which included the abolition of the committees and the restoration of officers' powers. Kerensky accepted his points defending some of Denikin's comments and agreeing with others. The other generals to a man supported Denikin. However, when Kornilov's views were read out they were less radical. The meeting closed but on his way back to Petrograd Kerensky, safely away from any retribution, announced the replacement of Brusilov by Kornilov as Supreme Commander in Chief with effect from 1 August.

With their return to Russian soil and the halting of the Austro-German advance the men's attitude changed. As an eminent authority on the period has stated, "The Germans could not be allowed to sweep into the interior of Mother Russia. A primordial peasant patriotism finally did reassert itself, but it did not transform attitudes to officers or the war in general."

The reintroduction of capital punishment was at first regarded by many officers and committeemen as the first step towards the reintroduction of the old style of discipline. Bolshevik and other agitators were rounded up in a massive exercise aimed at the restoration of order. Every front was

Above: During the retreat to the Russian border members of the RNACD were seconded to train Caucasians of the Savage Division in the use of machine guns. The machine gun troops attached to the Savage Division were Russians and felt to be unlikely to obey orders to fire on fellow Russians whether they were deserters or not. The Caucasians did not have such scruples and were frequently used to round up mutinous Russian troops.

Opposite: The regimental standard of the Tartar regiment one of the six regiments of the so-called Savage Division (official title Caucasian Native Cavalry Division). This division was part of the force that marched on Petrograd in support of Kornilov's move against Kerensky during the summer of 1917. To the right is Colonel Polovtsov, the regimental commander from September 1914 to April 1917. Though the majority of the officers of the CNC were Russian, Caucasian aristocrats also held high ranks.

affected by this movement but the desired outcome was not universal, particularly on N and W fronts where those believed to be harbouring suspect ideas merely went into hiding in the larger towns.

However, as conditions settled down the belief began to grow amongst the lower ranks that their superiors had purposely engineered the retreat as an excuse to restore pre-Revolutionary ways. Although with hindsight this might seem an absurd idea in early twentieth century Russia, it most certainly was not. Germans were virtually the only foreigners that the ordinary, semi-literate

An interesting group of officers, men and civilians who are both wearing helmets. The civilians are allegedly Bolshevik agitators visiting the front line. Agitation was carried on by all manner of political groups but none were as consistently successful as the Bolsheviks whose simple message of peace, bread and land found a ready audience.

Russian peasant soldier had heard of and they enjoyed a mixed reputation. The descendants of the German aristocracy, the so-called "Baltic Barons" in the Baltic provinces, were renowned for their complete loyalty to the Tsarist regime combined with a particular fondness for cruelty and repression in times of unrest such as 1905. A consequence of this was that despite proven loyalty over many generations of service, many of the senior officers who had German-sounding names and who had either a rudimentary or non-existent command of the Russian language were instantly marked out as being different and viewed negatively. During an engagement in 1914 a picket arrested a Baltic Baron serving with the Guards cavalry because of his abysmal Russian. German farmers had been encouraged to come to Russia during the eighteenth century and had settled across the western and southern provinces of the empire. Many of their descendants found work as estate managers and thus were viewed as oppressors of the poor. Furthermore the former Tsaritsa was German and her well-known sympathy for German and Austrian POWs (allegedly at the expense of Russians in a similar position) had convinced the bulk of the population of her disloyalty to her adopted country. Therefore it was unsurprising that such a rumour rapidly gained acceptance.

Mistrust between officers and men grew during the weeks of August as the front lapsed into inactivity and rumour mongering and gossip were the main occupation of the men as they struggled to come to terms with what was happening. Their leaders from Kerensky and the Soviet down to the committees at regimental level had all, apparently, begun to turn into counter-revolutionaries and were assuming the trappings of the old regime. Slowly but surely the appealing slogans of the Bolsheviks particularly the call for, "peace, bread and land", were beginning to sound more and more relevant to the mass of the frontline troops than Kerensky's histrionic patriotism and calls for revolutionary sacrifice. As a *Stavka* report for early August noted,

> In the more tranquil units the new measures served to create a healthy climate, but in undependable units they only magnify the unrest, since the soldiers regard the orders on discipline and the death penalty as a return to the old regime and blame officers for their publication. The situation of officers in many units is very bad, even critical.

The Kornilov affair

Born into a poor military family Kornilov had enjoyed an interesting career since being commissioned into the artillery in 1892 at the age of twenty-two. Having served in Asia he was promoted to General and given command of the 48th Infantry Division on SW Front in 1914. Captured by the Austrians in 1915 he escaped and returned to Russia in late 1916 where he became an overnight celebrity as the most senior escapee. After commanding the XXV Corps for some months Kornilov was invited to take command of the Petrograd garrison immediately following the revolution. One of his first duties, on 21 March, was to place the Tsaritsa under house arrest. This act may have accorded him some satisfaction as she had questioned him after his escape as to the nature of the treatment of meted out to Russian POWs: when he answered that they were treated "like dogs" she turned away obviously not believing his answer. During the disturbances of April, Kornilov, convinced that the Provisional Government was in danger, ordered artillery on to the streets only to have his order countermanded very publicly by the Soviet. Infuriated at their behaviour he resigned and returned to the SW Front as Eighth Army commander. His activities during the offensive are chronicled earlier.

Kornilov made his acceptance of the Supreme Command subject to three conditions:

1. He would consider himself responsible to his conscience and the nation as a whole.
2. There was to be no interference with his operational orders and consequently with his appointment of senior commanders.
3. Measures recently applied at the front, including the death penalty, should also apply behind the lines where the reserve troops were stationed.

Kerensky's agreement to this remarkable document was indicative of the weakness of his position at the head of a second, shaky coalition cabinet. However the "nation as a whole" was read to signify the Provisional Government. On 4 August Kerensky became the head of the cabinet, not just its apparent leader. With no obvious sense of irony Kerensky took up residence in the former Tsar's Winter Palace and gained the nickname "Alexander IV". It was unsurprising that the faith of the "poor bloody infantry" far away in the squalor of the trenches began to ebb away.

During early August Kornilov worked out his programme for reviving the army. His suggestions were radical and included the imposition of martial law not only in the armed forces but also on the railways and in munitions factories. The death penalty could be invoked for offences ranging from rumour mongering and public agitation to the publication of seditious literature.

Kornilov was also concerned about the military situation. SW Front was in no immediate danger and Denikin, its new commander, enjoyed Kornilov's confidence. But on N Front Riga was of particular concern as it defended the approaches to Petrograd itself and many of the troops were believed to be unreliable should the Germans launch a serious attack. Therefore Kornilov revived his idea for a dedicated Petrograd Army. This concept had received the approval of Alexeyev back in April but had subsequently been shelved. The Petrograd Army was to include the garrison of Finland, the Revel Fortified District, the two right flank corps of Twelfth Army and the Petrograd garrison. To bolster the loyalty of some of these formations III Cavalry Corps and the Caucasian Cavalry Corps (the expanded Caucasian Native Cavalry Division) with its attached brigade of Ossetian riflemen were to be transferred to the area. The new command was to be under General A. M. Krymov. At a meeting in Petrograd on 20 August Kornilov and Kerensky discussed the martial law issue at length but the threat to Riga and Petrograd only briefly. Nevertheless on his return to *Stavka*

Kornilov authorised the transfer of the two cavalry corps. As Kornilov later stated, "I wanted to have near Petrograd units capable of withstanding the corroding influence of the Petrograd Soviet of Worker's and Soldier's Deputies, which would adjoin the [Caucasian Native Cavalry] division." It was also clear that such troops could be used in Petrograd should the need arise, a point Kornilov did not deny when questioned about these moves by his Chief of Staff, General A. S. Lukomsky.

However, in Petrograd Kerensky was under severe pressure. The Soviet wished to abolish the death penalty while the left-wing and right-wing press were engaged in a war of words over Kornilov's proposals. Indeed Kornilov enjoyed increasing support from right-wingers desperate for a strong leader as their fears of a move to the extreme left had been growing despite the failure of the July Days and his championing of discipline and coercion made him the perfect man. Kerensky planned to, "obtain a mandate from the nation to carry the war on to a successful conclusion, without sacrificing any of the 'conquests of the revolution.'" To restore some semblance of unity a conference was planned that would take place away from the hothouse atmosphere of Petrograd. "The Moscow State Conference was therefore billed as a great event destined to restore national unity." There was only one group that refused to attend: the Bolshevik Party.

In the few days before the opening of the of the Moscow conference various right-wing activists sent Kornilov messages of support. When he arrived in Moscow on 26 August Kornilov did so in great style accompanied by his bodyguard, the exotically uniformed Turkmen Cavalry Regiment. Fawned over by officers and politicians alike Kornilov defied Kerensky's instructions to speak of nothing but the strategic position. Kornilov launched into a description of the steps that had to be taken to defend the country, reiterating his earlier proposals and expressing his hopes for their acceptance by the Provisional Government. He also outlined the decline in weapons production. Having spoken, Kornilov returned to Moghilev.

On 6 September Kerensky granted permission for the formation of the Petrograd Army which Kornilov endorsed two days later. But it was too late. In a three-day operation, 1–3 September, the Germans had taken Riga. (This operation will be dealt with in the next chapter.)

Almost before the last Russian had left Riga, Kornilov issued a statement claiming that once again hordes of cowardly, Bolshevised mutineers had abandoned their positions. The language and tone of his communiqué virtually duplicated those describing events at Tarnopol. However, the left including Kerensky, the Bolsheviks and the committeemen did not believe *Stavka's* version. Inevitably those on the right accepted it verbatim. The controversy raged for several days as newspapers of both persuasions tried to rally support for the groups they represented. Army newsheets carried the argument right into the trenches and the phrases like "stab in the back" and "taking advantage of sad events" became common currency.

During the first two weeks of September a remarkable series of events occurred. The details are out of place in a work such as this but the results are not. The forces of left and right fell in behind their respective figureheads Kerensky and Kornilov. Both groups proceeded to bluff and counter bluff each other in a deadly competition of words in which the prize was the leadership of Russia. With Kornilov at *Stavka* and Kerensky in Petrograd their discussions took place over the Hughes Apparatus, telegraph and telephone. As the words flew back and forth the Army of Petrograd slowly moved into place, some of the men believing that they were going to Petrograd to suppress a counter-revolution. But to Kerensky it looked as if Kornilov was positioning his forces for a military take-over. Kerensky's colleagues in the Provisional Government urged him to compromise but on 10 September an announcement from Kornilov ended all hope of that. Kornilov made a direct appeal to the country at large in which he declared, "the Provisional Government, under pressure from the Bolshevik[s]…is acting in full accord with the plans of the German General Staff…." With these words Kornilov immediately lost the support of two of his front commanders as well as many of his civilian supporters.

With compromise now impossible Kerensky acted. Political workers were despatched to the Caucasian Cavalry Corps where they convinced them their journey was unjustified and that extra land was reserved for loyal troops. Railway workers slowed the progress of III Cavalry Corps to virtually nothing and they too began to question their mission. Finally Kerensky authorised the Soviet to arm Petrograd's workers, thus resurrecting the Red Guards (banned since the July Days) to provide some muscle. As his military support faded away and with his civilian support dwindling, Kornilov waited on events at Moghilev.

Kerensky summoned Alexeyev from retirement and dispatched him to Moghilev to arrest Kornilov and assume command of the army. With Kornilov in custody Denikin and other senior officers were also arrested. The "conspirators" were all held in a monastery at Bykhov pending trial. What became known as Kornilov's Coup had fizzled out but it had the effect of weakening the Provisional Government and polarising opinion. Kerensky's position appeared more secure with the arrest of Kornilov but in reality he had few supporters left.

CHAPTER 10

Epilogue: September–November 1917, Russia's Exit

The fall of Riga

Having driven the Russians out of Galicia in July and early August the Central Powers turned their attention to the Baltic coast. Plans had been laid, in April 1917, for an attack on Riga but the Russian position was felt to be too strong for the available forces to deal with. Five months later Russian Twelfth Army (led by General V. N. Klembovski) was considered to be sufficiently demoralised to risk an attack. Furthermore it was hoped that such an operation so close to Petrograd would encourage the Russians to sue for peace whereas those on the Stokhod River and in Galicia had not.

The Russian line followed the course of the Duna River with a bridgehead on the western bank opposite Riga. The point the Germans chose to attack was upstream of the city and afforded them good landing areas as the assault troops would have to be ferried across the 366–457m (400–500 yards) wide river. The divisions used against SW Front earlier in the summer had been retained in the east for just such an opportunity. They were some of the best in the German army and included two Guards units. Infantry strength was roughly equal but the Germans had gathered every heavy gun on the Eastern Front. In round numbers they deployed over 400 field, and upwards of 250 heavy guns supported by more than 500 mortars of various calibres. Scores of pontoons were to be employed ferrying the men across the river and engineers were in place to build bridges as soon as possible. A boom was prepared to ward off any floating mines. Throughout August the German infantry were carefully trained in amphibious operations and briefed as to their specific tasks once ashore. However, despite strict security, the Russians became aware of the forthcoming attack and preparations for the evacuation of Riga were made.

At 0400 hours on 1 September the German bombardment began. It had been carefully planned with particular attention being given to the use of gas shells, and virtually no allowance had been made for registration shots so as not to alert the defenders. The Russian batteries were subjected to a mixed barrage of gas and high explosives, which continued intermittently for over two hours. The trench lines received similar treatment. Any counter battery fire after 0600 hours received a second dose. It is difficult to imagine what it was like for the Russian gunners. The filters on German, British and Russian gas masks were effective for an absolute maximum of two hours but the ability of a man to function began to drop rapidly before that limit was reached. The Avalov mask which was issued to the Russian artillery in 1917 was amongst the best available to sustain prolonged activity, however the Germans noted little defensive fire after 0700 hours. During this operation the Germans recorded firing a grand total of 116,400 gas shells. As the effectiveness of their masks wore off the Russian infantry in the riverside trenches began to make their way to the rear, but only to be greeted by the shells falling on the gun lines.

An early morning mist and smoke shells added to the confusion so that when the German pontoons started to cross at 0830 hours they encountered very little opposition. Within two hours a bridgehead of 2–3kms (1.2–1.9 miles) deep by 6kms (3.7 miles) wide had been established and the bridges were nearing completion: the Germans had achieved a stunning success. Unfortunately they were not prepared to exploit such a rapid victory. The approach roads to the bridges were clogged with unnecessary vehicles, a cavalry brigade tasked with sweeping into Riga got lost and the Russians re-established themselves beyond the range of the German artillery. Nevertheless Klembovski issued orders for a withdrawal from the western bank and the evacuation of the city. The Latvian Rifles did sterling work fighting rearguard actions and by 3 September the line stabilised 32kms (20 miles) north east of Riga.

The Germans claimed nine thousand POWs, which (by their recording methods) included the thousand dead who had been victims of gas. Over 200 guns were taken, many in fixed coastal batteries with many more abandoned as a result of the horses being gassed. Although a gas mask for horses was available one can only pity the driver trying to fit one with shells raining down and panicking horses. Kornilov seems to have been completely passive during this time. He issued no orders nor did he transfer reserves to the area despite the fact that they were available nearby. It was about this time that the word *Kornilovite* became a common insult for all those who wished to restore discipline or continue the war.

On 14 September the committee newsheet of Eighth Army accused *Stavka* of lying in its account of the fall of both Tarnopol and Riga. Apologising for having believed them it stated, "Fortunately the soldiers didn't believe us and they were the first to see that treason was behind it."

The shattered remains of a Putilov 76.2mm M1902 field gun in its shelter in the defence lines outside of Riga. Riga was the fourth city of the Russian Empire and its loss was a severe blow to morale.

Having achieved their objective, the Central Powers transferred the attack divisions to France and waited on events. Once again relative calm settled on the Eastern Front. Kerensky had weathered the Kornilov storm and the loss of Riga and emerged with apparently more authority than before. However, his support was rapidly fading away. September and October witnessed a revival in the fortunes of the Bolsheviks, as they appeared to be the only group untainted by the Kornilov affair and their consistent call for peace also enhanced their credibility. During September they gained majorities in the key Soviets of Petrograd, under the chairmanship of Trotsky, Moscow and Kiev. At the end of September Lenin declared that the time had come for, "decisions, not talk" and during the subsequent weeks pressed his supporters to spread the message of "bread, peace and land" to the soldiers and the workers.

General L. G. Kornilov, shown here shortly after being taken prisoner by the Austrians in 1915, became during the summer of 1917 the focus of those who wished to return the army to its pre-Revolutionary levels of discipline and efficiency.

Operation Albion

The loss of Riga had clearly not been enough of an incentive for the Russians to seek peace. Always wary that too great a victory might restore Russian martial ardour and also increasingly concerned lest they commit themselves too far east, the Germans prepared a small operation, code named "Operation Albion" to up the ante. The objective was a small group of islands at the mouth of the Gulf of Riga, in Moon Sound (which gave its name to the action), garrisoned by 25,000 men supported by a small naval flotilla with two battleships.

A German force of over 20,000 men with fifty-four guns was transported to the islands in the early hours of 12 October. The German naval presence was considerable and included several battleships and a seaplane carrier. Unrest in the German navy earlier in the year had caused some concern and activity such as this, it was believed, would be a useful morale booster.

The appearance of the German armada took the Russians completely by surprise as sightings of enemy ships were rare and could not be dismissed out of hand. During the course of the morning, German troops poured onto the shores of Oesel Island (the largest in the group) as if disembarking from a pleasure cruise. Cycle troops ranged far and wide securing coastal batteries, aerodromes and the radio station. There was some fighting on the smaller islands but by 21 October all were securely in German hands, as were thousands of POWs. The loss of ships on both sides was due in great part to the hundreds of mines which had been laid over the past three years. However, the loss of the islands was a major breach of Petrograd's defence network. It was the cause for much concern in the capital and led to rumours of the Germans imminent arrival.

On 22 October the Petrograd Soviet defeated a motion to support the Provisional Government in the war effort and adopted one which accused Kerensky of being ready to, "surrender Petrograd – the citadel of the revolution – to the Germans" as well as being, "in league with the bourgeoisie."

"Bourgeoisie" was a catch all insult like *Kornilovite*, used to against anyone who expressed politically unacceptable ideas and who was thus considered to be a counter revolutionary. The Soviet authorised the formation of a Revolutionary Committee of Defence. A confrontation was clearly in the air but between whom? It was sometimes difficult to calculate whether the greater threat came from within or without.

The November Revolution

Although Kerensky had announced that elections for the long anticipated Constituent Assembly would take place in mid-November and had proclaimed Russia a republic in September, the times for such populist measures had passed. With the Ukraine, Finland, several Cossack *voiskos* and various Caucasian nationalities on the point of declaring their independence a more radical solution than hysterical rhetoric and promises was called for.

Despite *Stavka* and the armies filing positive reports on the condition of the troops these had now assumed the nature of those which, a year earlier, were used to "calm" the Tsar. N, W and SW fronts were now witnessing disobedience, apathy and fraternisation on a scale unimaginable only six months before. Demands for the release of the over 40s poured in but desertion was not an issue. One source suggests that in,

> September and October desertions had not yet assumed massive proportions from the front lines, in part because of the expectation of an early peace (so why risk being branded a deserter?). On the other hand, there is every reason to believe that desertions from the garrisons, which had always been considerably larger than desertions from the front, were already massive.

Instances of officers being assaulted and even murdered, although not as common as some émigré literature would have one believe, increased. Although such events had happened ever since the March Revolution they were usually carried out quietly under the cover of an attack or barrage. Often such killings were the result of behaviour that was perceived as "provocative" such as orders to move into the line or undertake aggressive patrolling in no-man's land. What generated so much publicity and provoked such a degree of revulsion was the sadistic manner in which some officers were murdered. Officers had been shot, lynched, stabbed even crucified and often mutilated post-mortem, however, these acts were often as not the work of a group rather than an individual. Rumours of such occurrences, combined with a sense of frustration and disgust at the course of events in 1917 generally, led to the resignation or retirement of thousands of officers during the post-revolutionary period.

Until late October army committees managed to exercise some power and influence over the men but when rumours of Bolshevik plans to overthrow the Provisional Government leaked out in early November they chattered furiously but did nothing. The Military Governor of Petrograd, Polkovnikov, moved the remains of the Women's Battalion of Death and

The gloomy look on this staff officer's face tells the whole story of the demoralisation of the officer corps.

some officer cadets to the Winter Palace, possibly to avoid being accused of provocation. Kerensky, in conversation with the latest Supreme Commander in Chief, General N. N. Dukhonin, displayed tranquillity bordering on the soporific, saying that although the Bolsheviks were, "attempting to detach the troops from the command…I think we can easily handle it." Such sublime confidence in his own powers of persuasion and the assumed loyalty of the people and army was to prove grossly exaggerated.

On 7 November the Bolsheviks began their revolution. Well-armed Red Guard units took control of the main telegraph office and the power station. During the course of the next day the railway station to N Front was occupied and later that night, after a long stand off, the Winter Palace was occupied. The Provisional Government's cabinet, having waited patiently all day, was arrested. The Women's Battalion and the cadets left quietly. The Red Guards and sailors from Kronstadt then proceeded to get blind drunk in the former Tsar's wine cellars.

The first shots of civil war

Kerensky was not among the Bolshevik's prisoners. He had fled Petrograd to raise armed support to crush the uprising. Failing to find troops on his way Kerensky arrived at N Front headquarters in Pskov. However his fear of betrayal was so great that he hid himself in the rooms of his brother in law N Front's Quartermaster General. From there Kerensky issued a summons for loyal men. It was answered by General P. N. Krasnov who had replaced Krymov as commander of III Cavalry Corps when the latter committed suicide. Krasnov was authorised to marshal strong forces to regain control of Petrograd. Unfortunately strong forces were not forthcoming. Krasnov gathered roughly 1,000 Cossacks from his corps and a handful of infantry. Nevertheless they moved on Petrograd reaching Tsarskoe Selo on 11 November. Here they met up with the local garrison of 16,000 men who promptly laid down their arms and declared themselves neutral. Other units from other fronts were now moving on Petrograd but their progress was slow and the information they received contradictory as bulletins claiming victory for one group or another flooded the airwaves and telegraph wires. For most, neutrality was the order of the day as civil war was now a distinct possibility.

In Petrograd the Bolsheviks were spurred into action by an attempted counter coup mounted by officer cadets. The need to retain control of the city convinced them that they must take action against Kerensky. With the cadets suppressed Red Guard units backed by sailors and a few soldiers marched out and took up positions on the Pulkovo Heights on the Tsarskoe Selo–Petrograd road. Despite Kerensky's direct and increasingly hysterical

Technical units such as this armoured car *Divizion* tended to retain their discipline. This mix of vehicles includes a Garford armoured lorry mounting a modified 76.2mm mountain gun and two machine guns, two Sheffield Simplex-FIAT hybrids and an Armstrong Whitworth. The majority of Russia's armoured cars were imported from Britain.

orders Krasnov recognised the hopelessness of mounting an attack. Lacking artillery and infantry the workers and sailors, however poorly led and trained, could not fail to shoot his men to ribbons. As the day wore on, fraternisation between Krasnov's Cossacks and the workers and sailors increased. Eventually a compromise was reached and the Cossacks were allowed to leave for their homes on the Don River, an offer they promptly accepted. Kerensky went into hiding and left Russia for a life in exile. The only other significant battle took place in Vinnitsa where a pro-Kerensky infantry division routed a pro-Bolshevik force in a battle that involved artillery, aircraft and armoured cars. However, the refusal of railway workers to transport them north brought their progress to a halt. Similar activities, co-ordinated by the railway trade union which was anxious to

A company of the troops who accompanied the Red Guards and sailors to engage Krasnov's march on Petrograd at Pulkovo Heights. The majority of soldiers in the area adopted a neutral stance.

avoid civil war, stopped the few pro-Kerensky units almost before they got started. In Petrograd the Bolshevik take-over was an almost bloodless affair but in Moscow several days of vicious street fighting between 11 and 15 November, caused hundreds of lives to be lost until the Bolsheviks stamped out the opposition force which was mainly composed of officer cadets.

Armistice

Although the seat of government was in Bolshevik hands their position was not a strong one. There had been little fighting at Pulkovo Heights and elsewhere, yet the first shots of the civil war had been clearly and irrevocably

Unofficial truces and an atmosphere of live and let live permeated much of the Eastern Front during the late summer and autumn of 1917. Here Austrian and Russian troops pose together for the camera on the Romanian Front. The most senior participant appears to be the Austrian sergeant to the left, rarely were officers involved in such gatherings.

fired. Apprised of events by frequent radio broadcasts, the Central Powers eagerly awaited developments. Unlike the March Revolution none of the Allied ambassadors recognised the new government due to its continual demands for peace, particularly that made by Lenin on 7 November. They also hoped for a more sympathetic regime following the elections. However, when the other major left wing parties refused to be a part of a coalition the Bolsheviks immediately formed a cabinet called the Soviet of People's Commissars (*Sovnarkom*) and appointed a junior officer N. V. Krylenko as Commisar for War. As well as calling for "immediate peace" the Bolshevik programme anticipated international revolution and to this end a propaganda newsletter was put into production to undermine the loyalty of the armies of the Central Powers. It was passed across the lines during periods of fraternisation much to the chagrin of Austrian and German officers. Lenin was acutely aware that he now had to deliver peace and on 21 November Dukhonin was ordered to, "contact the enemy military authorities with an offer of the immediate cessation of hostilities for the purpose of opening up peace negotiations."

Dukhonin discussed the matter with the Allied representatives at *Stavka* and his front commanders. When Lenin demanded a reply that night Dukhonin tried to fob him off with excuses, which resulted in his immediate dismissal. As confirmation a radiogram was sent, uncoded, to all committees, at all levels of the army and navy. It announced that Krylenko was Dukhonin's replacement and that *Sovnarkom* gave, "each regiment on the front lines" the authority to undertake, "negotiations for an armistice with the adversary." Detailed instructions followed on how to conduct this delicate task.

On 24 November Krylenko set off for *Stavka* breaking his journey at Dvinsk (W Front) to select and despatch a team of negotiators to the Germans. This was followed up by an order to all committees to remove any general who hindered the peace process. Meanwhile Dukhonin had passed on a note from the Allied representatives to *Sovnarkom* reminding it of Russia's responsibility not to negotiate a separate peace as agreed by the Tsar in September 1914. The note included an enigmatic threat of, "the most serious consequences" should such talks take place. It was a futile gesture as the Germans had already replied to Krylenko's emissaries on 25 November offering to discuss terms at Brest-Litovsk on 2 December. All along the front elected negotiators crossed the lines and began their work. When Krylenko reached Moghilev Dukhonin had decided not to leave or to fight and was murdered by members of Krylenko's entourage who were enraged that their victim had assisted with the escape of Kornilov and his fellow prisoners from Bykhov. Many of the Allied representatives left for the relative safety of Kiev. The men of the RNACD, the French and British aviation missions had already received orders to make for Petrograd or Romania as best they could to avoid imprisonment. Equipment was destroyed, abandoned or handed over to any responsible body with a gun or requisition. In most cases they managed to leave with little difficulty but in considerably less comfort than on their arrival. The Belgian Armoured Car Division underwent an epic journey through Siberia.

The Bykhov prisoners split up and journeyed south to join Alexeyev who was in the process of forming an entirely new army with which he hoped to fight on against the Central Powers. Known as the Volunteer Army it would become the major threat to the Bolshevik regime during the coming years of civil war. The new "Revolutionary *Stavka*" that functioned into early 1918 was now concerned with ending the war.

During the early weeks of 1918 the Russian trenches emptied as the army demobilised. It was left to a force of screening units to maintain the line. Here a pair of guards keep watch by their dugout near to hand is a British supplied Lewis gun.

Brest-Litovsk

In the remains of the Russian fortress at Brest-Litovsk on 22 December representatives of the Central Powers, Turkey and Bulgaria met with Russia's delegation to discuss the peace treaty. Six days later the talks were adjourned until 8 January. However, when they resumed Trotsky found that a Ukrainian delegation had also joined the talks and were insisting on a separate treaty. The Ukrainians possessed one asset that everyone, particularly Austria, needed – grain. Trotsky now began to play a waiting game, hoping for revolutions to break out in Austria and Germany and for the triumph of pro-Bolshevik forces in Ukraine.

The talks dragged on for three weeks until, on 9 February, Ukraine's representatives signed a treaty although the question of who was in

power in Kiev was moot. The next day Trotsky made his now famous announcement: "We are going out of the war, but we feel ourselves compelled to refuse to sign the peace treaty." There was to be no peace but also no war. It was, as General Hoffman, the German commander on the Eastern Front said, "*Unerhort*" – unheard of. Trotsky concluded his remarkable speech with the sentence, "The Russian troops are receiving at the same time an order for a general demobilisation on all lines of the fronts." Later that night the Russian delegation left for Petrograd.

The German High Command was not happy with this solution and on 18 February resumed operations against the near deserted Russian lines. Without an army there was little the Bolsheviks could do. Although the propaganda machine worked overtime nothing could stop the Austro–German advance. Help from the west was unlikely as *Sovnarkom* had just repudiated £1.2 billion in war loans and confiscated the gold reserves of Romania. Therefore on 19 February Lenin and Trotsky agreed to the terms offered at Brest-Litovsk. The Central Powers declined and marched onwards, as Hoffman put it, "for the protection of Finland, Estonia, Livonia (Lithuania) and Ukraine." The reaction in Petrograd was remarkable: Red Guard units prepared to march out and fight, their ranks swelled by even more untrained workers incensed at the Central Powers apparent deceit. The press, of all political shades, attacked the Bolsheviks for their apparent cowardice. On 21 February German troops landed in Finland which had just been recognised as independent by *Sovnarkom*.

The Central Powers now offered harsher terms than before. Russia would lose thirty-two per cent of her agricultural land, thirty-four per cent of her population fifty-four per cent of her industry and eighty-nine per cent of her coalmines. Lenin, in the teeth of fierce opposition, pushed his argument for peace at any price through on the basis of one piece of simple, indisputable logic: Russia had no army left to fight with. Indeed as one sailor put it, "We haven't a fleet anymore; it's a wreck." The terms were accepted on 24 February and a delegation left Petrograd to make peace. On 27 February, while discussions were underway, the Germans bombed Petrograd by way of encouragement.

That which had begun with the signature of the most powerful individual in the world in a gilded palace during the balmy days of 1914 ended with the signatures of a group of international revolutionaries in the snowy, burned out shell of a Tsarist fortress. It was 3 March 1918. Russia's participation in the First World War was finally over but the first shots of the Russian Civil War had already been fired and that horror was to bring even greater misery than what became known as the German War.

APPENDIX 1

The Russian Navy

Peter the Great founded the Russian Navy in the early 1700s. The main fleet operated in the Baltic Sea with a squadron on the Sea of Azov which expanded later that century to become the Black Sea Fleet. During the Crimean War the sailors and guns of the Black Sea Fleet played a distinguished role in the defence of Sebastopol. However, the Baltic Fleet was reduced to passivity having proved itself incapable of breaking the Anglo-French blockade. When the empire expanded eastwards a Pacific Squadron was established with its base at Vladivostok. The remilitarization of the Black Sea at roughly the same time led to a further period of expansion but due to limited resources, the Baltic Fleet was somewhat overlooked. However, pressure from France following the 1894 treaty led to an increase in the strength of the Baltic Fleet to counter the growing naval power of Germany. As a result French companies received ship-building orders as Russian heavy industry did not have the capacity to build complete, modern warships.

The Russo-Japanese War was a disaster for the Russian Navy that lost virtually all of the Pacific Squadron as well as much of the Baltic Fleet which sailed to its doom at the battle of Tsushima. With severely limited resources the navy was faced with the dilemma of, "we must know what we want" in terms of ship types and whether it should concentrate on the Pacific Ocean, the Baltic or Black seas.

1906–1914

Although there had been a Navy Minister for decades his role was that of junior partner in the War Ministry where the army was regarded as the more important service. Strategically the navy's role was to support the army.

In 1906 a Naval General Staff was established under the new State Defence Committee but was almost immediately at loggerheads with the Navy

Minister Admiral A. A. Birilov who regarded the new body as an upstart creation of little value. Both the Navy Ministry and the Naval General Staff produced plans for modernisation and reform, but neither was acceptable on the grounds of cost. Furthermore the army and the Council of State Defence objected, complaining that they exceeded the Navy's defensive role. As the arguments and politicking dragged on the Tsar intervened. Nicholas II, in common with his cousins George V and Wilhelm II, liked ships and wished to expand Russia's overseas influence by the possession of a strong, modern navy. However, the Third *Duma* (1907–12) preferred to invest the money that was available in the army. Consequently the annual naval estimates became a matter of prolonged debate.

A series of emergency grants provided for the replacement of several ships lost at Tsushima and as money from increased state revenues and French loans filled the treasury and Turkey began to expand its fleet in the Black Sea, it was decided to increase the size of the fleet both there and in the Baltic. While a considerable proportion of this money was invested in capital projects such as shipyards, dry docks and improved port facilities, a large ship building programme was also approved. With the appointment of a new Navy Minister who was more receptive to reform, Admiral I. K. Grigorovich, in 1911 the *Duma* began to look more favourably on the naval estimates. On 6 July 1912 the Tsar signed a £42,000,000 expansion plan. The problem was that many of the ships laid down under this programme were not scheduled for completion for some time. Furthermore they were highly dependent on foreign expertise and equipment, and the overseas contracts were not placed with Russia's likely allies. As with heavy artillery procurement orders were made with German companies as well as those of Britain and France.

1914

At the outbreak of war two Russian cruisers, paid for and on the point of completion in German yards, were commissioned into the German navy. According to the 1914 edition of *Jane's Fighting Ships*, four Dreadnoughts and two cruisers were also under construction for the Baltic Fleet, as were three Dreadnoughts and nine cruisers for the Black Sea Fleet. These new capital ships were to be complemented by thirty-six new destroyers and a large number of submarines and auxiliary vessels. The majority of these ships were due for completion within the next few years. By 1914 Russian naval expenditure only lagged behind that of Britain and the USA having overtaken Germany and other potential enemies. Indeed Russia and Britain were on the point of signing a naval agreement when the war broke out.

Sailors of the Baltic Sea Fleet check a civilian's papers in Petrograd during the autumn of 1917. Such shore parties became a familiar sight in the capital during times of unrest and could be relied upon by the civilian administration to maintain order.

But the Russian Navy was not to be committed offensively during the war years and the majority of its operations were defensive.

1914–17

As noted in **Plan 19** both fleets were subordinated to *Stavka*. The HQ of the Black Sea Fleet was at Sebastopol, the headquarters of the Baltic fleet at Helsingfors (Helsinki) in Finland, having major bases at Kronstadt and Riga. The Navy Ministry at Petrograd acted as a clearing house for orders from *Stavka*.

As the Pacific Squadron took virtually no part in the war it is mainly the operations of the Baltic and Black sea fleets that concern us here and as little or no co-ordination was possible each will be dealt with individually.

A rating in the standard winter dress of the period. The cap tally shows that he was a member of the crew of the destroyer *Engineer-Mechanic Zverev*, which was part of the Baltic Sea Fleet, named after a hero of the Russo-Japanese War.

Baltic Sea Fleet

At the outbreak of war the Baltic Fleet put a carefully planned defensive mining programme into operation. Russian mines were reputedly the best and most effective used by any navy in the war. The objective of this was to prevent the movement of German naval units against the capital or the flank of NW Front. The officer in charge of mining was Captain A. V. Kolchak who was to advance swiftly to the rank of Admiral. The major achievement of the Baltic Fleet during 1914 was the capture of a set of German naval code books from the *Magdeburg* during August thus enabling Allied intelligence officers to monitor German movements.

For the next two years the Baltic Fleet's major units were preserved in anticipation of a decisive fleet action. The burden of offensive operations was undertaken by the eleven submarines of the Baltic Fleet and a small number of British submarines that reached Russia via the Arctic or by running the gauntlet of German patrols at the mouth of the Baltic. Although the submariners of both navies did sterling work against coastal traders plying the Baltic, the bulk of the Russian fleet remained in harbour. Such passivity had a dire effect on the officers and men leaving them prey to apathy and politicisation. Protected by the increasingly complex web of minefields the sailors' discipline eroded slowly. Cruises were limited due to the lack of British anthracite coal stocks which were in short supply (although interestingly enough, thousands of tons of coal had in fact been stockpiled at Archangel and Murmansk but were instead being used to ballast ships returning to their home ports after delivering munitions to Russia). The sailors' dockside work was also inhibited by the blanket of ice that built up on the harbours and the ship building programme was held up because many of the vessels under construction were designed only to take German-made turbines. The overall result of all these problems was a number of crews with little or nothing to do.

When the army's rifle shortage became critical in 1915 the navy exchanged its Russian rifles for the Japanese *Arisaka* to ease ammunition supply problems. Japan also salvaged ships from the Russo-Japanese War, which were re-commissioned by the Russians and a Separate Baltic Detachment was formed but it did not manage to return to the Baltic.

Problems

The first outbreak of trouble occurred on the cruiser *Rossiia* in Helsingfors during September 1915. The sailors protested about poor food, overly

The bearded British officer is Admiral Sir Richard Phillimore the Royal Navy's representative at *Stavka* from 1915 to late 1916. The Russian officers are a mixture of army and navy pilots escorting Phillimore on a tour of the Kilkond Naval Air Station on Oesel Island during 1916. The Russian officer on the left is the commander of the base Lieutenant V. A. Litvinov.

harsh discipline and "German officers". Rumours of the treachery of the "German officers" had been growing since the loss of the cruiser *Pallada* when on patrol duties in November 1914, though the fact that it went down with all hands did not enter into the gossip mongers' tales.

The navy seems to have had a greater proportion of officers with German sounding names than the army and being a smaller service they were more noticeable. Indeed the commander of the Baltic Fleet in 1915 was Admiral N. O. von Essen who apparently considered "russifying" his name during this period. Although the ringleaders aboard the *Rossiia* were arrested it did not prevent further problems in November 1915 when part of the crew of the battleship *Gangoot* rioted beyond their officers' control over poor food. More worrying for senior commanders was the refusal of neighbouring vessel's crews to train their guns on the mutineers. Finally the threat of a submarine putting torpedoes into the *Gangoot* put a stop to the mutiny. A series of arrests were made resulting in those men being assigned to disciplinary battalions. Disciplinary battalions, usually 200 men at a time,

The horse transport ship *Rivn* operated on the Black Sea in support of the forces in Anatolia. Such vessels were often converted from the cattle transports that plied their trade in the coastal waters pre-war. Such a method saved time and of course the animal's strength.

were often sent to NW Front until Twelfth Army complained that they more trouble than they were worth. Subsequently the disciplinary battalions were detained at the naval bases where they became progressively more difficult to control.

As 1916 wore on morale declined still further. Whenever ships changed commanders or officers transferred and attempts were made to tighten discipline where it was perceived to be too lax the men reacted with dumb insolence or worked at a snail's pace. That November Grigorovich expressed his concerns to the Tsar during an interview at *Stavka*. However, Nicholas refused to discuss internal security matters nor did he respond to written reports on similar matters. The situation was summed up in a report from the commander of the Kronstadt base to the navy's representative at *Stavka*. "Yesterday I visited the cruiser *Diana*...I felt as if I were on board an enemy ship.... In the wardroom the officers openly said that the sailors were completely revolutionaries.... So it is everywhere in Kronstadt."

In November 1916 the Russian defences claimed their greatest victory. A force of eleven German destroyers became entangled in minefields while hunting coastal traffic and within forty-eight hours seven were lost and one severely damaged. There was no Russian shipping in the area as they had intercepted radio transmissions and stayed away.

Boredom and lack of activity were not the only reasons for the men's increased disillusionment with the war and the regime. Service in the navy demanded a different sort of recruit to those of the army. The literacy rate amongst sailors was approaching seventy-five per cent, (in the army it was less than thirty per cent) a higher standard of proficiency with technology was vital as were teamwork and initiative, all qualities which fostered a more highly skilled and integrated body of men. The close proximity to urban, industrial centres inevitably led them to be exposed to extreme political viewpoints and the discussion of conditions ashore. Consequently when the revolution came in March 1917 the sailors of the Baltic Fleet were ready and willing to participate.

The Black Sea Fleet

The Black Sea Fleet (Admiral A. A. Eberhardt) followed a more aggressive policy, mounting operations against the Bosporus on 28 March 1915 and again the next month in support of the Gallipolli expedition. By way of drawing the Turks attention to the Black Sea coastline pretence was made of reconnoitring the shore for possible landing sites as had been agreed with the Western Allies. The Anatolian coastline slowly came to be dominated by the Russians which forced the Turks to rely more and more on the slower overland route to supply men and munitions for their Caucasian Front. When Bulgaria entered the war several raids were made against coastal shipping but the presence of German submarines limited such operations. However, it was in support of the right flank of the Caucasian Front that the Black Sea Fleet made its strongest contribution.

In August 1916 Kolchak was appointed commander of the Black Sea Fleet. In November the Black Sea Fleet suffered its greatest loss, the newly completed battleship *Emperatritsa Mariia* which blew up in Sebastopol harbour with over 400 casualties. For the remainder of the war the Black Sea virtually became a Russian lake and increasing use was made of the navy to ferry and escort supplies to the army. The reasons noted for the decline of the Baltic Fleet were much less pronounced amongst the Black Sea sailors. The simple fact that the men were more or less continually involved in an active war and were not subject to urban influences to the same extent as in the Baltic saved the Black Sea Fleet from the worst excesses of the March Revolution. Kolchak took many of his ships to sea

The government took the spiritual welfare of the armed forces very seriously. The image shows a water-borne church that was for use by units on the Black Sea. Whether the church was intended to be assembled on shore or to be used in situ is unknown. Similar places of worship were transported on railway wagons.

when the situation in Petrograd became serious and only returned to harbour when the Tsar had abdicated. Thus, when dozens of officers of all ranks in the Baltic Fleet were being murdered by their men the Black Sea Fleet remained comparatively quiet.

The navy and the revolutions

The speed with which the Baltic Fleet's sailors responded to the March events in Petrograd points to a sense of unity of purpose, although not necessarily a carefully tailored uprising guided by a single mind. When the revolution began the sailors supported it from the outset and were prepared to shoot any who stood in their way. This included their officers, although many were also killed as retribution for past behaviour. On 16

On 14 March 1917 the Guard Equipage, commanded and led by the Grand Duke Kyrill Vladimirovitch, marched to the Duma to show their support for the Provisional Government. The band is playing the Russian version of the *Marseilles*, which was often confused by western commentators for a poorly rehearsed version of the French original as it followed a different beat.

March Admiral A. I. Nepenin, commanding the Baltic Fleet, informed the Provisional Government, "The Baltic Fleet as a military force no longer exists." As far as he could see his ice bound ships had raised red flags.

In both fleets committees were established with powers similar to those in the army. The difference between the fleets was Baltic Fleet's greater degree of militancy and involvement with the affairs of Petrograd. During the July Days Baltic Fleet sailors were heavily involved but the actions subsequently launched to contain radicalism seem to have achieved little but the further alienation of the men. Despite this the sailors supported Kerensky during the Kornilov affair but by the end of September the Provisional Government exercised very little authority over them.

However, when the Germans launched Operation Albion Kerensky sent an inspirational message to the sailors, which elicited the reply, "We will fulfil our duty… [but] not by order of some kind of pitiful Russian Bonaparte…. Long live the world revolution."

The squadron in Moon Sound had been on station for over a month and knew the waters well. Although outnumbered the Russians inflicted considerable damage on the German capital ships but were unable to reach the transports. The British submarines were not called into action but from their commander's diary the commander of the Baltic Fleet (Admiral A. V. Razvozov), "expected to give battle with his big ships as the enemy try and force the outer minefields." The Germans ventured no further for the rest of the war. The ships of the Baltic Fleet had fought their last action and within a month the cruiser *Aurora* was to provide support for the Bolshevik coup. Ownership of the Black Sea Fleet passed to the Ukrainian *Rada* and Ukrainian sailors were transferred from the Baltic Fleet late in 1917.

APPENDIX 2

The Russian Military Air Fleet

In 1885 a military balloon school was opened near St Petersburg. The value of military balloonists was demonstrated during the Russo-Japanese War by the accurate observation of Japanese troop movements at distances up to 8km (5 miles). In 1906 it was decided to increase the number of balloon units from one to ten battalions within a time frame dictated by the military budget. During the next year three battalions and a training unit were established as were eight companies dedicated exclusively to observation from fortresses. Large airships with engines capable of speeds exceeding 40km (25 mph) and the capacity to carry bombs and undertake long-range reconnaissance were seen as the future of aerial warfare.

Airships

In July 1909 an order was placed with the Army Airship Works in St Petersburg for a semi-rigid airship. During October 1910 the airship was accepted into service. Over the next three years several powered airships were imported from France and Germany and a smaller number built domestically. By 1914 the Air Fleet possessed fifteen airships, only four of which were to see limited service. However, experience during the early war period had clearly demonstrated the vulnerability of such large targets that were difficult to manoeuvre and hugely expensive in material and human resources. Although the airships had carried out a few missions the results were negligible. On the other hand tethered balloons had demonstrated their worth as artillery observation platforms, they did not require the resources of the large ships and were easier to replace and maintain.

By the autumn of 1914 airships were being phased out of service and their equipment and their men reassigned to observation balloon units. The tiny Russian aircraft industry now devoted its limited capacity to the production of aeroplanes.

Above and opposite: A Lebed 12 reconnaissance machine has its Colt machine gun fitted in the observer's cockpit. This aircraft entered service in 1916 and over 200 were produced. Equipped with a 150hp Salmson engine the Lebed 12 was capable of 115–125kph (71–78mph). Later versions carried up to 91kg (200lbs) of bombs. Seated on the wheel is V. A. Lebedev the designer.

Aeroplanes

During the first decade of the twentieth century heavier than air machines were still in their infancy. When in 1909 Louis Bleriot flew the English Channel, the military began to take them seriously. If nothing else an aeroplane was capable of carrying out reconnaissance missions over a broader landscape than a tethered balloon with its limited horizon.

The driving force behind the use of aeroplanes was the Grand Duke Alexander Mikhailovitch, a cousin of the Tsar. In January 1910 the Section of the Air Fleet was formed. By 1914 this department would be known as the Russian Military Air Fleet headed by the Grand Duke Alexander. A Bleriot monoplane was bought from France and six officers went there to

learn about aviation. During 1911 the St Petersburg balloon facility was expanded to include aeroplane pilot training. To enable all-year-round training another base was opened in the sunnier climes of the Crimea near Sebastopol. A plan to create ten air detachments by the end of 1912 failed as pilot recruitment and training was slow. Therefore it was agreed that non-commissioned officers and other ranks could be trained as pilots. The majority of the first volunteers were from the artillery as observation for the guns and reconnaissance were the prime remit for the Air Fleet.

Pilot training was rudimentary and involved courses in flight theory, mechanics and practical flight training. During the latter the student would sit behind the instructor and simply watch what he did. Having accompanied an instructor for three or four hours the student would then fly solo for thirty minutes and, having performed several figures of eight, attempt to land. If the student passed the theory and survived the practical he graduated as a pilot.

Lieutenant P. N. Nesterov performed the world's first full loop of an aircraft on 8 September 1913 in a Nieuport IV. Although placed under arrest for endangering, "…a machine, the property of his government," Nesterov was soon promoted to Staff-Captain.

Domestic production and imports

The machines available to the Air Fleet were, almost without exception, imported from France or made in Russia under licence. Various types made by Henri Farman, Morane Saulnier, Nieuport, Bleriot and Deperdussin were issued to flying units with little or no thought given to the problems of having such a miscellany in one formation.

There were four major Russian aircraft manufacturers: Dux in Moscow, Antara in Odessa and Lebedev and the Russo-Baltic Railway Wagon Company (RBVZ) in Petrograd. Before the war approximately 600 aircraft had been built in Russia, some of these were one-off, experimental machines, but the majority were licensed copies or the machines noted above. During the war over 5,500 aircraft were produced under licence of which 1,100 were seaplanes for the navy that operated a separate air fleet. The numbers are low in comparison with Allied and German production figures but the Russian aero-industry was hamstrung by its limited ability to manufacture engines. Virtually all the engines were imported from France for final assembly in Russian factories.

Repair, maintenance and the provision of spares were, within a short space of time, to assume nightmarish proportions. Although flying the aircraft was relatively simple the mechanical work was not. A pilot required little time to convert between aircraft types but the ground staff needed to know as many as five or six different engines and airframes. During autumn and winter aircraft had to be fitted with skis which, given the often unmade nature of airfields, made take-off and landing risky in the extreme.

Organisation

By the summer of 1914 the Air Fleet's inventory numbered some 250 aircraft and a little over 200 pilots. Of these aircraft, 145 were frontline types and of the pilots thirty-six were NCOs. Germany and Austria had roughly 300 aircraft divided between the Eastern, Western and Serbian fronts. On paper the Air Fleet was a formidable protagonist and certainly capable of waging the short war that was generally anticipated.

The organisation was based on six aviation companies that acted as depots for twenty-eight Air Detachments attached to individual army corps with nine in the major fortresses. The HQ of the Air Fleet was eventually established in Kiev. The Grand Duke Alexander commanded the units supporting SW Front, General A. V. Kaul'bars those on NW Front.

Above and below: One of First Battle Group's Nieuport XIs (*Bebe*), numbers of which were built by the Dux factory in Moscow. Designed purely as a fighter, the *Bebe* was popular with Russian pilots. On the upper wing is the stripped down air combat version of the Lewis gun. The maximum speed was 155kph (96mph).

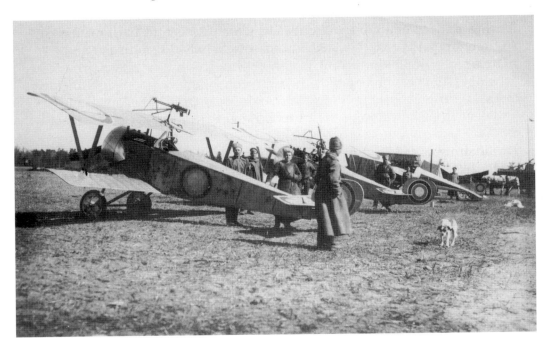

This Morane Saulnier 1 is armed with a water-cooled Maxim, positioned to fire directly through the propeller. It is possible that this was the machine flown by Staff Captain K. K. Vakulovsky, one of Russia's aces who achieved six confirmed victories but disappeared in the maelstrom of revolution and civil war.

There was no attempt to standardise the six machines within a detachment. Initially the task of the Air Fleet was observation and reconnaissance.

It rapidly became obvious that it was necessary to intercept enemy machines similarly employed. Although various engineers had experimented with interrupter gear nothing satisfactory had been developed and the problem of firing through the propeller remained. Therefore it was only possible to arm the observer behind or in front of the pilot. At first only carbines or pistols were carried but the chances of hitting the enemy pilot were negligible. So other, equally lethal, methods were experimented with such as swinging hooks on ropes or throwing hand grenades and darts. But it was Staff Captain P N Nesterov's ramming of an Austrian aircraft that was to gain him a second entry in the history books. Austrian fliers had attacked the airfield of Nesterov's 11th Aviation Detachment on 8 September 1914, so it was necessary to regain the unit's honour. Nesterov took off in his Morane-Saulnier G and rapidly gained altitude. Flying above the Austrian, Nesterov put his aircraft into a dive, his propeller slashed into his enemy's wing and both aircraft plunged into the ground. Both Nesterov and the Austrians were killed. This dramatic act of self-sacrifice caught the mood of the time and the imagination of the public and service alike. As the citation of his Order of St George 4th Class read, "Nesterov died the death of a hero in that battle."

Although notable for its lack of aerial combat, 1914 was remarkable for the attrition rate caused by the inexperience of the pilots and incidents of damage by friendly fire. Russian troops, unaccustomed to innovation being anything other than foreign, automatically assumed all aircraft to be hostile and consequently opened up with everything they had despite orders to the contrary.

By the end of 1914 the Air Fleet had lost 146 planes and the units on SW Front had been reduced to eight serviceable aircraft, resulting in the majority of frontline units being withdrawn for repair and re-equipping. Nonetheless the Air Fleet had performed its task well. General A. A. Brusilov, not initially an aviation enthusiast, commented on the effect of aerial reconnaissance at the battle of Gorodek in September 1914 thus. "This report [produced by aerial reconnaissance] could not have been made except by aeroplane...it gave me time to bring all my reserves to the assistance of the VII and VIII Corps."

During the course of the winter 1914–15 the fragility of the machines and the severity of the weather precluded much flying by either side. Indeed the lack of good, weatherproof shelter for the aircraft caused many problems particularly damage to the fabric covering of the wings.

The Russian retreat from Poland led to a restructuring of the Air Fleet bringing the number of detachments up to fifty-eight. The fortress units became Corps Detachments. When Novo-Georgievsk fortress surrendered during August 1915 pilots of its aviation detachment broke the news to *Stavka*. The pilots flew out the garrison's standards and were redesignated the XXXIII Corps Detachment. The speed of the retreat resulted in the loss of aircraft on the ground as unserviceable planes were often abandoned.

By the autumn of 1915 the Air Fleet had re-established itself along the length of the front. In the rear four or five training schools were now producing pilots who were able to draw on the combat experience of men such as Military Pilot Y. N. Kruten. Kruten wrote six pamphlets with titles such as "Air Combat" and "Manual of a Fighter Pilot" and defined the classic sequence of aerial warfare as altitude, speed, manoeuvre and attack.

Captured aircraft

As many of the early planes were unarmed and mechanically unreliable pilots were sometimes driven down inside hostile territory. If the crew were unable to destroy the plane it would be captured. The Russians made

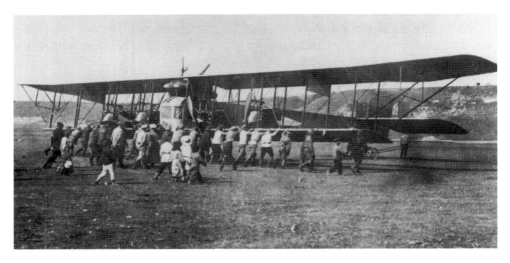

The *Illya Muromets* shown here is a Type B, the *Kievsky*, at Yablonna airfield near Warsaw during spring 1915. Yablonna placed the heavy bombers in an ideal position to undertake raids in support of Northern Front. Just visible on the fuselage is a chevron in the Russian national colours of, from the top, white, red and blue.

extensive use of captured *Albatros* and *Aviatik* two-seaters. Another bonus of capturing enemy planes was the opportunity to copy their technology. One such instance was the *Lebedev* 12 that incorporated features from the L.V.G C. II and the *Albatros* BI. Engines were taken from enemy aircraft and installed in Russian machines, as were any other useful parts. At the end of 1917 about seventeen captured aircraft were in Russian service, the number captured throughout the war is estimated at between 120 and 150, many of which were cannibalised for parts.

Imported aircraft

Between 1914 and 1917 the Allies supplied Russia with 1800 aircraft but many of these were left to rot on the quaysides of Murmansk and Archangel due to limited transport and storage facilities. The quality of these (mainly French) aircraft was variable. Naturally the French government was not going to provide the Russians with the most up to date models, and so it was that the Air Fleet received a number of obsolete or unpopular machines. A prime example of the latter was the Spad A.2, a remarkably hideous design. Heartily disliked by its French crews approximately fifty A.2s were shipped to Russia in 1917 where they rapidly gained a reputation as death traps. Later that year the French supplied the Spad VII, one of their best fighters of the period.

From late 1916 Britain supplied 251 aircraft amongst which were the B.E.2e, Vickers F.B.19 and Sopwith 11/2 Strutters, a combination of reconnaissance, fighters and bombers respectively.

The E.V.K.

The Russian Military Air Fleet in 1914 was the only air force to possess the four-engined long-range aircraft, the *Il'ya Muromets* (IM) named after a legendary Russian folk hero. The first IM had flown in early 1913. It was an immense machine with a wingspan of 27m (88 feet) and a fuselage length of 19m (65 feet). During the next year redesign and modifications were undertaken and the War Ministry placed an order for ten IMs to undertake long-range reconnaissance and bombing missions, followed by a second for thirty-two machines of an improved type. The IM had an enclosed cabin with windows and a glass floor section that provided excellent vision for the pilot, cameraman and bomb aimer, at a height of 2,000m (6,562 feet). Ideally it was suited for the bomber role. By August 1914 only two IMs had been completed, IM I and IM II. IM I was sent by rail to Brest-Litovsk whilst IM II flew to the same destination. Unfortunately IM II was damaged by friendly fire, forced to land and complete the journey by train.

Between October 1914 and January 1915 IM I carried out several reconnaissance missions but these were not entirely satisfactory. Consequently *Stavka* cancelled the second order. M. V. Shidlovsky, chairman of RBVZ, travelled to *Stavka,* pleaded his case and the order was reinstated. In January 1915 the Command of the Squadron of Flying Ships, better known by its Russian acronym of UEVK, was established at Jablonna north of Warsaw. The first commander of the UEVK, with the rank of Major General, was Shidlovsky himself.

The first bombing mission against German positions on 15 February 1915 went well. The next five months were very successful for the UEVK. Better cameras were installed, as were rudimentary bombsights. On later models 1,000 kg (2,200 lbs) of bombs could be carried. The defence of an IM rested with three to four machine gunners, although on a bombing mission the norm was three. The machine guns carried were Madsen, Maxim, Lewis and Colt. Often a mixture of guns was carried on each plane, and as the reliability of each one varied considerably this probably enabled the gunners to choose the most suitable weapon for them. The final IM series, the E, featured a retractable belly gun bay and a tail gunner. One early IM had been armed with a 37mm Hotchkiss gun for shooting down Zeppelins but it was never used.

In May 1915 the UEVK became the EVK. Interestingly, it was a tail-gunner with the EVK named Marcel Pliat from the French colony of Tahiti who was to become the first black aviator to shoot down an aircraft in combat.

As more IMs, improved with experience gained in combat, rolled off the production line a detachment of two IMs was established to operate on the SW Front to be based at Wlodowa. The retreat from Poland had forced the relocation of NW Front's IM base from Jablonna to Pskov with another at Minsk. Such was the success of IM production from mid-1915 to early 1916 that a Third Combat Detachment was formed at Minsk to fly in support of the Russian summer offensive of 1916. The fourth and final IM detachment became operational in March 1917 at Belgorod on the Romanian Front.

During the 1917 summer offensive the First, Second and Third Detachments shared an airfield with Kozakov's First Fighter Group that often flew escort for the IMs. The collapse of the SW Front forced the EVK to relocate to Vinnitsa in the Ukraine where the bulk of its equipment was taken over by nationalists towards the end of 1917.

By the end of the war the EVK had dropped 20,000kg (53,580lbs) of bombs and taken thousands of reconnaissance photos. Out of eighty-eight IMs of various types completed only three were lost to enemy action, one to fighters and two to ground fire all during 1915. Several were lost through mechanical failure or accident.

The Caucasian Front

The fighting on the Caucasian front began in November 1914. The pre-war establishment comprised the 1st Caucasian Corps Air Detachment based in the fortress of Kars in Russian Armenia. Details of operations during 1914–1915 are scarce but there is a reference to some twenty aircraft carrying out reconnaissance during the Russian offensive of early 1916. The 1st Siberian Air Detachment operated on this front. Certainly at least one aeroplane operated with the Russian forces in Persia as a photograph exists of the Shah inspecting one in Teheran during 1916.

Overview

The air war on the Eastern Front was less intense than that in the west. The sheer scale of the combat zone played a part as fewer aircraft had to cover such a huge area. However, the Air Service did have several pilots of note. To achieve the status of "Ace" it was necessary to have five kills confirmed by the men on the ground. Each member of a plane's crew that destroyed an enemy machine was credited with that victory.

APPENDIX 3

TAON: The Heavy Artillery of Special Duty

Information on the TAON, the Heavy Artillery of Special Duty or Special Purpose as it was sometimes known, is not easily accessible and until recently this topic has received scant if any coverage in the west. Apart from vague references in Brusilov or Denikin's works it is a subject that history has overlooked.

Heavy artillery 1914–15

The Imperial Army's artillery branch of service was divided into field, mountain, horse, field howitzer and heavy sections. All the artillery was horse drawn and subject to the clemency of the weather allowing good roads.

A rough rule of thumb classified heavy artillery as any gun or howitzer over 152mm (6 inches) and 203mm (8 inches) in calibre respectively. In August 1914 the official total number of heavy pieces was 240 but this figure included several batteries of lighter howitzers that made up for the shortfall in the tables of establishment in some units. Furthermore within days of the outbreak of war obsolete stock was re-activated to create heavy batteries for the newly mobilised infantry corps. There was no standard number of guns per battery in these new formations as this ad hoc organisation depended on the weapons available. Simply put, the staff responsible concentrated on getting weapons swiftly into place rather than adhering to a system. The result was that some new batteries had two pieces and others four. Establishing an accurate figure for the number of heavy guns and howitzers therefore becomes difficult.

With the armies advancing in relatively compact groups the concentration of such weapons did not pose too many problems as the roads were dry. Nor was there much need for them, for by the time they were brought into action the moment had usually passed. Indeed the Russian gunners were often unenthusiastic about using their expensive and sophisticated

In contrast to the generally modern weapons concentrated in the TAON this battery of Obuchkov M1904 152mm gun was obsolete almost before it left the drawing board. Nevertheless it was heavy gun and saw service throughout the war.

equipment in a situation where it might be put at risk if they had to retreat. However, with the advent of positional warfare and wetter conditions in late 1914 the situation began to change. The siege lines that grew up around Przemysl illustrate this point clearly. The second line forces (Ninth Army) detailed to undertake the investment of Przemysl did not have suitable artillery to bombard the fortresses, resulting in the importation of guns from the naval arsenal at Kronstadt. Once they had left the railhead the weight of these guns and their specialist platforms reduced the speed of movement to a snail's pace and the bombardment proper did not commence until late January. When Przemysl fell in March the siege train was retained under the control of SW Front for possible use against Cracow or better still Budapest.

As an almost continuous line from the Baltic coast to the Carpathian Mountains grew, the spread of heavy artillery along the front became increasingly sparse. When the Central Powers unleashed their offensive at Gorlice-Tarnow in May 1915 they demonstrated the value of concentrated artillery power to the Russians who determined that the lesson would not be forgotten.

1915

When the dust had settled following the retreat from Poland *Stavka* took its first steps towards re-organising the army's heavy artillery. Each of the three fronts was authorised to gather its heavy guns into Separate Heavy Artillery *Divizions* (a half regiment with an indeterminate number of batteries) that would be placed at the disposal of the front commander to allocate as he saw fit. Thus were created three "heavy artillery fists."

To simplify ammunition supply, repair and maintenance batteries and *divizions* were to be formed of the same type of gun. Additional batteries were formed by removing guns from fortifications such as those near Odessa and Riga but the number was limited as these weapons were often designed to be used from specially prepared mountings and were not easily adapted to field carriages. Another useful source of heavy guns and howitzers were foreign suppliers. France, Britain and Japan had all sold heavy artillery to Russia and late in 1915 some of these weapons began to appear.

Imported artillery

Japanese sales to Russia are often overlooked yet they supplied considerable numbers of weapons between 1914 and 1917. Amongst these were 350 guns including twelve Krupp 280mm (11 inch) coastal defence guns similar to those used at the siege of Port Arthur. Most of these heavy guns arrived during early 1915. Unfortunately several were captured by the Germans who had no difficulty taking them into service.

Between 1915 and 1917 the British and French sold the Russians 442 heavy guns. However, delays in moving these weapons from the ports in northern Russia or Vladivostok meant that not all of them arrived at the front promptly, sometimes they were held up for months at the quayside, in transit or became separated from their carriages, wagons or harness causing further delays. Where necessary, such as in the case of the Vickers 305mm (12 inch) howitzers, caterpillar tractors were also supplied. To speed up the familiarisation of the Russian crews with these new weapons specialists were sent from the manufacturers to act as instructors as were groups of artillery advisers from the French and British branches of service. As French was the most commonly spoken foreign language amongst the Russian staff they were more often listened to than the British whose linguistic skills were sadly lacking.

Britain supplied at least twenty-four of these Vickers Mark VI 203mm howitzers to Russia. They were concentrated in six batteries within the TAON. To provide cover they were often emplaced in pits with a track such as this one at the rear to aid traverse.

1916–17

Towards the end of 1916 an analysis of the summer offensive concluded that it was necessary to reform the heavy artillery organisation to overcome the front commanders' hoarding of resources which it was felt had impaired following up the successes achieved by Brusilov's SW Front. Logic dictated that *Stavka* itself should have its own heavy artillery force, to dispose of as it would. As part of the army reforms authorised in December 1916 it was decided to create XLVIII Corps which would consist entirely of heavy artillery under the direction of the Supreme Commander in Chief, the Tsar himself. Two orders were issued, the first on 2 January 1917 to form the corps and its staff and the second two days later creating an entirely motorised mobile supply depot for them. The corps was to be commanded by General G. M. Scheidemann and secrecy was to surround it from the outset, for if word reached the Germans of its nature then its deployment

A Russian manufactured Lender M14 76mm anti-aircraft gun mounted on what is possibly a Russo-Balt or a White lorry. Ammunition was carried in the storage bins on the flatbed and stability provided by the outriggers to the rear. The Tsar is being shown the sighting mechanism. Several such batteries were deployed in support of the TAON during 1917.

would point a finger directly at the area to be attacked. So successful was this that German intelligence's order of battle for the Russian Army dated May 1917 comments that "Details of 48 Corps are lacking". Given the situation at the time and the degree of accuracy evident throughout the document that the corps' details remained secret is remarkable.

XLVIII Corps

The corps' HQ was to be based at Smolensk with a supply depot at Mozhaisk and the transport depot at Karachev: all points with good access to the rail network. Orders were sent out to the four front commanders to make arrangements for their contributions to XLVIII Corps to make their way to the various assembly points in the rear. At the same time it was decided that future shipments of heavy guns from the British and French would be allocated to the corps, these to include those waiting to move out of the ports in Russia, those on order and any subsequently ordered. None of the front commanders were enamoured with the idea of handing over these assets and their attitude can be summed up by Ruzski who noted that such a withdrawal of heavy guns, "…would undermine the morale of the army." Despite such comments the transfers went ahead albeit slowly due to the problems of transporting such equipment at that time of year. From the First, Fifth and Twelfth armies of N Front seventy-two guns were transferred. The list included thirty-six 152mm (6 inch) M1909 fortress howitzers, thirty-two 152mm M1904 guns and four Schneider 280mm (11 inch) howitzers with more from W and SW fronts. The Romanian Front lost fewer than the others possibly due to the intervention of the Romanian King. Motor transport was to be provided by the Allies from orders already in transit. Although in theory XLVIII Corps was to be one unit, the batteries and *divizions* retained the word Separate in their titles. The Corps was divided into six brigades numbered 200–205.

By the end of February almost 300 heavy guns had arrived at the assembly points. Plans were also in hand to set up aerial observation units, one based at Kiev the other at Smolensk. These would train artillery observers who would supplement the observation work carried out by the corps' fifteen balloons.

The abdication of the Tsar and the installation of the Provisional Government had little effect and XLVIII Corps continued to expand as the coming of spring allowed the movement of guns from the northern ports to speed up. On 26 May General M. V. Alexeyev, now the Supreme Commander in Chief, ordered that the HQ of XLVIII Corps be reformed into the TAON. The same order recognised the need for an officer's school to be established to familiarise the battery and *divizional* commanders with the new weapons. However, specialist training for the men appears to have been given a lower priority. It had become apparent that although the front commanders had released guns and equipment the personnel were not of the best quality. Nevertheless arrangements now began to move elements of the TAON into position for the forthcoming offensive.

Summer offensive, 1917

The brigades were divided between the fronts in the following manner: 203rd to the N Front; 201st to the W Front and the remainder to the SW Front. Unfortunately it was at this point that matters began to go awry and the unified, independent command that had been envisaged six months earlier began to place demands on the fronts to which its brigades were attached. Any shortfall in man or horse-power was to be made good

The TAON was the most highly mechanised formation in the army. Here a Ruston tractor is towing what is possibly a Vickers 127mm 60-pounder gun on a Mark 2 carriage. The barrel was transported separately. Similar tractor units were provided by Bullock Lombard, Clayton and Holt along with tracked trailers.

by the front concerned as were gunner's sidearms, engineering, veterinary, sanitary and transport needs. However, the commander of the TAON retained control over spare parts and munitions allocations as well as special vehicles which included all the tractor units and lorries.

Owing to the lack of weaponry in the armouries when the corps was formed many men had not received their personal weapons. In one *divizion* less than one third of the 1,100 men had revolvers. When they arrived at the front positions it was not possible to issue all that were required. Even more worrying was the fact that several batteries arrived at the front without any ammunition or with uncharged shells. One notable example of this is the four, two-gun batteries of *Divizion T* (all *divizions* were known by a letter) which was equipped with Vickers 234mm (9.2 inch) howitzers. Considerable effort went into preparing one of these monsters for action including the filling of a base box with eleven tons of earth. The frustration of the crew and labourers when the weapons were found to be useless can only be imagined and doubtless fed the general air of discontent and mistrust of the officer corps. Furthermore the deployment of TAON units had not been thought out beforehand therefore batteries were allocated to points where they might just prove useful.

A very clear image of a Schneider M1910 152mm gun just on the point of being reassembled. The chute for fitting the barrel can be seen on the trail. Putilov produced this piece under licence in Russia and forty-six were allocated to the TAON. The tractor unit is out of shot to the left. Served by a crew of eight with an effective range of 17,000m (18,590yards) it was a highly effective weapon.

The situation at the depots in the rear was not much better. The main ammunition storage facility at Mozhaisk, in an old brick factory, was simply too small and undermanned. There were insufficient personnel available to unload the ammunition trains consequently although stocks grew it proved near impossible to store and transport them let alone prepare the munitions. Therefore the charges were stored under cover whilst the shells were left in the open.

Although over 1,000 guns were sent forward by the TAON, their contribution was negligible. However, it was vital that such a formidable array of heavy guns be seen "to do something" even if conditions were not ideal, such was the parlous condition of some of the infantry units' morale. In one case several batteries of 152mm M1904 guns were ordered to fire using incorrect charges. As they required a special *Shukov* platform to give them stability, such charges caused them to bounce which inevitably damaged the platform and impaired further shooting. Despite this the guns were ordered to continue firing until they were virtually useless. Firing the guns to improve the infantry's morale even when it was causing obvious damage was not uncommon and led to a very high number of weapons being put out of commission. Some sources put this figure as high as fifty per cent of TAON's establishment. Given the performance of the infantry it was total waste of resources.

When the retreat on SW Front began the TAON batteries had to move out (sometimes very rapidly), which was not something they were designed to do. Two batteries of Vickers 305mm (12 inch) howitzers were captured, as they proved too heavy to be shifted quickly. Two batteries of unidentified "152mm positional guns" (ex-fortress) were also lost. Some worn out pieces were abandoned but the vast bulk of the TAON withdrew safely.

Aftermath

The post-offensive analysis of the TAON's performance identified several areas of weakness:

1. The lack of overall control.
2. Too many targets, few of which were properly identified and ranged in on.
3. The damage caused to the guns by firing to boost morale.
4. The disorganisation of ammunition supplies and repair services.
5. The uncoordinated retreat of supporting units.

To remedy these shortcomings in the future it was decided that the TAON would have its own scouting troops, engineers and machine gun units so that in the event of another precipitate withdrawal there would be dedicated covering fire that would allow the gunners to dismantle their equipment. Officer training would be modified to include camouflage, maintenance and positioning. Time would also be given to improving the abilities of the men but how was not specified.

The deterioration in the condition of the army now began to have its effect on the TAON, which had been moved into reserve. By September several batteries were becoming restive and interpreting the title of Separate to mean that they did not have to obey orders from *divizional* or brigade staffs. One officer reported, "My orders are partly executed, and partly ignored completely…. With my rights and responsibilities being totally undetermined, as the *divizioner* of two "separate" batteries, and respecting my dignity, I am forced to refuse to give any orders to the batteries I am in charge of…." Another wrote, "…the committees in Separate batteries are pursuing separatism; when it comes to mutual assistance, the *divizion* is divided even more…" The resulting order to remove the word Separate from the batteries' titles had little effect. A report submitted to *Stavka* commented on the lamentable condition of the repair and maintenance workshops and warned, "…if we don't take urgent measures to restore (these services) the total loss of TAON's fighting efficiency will be only a matter of days away."

During October it was decided that to preserve the guns the TAON should be divided up and sent deeper into Russia. However, when some units began to move across Ukraine in early December they were ordered to leave the area or begin to "Ukrainianise". As there was no where else to go Scheidemann, at gunpoint, was forced to sign away nearly all the guns and equipment of the TAON to the Ukrainians. The men were told to return to their recruiting areas but the officers were to remain at the disposal of the TAON staff.

What followed was rather a tragi-comedy. The TAON was abandoned to its fate. Harness and draught animals were stolen by the local farmers; tents and other such useful and portable equipment were sold off by the men; and the guns, many of which now lacked the specialist vehicle drivers to move them, were left to rot where they stood.

One of the last reports written on 12 March 1918 by an officer with the 12th Siege Artillery *Divizion* isolated in Chernigov sadly notes that his unit,

> ...owes...17,000 roubles for provision it's acquired in 1917... Since we are unable to pay it back, I was arrested and released only on bail. Please pay 30,000 roubles for forage and provisions...otherwise the local authorities won't let us go and we'll have to stay in captivity with Ukrainian and Austrian forces.

It is indeed tragic that a formation which had cost millions of roubles to create was reduced to this condition and in some ways it was a direct reflection of the demise of the old Imperial Army.

APPENDIX 4

Conscription and Casualties

Since the end of World War I analysis of Russia's call up and casualty figures have been the subject of much debate. The confusion and disruption resulting from two revolutions, civil war and internal upheaval inevitably played havoc with the compilation of accurate statistics. Consequently it is impossible to provide a definitive set of numbers. Therefore I have chosen to include those most generally accepted, which were compiled during the 1930s.

In 1914 the standing army numbered just under 1,500,000 officers and men and by the end of 1914 5,100,000 recruits had been mobilised. However, this was still considered to be too few and it was deemed necessary to issue the *Opolchenie* mobilisation *Ukase*. This was done, calling up two categories of *Opolchenie* during 1915. These measures brought in a further 5,600,000 men but these included men who had not expected to serve, such as the over 40s. The ill-will caused by these orders was to simmer away, especially amongst the peasantry, which was affected by the loss of its manpower. Resentment was also very bitter towards those sprigs of the richer, more influential classes that worked for the volunteer organisations behind the lines. Dubbed the "*Zemstvo* Hussars" due to the semi-military dress they affected such men were held in low esteem regardless of the good work they carried out.

During 1916 a further 3,000,000 men were drafted, followed by 2,700,000 in 1917. In all some 18,600,000 men passed through the armed forces during the war. Of those called to the colours almost 700,000 were killed in action; 970,000 died of their wounds; 155,000 died of disease and 181,000 POWs died of various other causes, giving a total of 2,006,000 dead.

With over 5,000,000 men passing into captivity (the majority during 1915) and a slightly lesser figure, 5,000,000 wounded or sick there is no doubt that the Russians suffered to the same extent in percentage terms as the British Empire which lost roughly five per cent of its male population in the fifteen to forty-nine age group.

Judging by his grizzled appearance and equipment this soldier is clearly one of the over 40s men, the *Opolchenie* category called up in 1915. The army included thousands of such men who were regarded with disdain by many senior officers.

Civilian casualties were particularly heavy during the first two years of the war, estimates varying between five and six hundred thousand. When the population began to move east the statisticians appear to have been overwhelmed by the sheer numbers and the impossibility of keeping an accurate tally. Therefore civilian losses of over 1,500,000 do not seem unlikely.

APPENDIX 5

Chemical Warfare

Before the outbreak of the war in 1914 Russia's economy relied almost completely on Germany for all its chemical needs as it proved easier to import products than to exploit the empire's natural resources. With the cessation of such imports the need to make up the shortfall became acute. However, it was only with the advent of gas as a weapon that work had to be undertaken on an industrial scale.

Although it was rumoured that the Austro-Hungarians had used an acid spraying device during the siege of Przemysl, chemical warfare properly began on the Eastern Front on 31 January 1915 at the battle of Bolimov. The Germans fired over 18,000 tear gas shells at the Russian positions confident in the belief that their new weapon would neutralise their opponents and grant them a bloodless victory. However, the advancing Germans were not met by a weeping mob but by heavy gunfire. The gas, xylyl bromide, had frozen instead of evaporating and thus became useless. Unlike the British who had undergone a similar experience several months earlier, the Russians were aware that gas had been used against them. Following the Bolimov attack information reached *Stavka* that the Germans had used poison gas at Ypres. As a result. a simple form of protection, bandages saturated in chemicals, was prepared but tragically it was not issued.

During May 1915 the Germans released chlorine gas from cylinders placed in the frontline on the Rawka River near Warsaw. This time the attack was successful and Russian fatalities numbered between seven and eight thousand. *Stavka* responded immediately, ordering 600 *poods* (9,828kg – almost ten tons) of phosgene gas for shells with which to retaliate. It was at this point that the curse of the Russian war effort intervened and within a short space of time eight committees, representing various bodies, sprang into existence all competing for scarce plants and materials to manufacture masks and gas. Fortunately for the men in the trenches the Germans did not use gas again for over a year by which time some sort of order prevailed in the Russian bureaucracy. In April 1916 the Chemical Committee (CC) was formed under the leadership of Lieutenant-General

V. N. Ipatiev, an eminent chemist. The CC was composed of five branches, which were:

1. Explosives
2. Poison gases
3. Incendiaries and flame-throwers
4. Gas masks
5. Acids

The Chemical Battalion was also formed which recruited officers and men who studied poison gases and chemical warfare under special instructors and then in their turn acted as teachers of chemical warfare to the rest of the army.

As well as producing the bandage mask some two million Mining Institute masks were ordered which were similar to those used by mine rescue teams. However, two scientists, Kumant and Zelinsky, were also working on masks and their designs were also ordered. With several types of mask in production a rolling programme of improvement and replacement was undertaken. Each front had a special laboratory-equipped train to study masks under combat conditions. Furthermore a specialist Director of Chemical Warfare was allocated to each front HQ. Such directors were all artillery officers who had passed through the Chemical Battalion's training regime.

By late 1916 two more gas masks were in production: the Prokofiev, similar to the original bandage type and the Avalov which was an improved version of the Kumant-Zelinsky model. A gas mask for horses was also under development.

The testing of gas masks was carried out near Petrograd using men from the Guards reserve regiments. The men entered gas chambers and carried out a series of tasks timed to last an hour. As Ipatiev recorded,

> The efficiency of the various masks was judged by the number of men who could keep working masked in the gas filled room. In repeated tests only 5 or 6 per cent of the men wearing the Avalov mask fell out of line as compared with 20 to 30 per cent of the others.

One can only hope they were volunteers. As a consequence of these tests one million Avalov masks were ordered.

Although production, distribution and effectiveness were improving, training and awareness were still inadequate. One simple reason was the fact that the majority of the men, recruited from the peasantry, had little or no idea what gas was. Furthermore the infrequency of gas attacks made it appear to be a less than serious threat. This situation maintained even after

Stavka, following a devastating gas attack at the junction of Second and Tenth armies, on the Western Front, issued an order that instruction in the use of gas masks was obligatory in all formations whether in or out of the frontline. Sadly, as Dr M. C. Grow, an American surgeon serving with the Russian Army recalled,

> Although it was a rule that officers and soldiers should always wear gas masks when within two miles [3km] of the trenches, we were all rather careless in that last respect. Indeed, we frequently found upon examining the soldier's masks that the box containing the chemicals designed to neutralize the gas had been emptied and contained instead tobacco, bread or similar articles. Our corps [I Siberian] had never experienced a really severe gas attack and our carelessness was more or less natural.

Grow described the attack as a, "…swirling bank of fog rolling down on us. It was only 50 feet [15m] high and it crept slowly and heavily, seeming to flow along the surface of the earth with a hideous writhing motion." Three such yellow clouds were released killing 2,000 Russians but the line held. The gas penetrated some 16km (10 miles), "like a river flowing through a valley." There is no information presently available on the use the Russian's made of gas but both cylinder and shell delivery systems were available. Production of gas and masks continued throughout 1917.

Following the March Revolution the Germans made three significant gas attacks. The first in April resulted in the elimination of the Russian bridgehead at Chrevishe-Golemi on the Stokhod River. The Russian defenders, enjoying the post-revolution period of calm that pervaded the front from north to south, were caught completely unawares by a heavy bombardment that included a high proportion of gas shells. The bridgehead fell with the Germans claiming to have taken over 10,000 prisoners.

The second attack resulted in the capture of Riga and was remarkable insofar as the preliminary barrage included the use of 116,400 gas shells many charged with the lethal mustard gas. Lieutenant-Colonel Bruchmuller designed the German fire plan designating Russian artillery positions and infantry concentration points as the priority targets. These locations were intermittently saturated with a mixture of HE and gas shells for over three hours. Faced with such a combination barrage the Russian lines broke and after two days Riga was taken on 3 September. Bruchmuller's plan had worked remarkably well and was to be repeated with equal success against the British in March 1918. The last attack was again to reduce a Russian bridgehead 51km (32 miles) upriver from Riga at Jakobstadt. Again the attack was a success but the Germans also employed the 3rd Guard Pioneer Battalion that was responsible for operating flame-throwers.

Although flame-throwers had first been used in France during 1915, they did not appear on the Eastern Front for some time. The reason for this was that the distance between the trenches precluded the use of trench mounted equipment: the range, 27m (30yards), was too great. Man-portable flame-throwers were more in demand in France. The Austro-Hungarians used both man-portable and positional flame-throwers in Galicia. The Russians obtained various British flame-throwers to experiment with during 1916. The CC's third section demonstrated a modified Austrian M1915 to the Tsar during May 1916 and this weapon, the *Tovornitsky*, was adopted for front line deployment. Several flame-thrower units were trained by the Chemical Battalion and sent to the front in 1917 but production difficulties limited the number available.

Following the March Revolution the CC continued its work but to little effect as the supply chain and production facilities were slowly grinding to a halt. A year later few of the specialist officers, scientists and technicians remained in post and their work was only carried on to a limited extent.

However, the work of the CC during the war years had laid the foundations of an independent Russian chemical industry, which was to stand the USSR in good stead during the next world war.

Bibliography

When compiling this bibliography it rapidly became clear that there is very little currently in print on this subject. Many of the titles listed here are only available through antiquarian bookshops but at a tremendous price. I was lucky to have purchased several titles from the estimable Gareth Simmon who, until recently, reissued obscure works of military history in an affordable format. Sadly this excellent service is no longer available.

Believed to be in print

British General Staff, *The Russian Army Handbook 1914*, reprinted Battery Press, Nashville, 1996.

Figes, O. and Kolonitskii, B., *Interpreting the Russian Revolution*, Yale University Press, Yale, 1999.

Stone, N., *The Eastern Front 1914–17*, Hodder & Stoughton, London, 1975.

Bruce Lincoln, W., *Passage through Armageddon*, Simon & Schuster Ltd, London, 1988

Hogg, I. V., *Allied Artillery of World War One*, Crowood Press, Marlborough, 1998.

Bariyatinski. M and Kolomets M., *Armoured Cars of the Russian Army 1906–1917*, published privately, Moscow, 2000. (Russian text)

Markov, O. D., *The Russian Army 1914–17*, published privately, St Petersburg, year of publication unknown (Russian text)

Solzhenitsyn, A., *August 1914*, Penguin Books, London, 1974.

Solzhenitsyn, A., *November 1916*, translated by Willetts, Farrar, Straus & Giroux, New York, London, 1999.

Muratoff, P. and Allan, W. E. D., *Caucasian Battlefields*, reprinted Battery Press, Nashville, 1999.

Menning, B. W., *Bayonets before Bullets*, Indiana University Press, Indiana, 1992.

Gatrell, P., *Russia's First World War*, Pearson, London, 2005.

Jahn, H. F., *Patriotic Culture in Russia during World War One*, Cornell University Press, Cornell, 1995.

Massie, R. K., *Dreadnought*, Pimlico, London, 1991.

Believed to be out of print

Bezobrazov, General V.M., *Diary of the Commander of the Russian Imperial Guard* (ed. M. Lyons), Dramco Publishers, Florida, 1994.

Wrangel. A, *The End of Chivalry: The last great cavalry battles, 1914–18*, Hippocrene Books, New York, 1982.

Bruin, A.H., *Troublous Times*, Constable Ltd., London 1931.

Lord, A. and Perrett B, *The Czar's British Squadron*, William Kimber & Co., London, 1981.

Brusilov, General A.A., *A Soldier's Notebook*, Macmillan & Co. Ltd., London, 1930

Golovin, General N. N., *The Russian Army in the World War*, Yale University Press, Yale, 1931

Knox, General Sir A., *With the Russian Army 1914–17*, Hutchinson, London, 1921

Denikin, General A. I., *The Russian Turmoil*, Hutchinson & Co., London, c.1918

Lloyd George, D., *War Memoirs*, Odhams Press Ltd., London 1938

Gourko, General V.I., *Memories and Impressions of War and Revolution*, John Murray, London, 1918.

Kerensky, A.F., *The Catastrophe*, D. Appleton and Company, London, 1927

Wildmann, A. K., *The End of the Russian Imperial Army (vols. I and II)*, Princeton University Press, Princeton, 1987.

Kournakoff, S., *Savage Squadrons*, Hale, Cushman and Flint, New York, 1935.

Polovtsoff, General P., *Glory and Downfall*, Longmans, London, 1935.

Mollo, A., *Army Uniforms of World War One*, Blandford Press, London, 1977.

Darcey. T. Durkota. A and Kulikov V., *The Imperial Russian Air Service*, Flying Machines Press California 1995.

Compton, Major T. E., *The Romanian Campaign*, RUSI, London, 1922

Kirke, Major General W. M. St G., *An Outline of the Romanian Campaign*, RUSI, London, 1924.

Farmborough, F., *A Nurse at the Russian Front*, Constable Ltd., London, 1974.

Wheeler-Bennett, J. W., *Brest-Litovsk*, Macmillan, London, 1938.

Gronsky, P.P., and Astrov, N.I., *The War and the Russian Government*, Yale, 1929.

Sack, A. J., *The Birth of Russian Democracy*, Russian Information Bureau, New York, 1918.

Katkov, G., *The Kornilov Affair*, Longman, London, 1980.

Saul, N. E., *Sailors in Revolt*, University of Kansas Press, Kansas, 1978.

Gatrell, P., *Government, Industry and Re-armament in Russia 1900–1914*, Cambridge University Press, Cambridge,1994.

Index

Page references in *italic* refer to captions.

A

Akardahar River, 84
Albion, Operation, 186, 212
Alexander I, Tsar, 1
Alexander II, Tsar, 1, 5
Alexander III, Tsar, 6
Alexandra, Tsaritsa, *111*, 6, 50, 66, 74, 110, 113, 137, 143, 144, 179
Alexeyev, General M.V., *59*, 12-13, 24, 41-2, 45-6, 48, 51, 55, 58, 65-6, *71*, 89, 99, 105, 108-10, 113, 118, 122, 125, 127, 129-130, 136-137, 139, 148, 151, 153, 157, 161-162, 170, 175, 182, 194, 230
Anatolia, 75
Ankara, 75, 90
Archangel, 115, 207, 222
Ardahan, 82, 84-5
Armenia, 64, 75, 77, 85, 94, 167, 224
Augustow Forest, 40
Austria (Hungary), 1-2, 12, 21, 30, 34-5, 42, 57, 119, 199
Austrian Army, 27, 32, 63, 103, 105, 116, 123
Austrian armies
    First Army, 28, 31, 33, 44, 125
    Third Army, 35, 173
    Fourth Army, 105, 107
    Seventh Army, 106, 125, 174
    Ninth Army, 168
Austrian Corps
    XXVI Corps, 165
Austrian Divisions
    51st Infantry Division, 124
Avalov gas masks, 184, 238 (See Appendix 5)
Azerbaijan, 78, 81, 85, 89, 94

B

Baghdad, 97-98

Baku, 77
Baltic Fleet, *205, 206, 208, 212*, 8, 10, 166, 203, 205-6, 208, 210-13 (See Appendix 1, pp. 203-13, also Russian Navy)
Black Sea Fleet, *209, 211*, 85, 122, 162, 210-11, 213 (See Appendix 1, pp. 203-13, also Russian Navy)
Baranovitchi, 24, 110
Bardiz Pass, 83-4
Baratov, General N. N., 81, 97, 98, 134
Batum, 75, 81, 93
Bayburt, 92-3, 95
Belgian Armoured Car Unit, *64*, 65, 164, 194
Beliaev, General M. A., 37, 141
Berdichev, 103
Bergman, General, 82-3
Berlin, 34-5, 79
Berthelot, General, 127
Bessarabia, 79, 119, 198
Bezobrazov, General V. M., 65, 108, 110-13
Bialystok, 40
Bingol Dag, 88
Birilov, Admiral A.A., 208
Bitlis, 86, 92-4
Blizniki, *70*
Bobrinsky, Count A., 131
Bolimov, 39, 237
Bolshevik Party, 96, 149-50, 152, 157, 159, 163, 166, 174-5, 178, 181, 188, 190, 192-3, 197, 201
Bran Pass, 125
Brasov, battle of, 125
Brody, 112
Brest Litovsk, 4, 48, *59*, 96, 194, 199, 201, 223
British, 43, 58, 78, 85, 99, 164

British supplies, 118, 134, 141, 142, 144, 164, *166, 191, 199*
British Armoured Car Unit (RNACD), 65, 96, 129, 164, 165, 176, 194
British Submarine Unit, 207, 213
Brusilov, A. A. General, *100*, 27, 31, 35, 44, 55, 63, 99, 101, 103-5, 107, 108, 110-11, 113, 116, 130, 132, 153, 158, 162, 165, 170, 173-5, 221, 225, 228
Buchanan, Sir George, 21, 37, 141, 147
Bucharest, 22, 119, 125-8, 128, (Treaty of) 198
Budapest, 34
Bulgaria, 119-20, 122, 199, 210
Bukovina, 28, 42, 44, 60, 106-7, 109, 122

C

Carpathian Mountains, *40*, 14-5, 31, 33-4, 35, 41, 44, 116, 120, 122, 126, 132, 134, 226
Castelnau, General, 143-4
Cavalry
    Cossack (All Hosts/ *Voiskos*), *5, 29, 126*, 4, 7, 60, 63, 79, 84, 86, 91, 97, 107, 114-5, 147, 174, 188, 191
    German, 45, 48, 55, 124-7
    Russian, *11, 123*, 4, 25, 48, 57, 63, 67, 107, 134
    Austrian (Hungarian), 13, 124, 126
Caspian Sea, 75, 77, 97
Caucasus, 7, 37, 52, 63, 79, 114, 167, 188
Chemical Committee (CC), 237–40 (See Appendix 5 237–40)
Cholm, 31, 46, 60
Christmas battle, 136, 141

Committees, soldiers and units, 151-2, 159, 162, 179, 188
Constanza, 119, 122, 125
Constituent Assembly, 148, 150, 188
Courland, 45, 64, 136
Cracow, 14, 27, 31-5
Craiova, 126
Crimea, 78, 217
Czechoslovakian Units, 63, 164-5

D
Dalan Goz Fort, 91
Danilov General I. N., 13, 61
Danube, River, 34, 120, 122, 125
Denikin, General A. I., 130, 151, 159, 162, 169, 175, 180, 182, 225
Dilman, 86
Dnieper, River, 52
Dniester River, 106
Dobrudja, 120, 122, 125
Dragomirov, General A. M., 153, 158, 175
Dukhonin, General N. N., 129, 190, 194
Dubno, 106
Duna River, 183
Duma, 9-10, 18, 21, 37, 50-1, 74, 113, 137, 139, 141-2, 144, 148, 151, 157, 204, 212

E
East Prussia, 2, 13-4, 22, 24, 31-2, 35, 37, 39, 66
Eberhardt, Admiral A. A., 85, 93, 210
Eleskirt Valley, 79, 83
Enver Pasha, 78, 81, 83-6, 91, 92, 95, 97
Enzeli, 75
Erzinan, 92-3, 95
Erzurum, 77, 81, 85, 88-93
Essen, Admiral N. O. von, 208
Evert, General A. E., 51, 99, *101*, 105, 107, 108, 109, 113, 116

F
Falkenhayn General, 39, 43, 52, 55, 106-7, 124-6
Fedotov, General I. I., 173
Finland, 14, 27, 153, 188, 201
Flamethrower, *71*, 239–40
Flug, General V. E., 39-40
France, 6, 10, 12, 13, 14, 37, 43, 57-8, 65, 72, 99, 117, 144, 153
    Military Mission, 127-8, 164-5
    Ambassador (M. Paleologue), 22, 37, 52, 60, 74, 144
    Supplies, 65, 118, 141-2

G
Galatz, 120, 122
Gallipoli, 88-89
Galicia, 2, 13, 27-8, 39, 46, 48, 60, 80, 88, 173, 183, 240
Georgia, 77, 82, 94, 167
Germany, 2, 12, 21, 80, 119, 199
German armies
    Eighth Army, 24, 26, 32, 34, 39-40
    Ninth Army, 32-4, 124, 125
    Tenth Army, 39
German Corps
    I Corps, 24
    XVII Corps, 24
    XI Corps, 33
    Alpine Corps, 124-5
German Divisions
    76th Infantry Division, 124
    89th Infantry Division, 124
    187th Infantry Division, 124
Great Programme, 18
Gorlice Tarnow, 43-4, 226
Gourko, General V., 26, 67, 113, 116, 130-1, 133, 141, 142, 144, 148, 153, 158, 162
Grigorovich, Admiral I. K., 205, 209
Grodno, 40, 67
Grow, Dr M. C., 239
Guchkov, A. I., 152-3, 157-8
Gumbinnen, 24
Gutor, General A. E., 162

H
Hafik Hakki Pasha, 82
Hassan Izzet Pasha, 82, 92, 94
Helsingfors (Helsinki), 205, 207
Hermanstadt, 124
Hindenburg, General Paul von, 32-3, 39, 45
Hoffman, General Max, 200-1
Hotzendorf, Field Marshal Conrad von, 28, 31, 33-4, 39-41, 55, 79, 107,
Hungary, 14

I
Ihsan Pasha, 82
Italy, 21, 42, 44, 58, 103, 105, 107, 117, *129*, 142
Ipatiev, General V. N., 238
Ivangorod Fortress, 4, 31-3, 47
Ivanov, General N. I., 24, 28, 31, 34-5, 37, 41-2, 47, 63, 99

J
Jassy, 120, 127-8
Jaroslawice battle of, 28
Japan, 7, 12, 36, 52
Jews, 50, 60

K
Kaiser Wilhelm II, 21, 52, 204
Kaledin, General A. M., 103, 107, 162
Kampulung, 125
Kara Gobek Fort, 91
Kara Su Plain, 91
Kara Su River, 91, 92
Kars, 75, 82-4, 89, 218,
Kaul'bars, General A. V., 216, 218
Kerensky, A. F., *160, 164*, 94, 157-9, 161-3, 167, 169, 174-5, 179, 180-2, 185, 187-8, 190, 212
Kiev, 60, 167, 185, 194, 200, 230
Kirmanshah, 97
Klembovski, General V. N., 99, 130, 175, 183-4
Kolchak, Captain (later Admiral), 207–210
Konigsberg, 14, 25
Koprukoy, 88
Kornilov, L.G. General, *186*, 150, 153, 162, 165, 171, 174-5, 179-82, 184-5, 194, 198, 212, 248
Kotur Pass, 81
Kovel, 107, 109-11, 113, 116, 132
Kovno, 24, 26, 31, 39, 45-6, 51, 67
Krasnik, battle of, 28
Krasnov, General P. A., 190-2
Kronstadt (Romania), 123-4
Kronstadt (Russia), 169, 190, 205, 209, 226
Kruten, Military Pilot Y. N., 221
Krylenko, Ensign N. V., 193, 194
Krymov, General A. M., 180, 190
Kumant-Zelinsky gas mask, 238 (See Appendix 5)
Kurds, 75, 81, 86, 89, 92-3
Kuropatkin, General A. N., 8, *35*, 66-7, 99, *101*, 109-10, 113-4
Kut, 97

L
Latvia, 136, 167, 201
Lebedev, V. A., *216*
Lechitski, General P. A., 22, 57, 106-7, 109, 125-6
Lesh, General L. V., 44, 61
Lemberg (Lvov), 13, 28, 31, 48, 112, 132, 161, 165
Lenin, V. I., *195*, 155, 157-8, 166-7, 185, 193-4, 201
Libau, 46
Linsingen, General Alexander von, 155

Lithuania, 45, 48, 62, 64, 201
Locker-Lampson, Commander Oliver MP, 96
Lodz, 34-5
Lublin, 27, 31
Ludendorff, General Erich von, 39, 52, 55
Lutsk, 55, 103, 105
Lyakhov, General, 89, 92–93

M
Mackensen, General August von, 44, 125, 127-8, 169
Maklakov, N. A., 37
Malazgirt, 90
Manchuria, 7, 9
Marashti, battle of, 169, 198
Marasheshti, battle of, 169, 198
Maskirovka, 88
Masurian Lakes, 24, 39
Mecinkirt, 82
Mesopotamia, 97-8
Miliukov, P. N., 139, 157
Miliutin, General D. A., 1, 2, 5, 14
Milner, Lord, 142-3
Mikhailovitch, Grand Duke A., 216, 218
Minsk, 159, 224
Mitau, 136
Moghilev, 52, 66, 149, 151, 157, 175,
Moldavia, 119, 127, 129, 198
Molodetchno, 55
Moon Sound, 187, 212
Moscow, 218-19
Murmansk, 96, *114*, 115, 141, 222
Mush/Mus, 77, 89, 92-3, 95
Myshlayevski, General A. Z., 76, 82-5,

N
Narew/v River, 39
Narotch, Lake, *69*, *70*, 58, 65, 72
Nazarbekov, General, 94
Nepenin, Admiral, A. I., 212
Nesterov, Lt later Staff Captain P. N., 217, 220, 221
Nezmanov, Colonel A. A., 17-19, 31
Nicholas I, Tsar, 1, 6
Nicholaevich, Grand Duke N., 3, 10, 21-2, 24, 26-8, 31-2, 34, 37, 46, 50-2, 60, 130, 136, 149-51
Nicholas II, Tsar, *viii*, *49*, *64*, *71*, *111*, *142*, *229*, 6, 9, 18, 21-2, 26, 31, 37, 49-52, 60, 65-7, 76, 88, 89, 94, 98-9, 101, 105,

109-10, 113, 116, 130, 137, 139, 141, 144, 147, 149, 204, 209, 211, 216, *229*, 240,
Niemen River, 45
Novo Georgievsk Fortress, 4, 31, 47-8, 221

O
Obruchev, General N. N., 2
Odessa, 78, 80, 85, 218, 227,
Oesel Island, 187, 208
Ognot, 94
Okhrana, 146-7
Oltu River, 127
Oltu, 82, 84, 85
Opolchenie, 53, 236, 2, 7, 15, 41, 44-5, 48, 52, 60, 65, 89, 115, 131, 139, 141, 143, 146, 149, 153-4, 159, 166, 182, 187, 190, 194, 201. 235-36
Oranovski, General V. A., 24
Order Number One, 151-2
Ossoviets Fortress, 40, 47-8

P
Partisans, 63, 67-8
Persia, 75, 78, 81, 88, 97, 134, 113, 224
Petrograd (see also St. Petersburg), *19*, 37, 48, 52, 60, 65, 95, 98, 115, 131, 139, 141, 143, 146-7, 149, 153-4, 159, 166, 182, 187, 190, 194, 201, 238
Petrograd Soviet, 148-9, 151, 152-3, 15-9, 179, 181, 182, 185, 187
Pinsk, 55
Plan, 18 12
Plan 19, 12-3, 208
Plan 19 (revised), 13
Plan 20, 13-4
Plevna, 4-5, 14
Pleve, General A.E., 27-8, 39, 66
Pliat, Marcel, 224
Ploesti oilfields, 119, 127-8
Poland, 2, 7, 9, 12, 14, 27, 31, 32, 34, 39, 46-8, 60
Polish Units, 63, 164, 198
Polivanov, General A. A., 51, 57, 65, 74, 99, 152
Polovtsov, General P. A., *154*, 167, 177
Poole, General, 144
Port Arthur, 7, 8, 14, 227,
POWs, *114*, 115, 170, 179, 235
Predeal Pass, 124, 125, 127
Pripyat Marshes, *73*, 52, 58, 66, 99, 103
Protopopov, A. D., 137, 143-4

Provisional Government, 94, 148-50, 153, 155-8, 166, 174-5, 179, 180-2, 187-8, 190, 212, 230
Pruth River, 120
Przemysl Fortress, 14, 27, 31, 33-4, 39-41, 44, 47-8, 226, 237
Przevalski, General M. A., 84, 91, 95
Pulkovo Heights, 190, 192

R
Radko-Dimitriev, General, 34, 43
Rasputin, G., 51, 116, 139, 141
Razvozov, Admiral, A. V., 213
Red Army, 18
Rediger, General G. F., 10
Refugees, 59, 60, *170*
Rennenkampf, General P., 24, 26, 39
Revolutions
  1905, 9, 17, 43, 148, 178
  March 1917, 94, 145-6, 174, 188, 210-11, 239
  November 1917, 95, 190-3, 210, 213
Riga, 46, 48, 55, 71, 110, 153, 180-1, 183-5, 187, 205, 227, 239
Rodzianko, M., 113, 137, 147
Rise, 92-3
Romania, 4, 14, 21, 42, 55, 103, 112, 116, 118-19, 122, 142, 173, 194, 201
Romanian Army, 117, 120, 128, 132, 198
Romanian armies
  First Army, 122-5, 127-8
  Second Army, 122, 124, 127-8
  Third Army, 122
  Fourth Army, 124-5
  Infantry Divisions
  1st Division, 126
  2nd Division, 123, 128
  3rd Division, 123
  4th Division, 123, 126, 128
  5th Division, 123
  6th Division, 123
  7th Division, 123, 127
  8th Division, 123, 127
  9th Division, 122
  10th Division, 120, 127
  11th Division, 120, 123, 128
  12th Division, 120, 123
  13th Division, 120, 123, 127
  14th Division, 120, 123, 127
  15th Division, 120
  16th Division, 120, 122
  17th Division, 120, 122, 127

18th Division, 120, 122, 127
19th Division, 120, 122
20th Division, 120, 122, 126
21st Division, 123, 127
22nd Division, 123
23rd Division, 120, 122, 126
9/19th Division, 126, 127-8
2/5th Division, 126-7
1/7th Division, 127
Cavalry Divisions
1st Division, 123
2nd Division, 123
Russian Army,
    Army of the Caucasus, 14,
        75-6, 79-82
    Army of the Danube, 127, 130
    Army of Descent, 85
    Army of Petrograd, 180-1
    First Army, 13-4, 24, 26, 28,
        31-2, 34, 67, 230
    Second Army, 13-4, 24-6, 28,
        31-4, 55, 67, 69, 239
    Third Army, 13, 24, 27-8, 31,
        34-5, 42-4, 47, 61, 110-11, 113,
        116, 132, 173
    Fourth Army, 13, 24, 27-8,
        31-3, 168
    Fifth Army, 13, 24, 27-8, 31,
        32-4, 67, 71, 161, 230
    Sixth Army, 14, 48, 168
    Seventh Army, 14, 57, 106,
        112, 85, 132, 161, 163-5, 168,
        173-4
    Eighth Army, 13, 24, 27, 28,
        31, 33-5, 42, 55, 99, 101, 103,
        105, 107, 109, 111, 132, 162,
        165, 171, 174, 179, 184
    Ninth Army, 22, 28, 31-4,
        42, 44, 57, 106, 109, 112, 122,
        125-6, 128, 130, 167, 226
    Tenth Army, 22, 26, 31, 32,
        39, 55, 161, 169, 239
    Eleventh Army, 41-2, 105,
        112, 132, 159, 161, 163, 173
    Twelfth Army, 39, 67, 136,
        180, 183, 230
    Guards Army, 65, 108,
        110-11
    Special Army, 113, 116, 132,
        148
    Corps
    I Guards Infantry Corps,
        111-12, 164, 174
    II Guards Infantry Corps,
        111, 174
    Guards Cavalry Corps, 25,
        108, 111, 150, 177
    I Corps, 111

V Corps, 173
VI Corps, 25
VII Corps, 221
VIII Corps, 221
IX Corps, 30
XII Corps, 117, 165
XIV Corps, 169
XV Corps, 26
XVI Corps, 165
XVII Corps, 173
XX Corps, 40
XXV Corps, 61, 179
XXX Corps, 111
XXXI Corps, 161
XXXIII Corps, 165
XXXIV Corps, 165
XXXXI Corps, 161
XXXI Corps, 164
XLVIII Corps, (See
    Appendix 3)
XLIX Corps, 173
I Siberian Corps, 169, 239
II Siberian Corps, 136
VI Siberian Corps, 136
II Turkestan Corps, 79, 83,
    89, 91, 93
I Caucasian Corps, 42, 79
II Caucasian Corps, 90
IV Caucasian Corps, 86, 90
V Caucasian Corps, 85, 93
VII Caucasian Corps, 98
III Cavalry Corps, 180, 190
Caucasian Cavalry Corps (aka
    Wild/Savage Division), 63-4
Infantry Divisions
1st Grenadier, 2
6th Grenadier, 174
3rd Siberian, 136
4th Infantry, 25
20th Infantry, 79
39th Division, 79
48th Infantry, 179
61st Infantry, 122
163rd Infantry, 197
172nd Infantry, 171
Serbian Division, 122, 125, 164
4th Caucasian Rifle, 89, 92
Cavalry Divisions
Caucasian Native Cavalry
    Division (CNC, Wild or
    Savage Division), 63-4, 175,
    176, 180-2
Caucasian Cavalry Division,
    86, 97-8
3rd Cavalry, 122, 150
Infantry Brigades
First Caucasian Rifle, 42
Fourth Turkestan Rifle, 79

Fifth Turkestan Rifle, 79
First Kuban *Plastun*, 79, 92
Second Kuban *Plastun*, 79, 93
Third Kuban *Plastun*, 79, 94
Siberian Cossack, 79
Transcaspian Cossack, 79
Second Caucasian Cossack,
    79
Fourth Caucasian Cossack, 79
Third Transbaikal Cossack, 79
Second Siberian Artillery, 72
First Russian Special, 65, 143
Second Russian Special, 65
Infantry Regiments
Pavlovski Guards, 16
Preobrazhensky Guards, 9
13th *Belozerski*, 25
17th *Arkhangelogorodski*, 30
73rd *Krimsky*, 117
99th *Ivangorodsky*, 47
490th *Rhzevski*, 146
Cavalry Regiments
Tekinsky/Turkmen Cavalry
    Half Regiment 113, *150*, 181
3rd Don Cossack, 29
Miscellaneous Formations
Armenian Rifles, 64, 79, 95-
    6, 98
Azerbaijan Rifles, 64,
Georgian Rifles, 64, 79, 95, 98
Grenadier platoons/
    companies, 61, 105, 112, 170
1st Machine Gun Regiment,
    166
Women's Battalion of Death,
    161, 171, 188
Chemical Battalion, *71*, 238-
    240 (See Appendix 5)
Death/Shock battalions, 169,
    171, *172,*
Frontier Guards, *76*, 79, 83, 97
Latvian Rifles, 64, 71, 110,
    136,184
Armoured cars, *17*, 22, 65, *191*
Artillery, *18*, *33*, *134*, *185*,
    226, *228-9*, *231*, 232
Russian Military Air Fleet, (See
    Appendix 2)
EVK (UEVK), 223–224
Aircraft
Albatros B1, 222
Aviatik, 222
BE 2e, 223
Bleriot monoplane, 216, 218
Deperdussin, 218
Farman, 218
Illya Muromets, 222-3
Lebed 12, 216

Morane Saulnier, 218, *220*
Nieport IV, 217
Nieuport XI, 219
Sopwith 11/2 Strutter, 223
Spad A2, 222
Spad VII, 222
Vickers FB, 19, 223
Aircraft manufacturers
Antara, 218
Dux, 218-19
Russian Navy, (See Appendix 1)
Ships
Aurora, 213
Diana, 209
Emperatitsa Mariia, 210
Gangoot, 208
Pallada, 208
Panteleymon (formerly
Potemkin), 92
Potemkin, 9
Rivn, 209
Rossia, 207
Rotislav, 92
Russian Fronts
North Western Front, 13, 14,
24, 31, 40-2, 45, 48, 59, 64,
209, 218, 224
South Western Front, 13, 24,
27-8, 31, 34, 40-6, 57-8, 64-5,
99, 101, 103-5, 107, 109-11,
113, 116, 118, 132, 136, 153,
158-9, 161-2, 169, 171, 173-4,
179, 188, 196, 218, 224, 228,
230, 233
Northern Front, 48, 58, 66, 67,
99, 101, 108, 109, 113, 136, 143,
153, 159, 161, 166, *168*, 169,
176, 180, 188, 190, 230
Western Front, 48, 51, 61,
66-7, 71, 99, 101, 108-10, 113,
116, 153, 159, 161-2, 166, 171,
176, 188, 194, 230, 239
Caucasian Front, 64-5, 74,
77, 90, 94, 96, 134, 210, 224
Romanian Front, 64-5, 96,
130-1, 136, 159, 167, 169, *193*,
197, 224, 230
Russo-Baltic Railway Wagon
Company (RBVZ), 218
Russo-Japanese War, 4, 7, 15,
36, 66, 203, 206-7, 215
Russo-Turkish War, 4
Ruzski, General N.V., *100*, 26,
27-8, 30-1, 33-4, 37, 39,
41-2, 48, 113, 153, 175, 230
S
Sakharov, General V. V., 105, 125
Salonika, 120, 122

Salza, General Baron A.E., 27
Sarikamish, battle of, 75, 82-5, 89
Samsonov, General A.V., 24-6, 50
San River, 31-2, 44
Scheidemann, General G. M.,
228, 234
Serbia, 28, 55, 57, 80, 119
Sereth River, 128, 169
Sevastopol, 203, 205, 210, 217
Shcherbachev, General D. G.,
57, 106, 158, 167, 175, 198
Smirnov, General V. V., 45, 67
Somme, battle of, 69, 107, 110
Stokhod River, 105, 107, 109,
112, 116, 155, 183
Stokhod River, battle of, 153, 239
Silesia, 22, 31, 33, 35, 49
Silistria, 120, 122
St. Petersburg (see also
Petrograd), *19*, 1, 6, 8-10, 14, 21-2,
24, 37, 215, 217
Stavka (see also Moghilev), 13, 24,
31, 34, *35*, 35, 37, 40-2, 44-6,
48-50, 52, 57-9, 65-6, 94, 99, 105,
107, *108*, 116, 127, 129, 136, 139,
141, 155, 157, 159, 174, 179, 181,
188, 194, 205, 209, 223, 227, 237
Sturmer, B. V., 137, 139
Sukhomlinov, General V.A., 10,
12, 14, 19, 27, 50-1
T
Tabriz, 85, 98
Taflet Fort, 91
Tannenberg, battle of, 24, 26,
50, 173
Tarnopol, 27, 155, 171, 173-4,
181, 184
TAON, 161, (see Appendix 3)
Tiblisi (Tiflis), 75, 79, 82, 84, 95
Trans-Siberian Railway, 8, 115
Transylvania, 119, 122-3, 125
Trebizond (Trabzun), 77, 92-3. 96
Trotsky, L., 166-7, 185, 199-
201
Tsarskoe Selo, 6, 51, 66, 141, 190
Tsushima, battle of, 9
Turkestan, 79, 113-14
Turkey, 4, 14, 37, 80, 96, 199,
204, 210
Turkish Army, 77, 80
Turkish armies
Second, 92-3, 96
Third, 77, 80, 82, 85-6, 92-
94, 96
Sixth, 97
Corps
V, 92-3
IX, 80, 82, 84, 85-6

X, 80-1, 83-6, 88-9, 91
XI, 80, 81-2, 84-6, 88-9
XIII, 97-8
Infantry divisions
17th Division, 82-3, 89
28th Division, 82
29th Division, 82-3
30th Division, 82
31st Division, 82
32nd Division, 82
36th Division, 86
37th Division, 89
Cavalry divisions
2nd Cavalry, 80, 89
Other Units
Frontier Guards, 89
Gendarmerie, 89
Turtukai Fortresses, 120, 122
U
Ukraine, 55, 167, 173, 174, 188,
197-199, 201, 224, 234
Ukrainian *Rada*, 167, 213
V
Vakulovsky, Staff Captain K. K.,
220
Van, 75, 86
Van Lake, 75, 86, 89
Variant A, 13
Variant G, 13
Verdun, 65-6, 107
Vilna, 52, 55, 99, 161
Vinnitsa, 191, 224
Vistula River, 2, 14, 25, 32, 34, 48
Vladimir Volyinsk, 112, 132
Vladivostok, 78, 115, 203, 227,
W
Wallachia, 119, 125-6
Warsaw, 2, 4, 12-13, 24, 27-8,
34, 48, 222, 237
Western Allies, 99, 131, 141-2,
144, 158, 210
Western Front (Belgium and
France), 33, 55, 65, 69, 110, 131,
185
Wilson, General Sir Henry, 142-3
Y
Yanushkevitch, General N.N.,
21-2, 60
Yudenitch, General N. N., 7,
82-5, 88, 91-4, 98
Z
Zaionchkovski, General A. M.,
122, 125
Zhilinski, General I. G., 24, 26,
50, 58, 99

Cyclist units were popular with all armies during World War One and they were often used as scouts or semi-mobile reserves. The lack of good roads in Eastern Europe limited their role due to the wear and tear on the tyres. During the retreat of SW Front during the summer of 1917 cycle troops were often used to provide punitive detachments and were complimented by Kornilov for their devotion to duty.